DESTINATION ARCHITECTURE

THE ESSENTIAL GUIDE TO 1000 CONTEMPORARY BUILDINGS

Destination Architecture presents 1,000 of the most compelling works of architecture completed in the last 30 years in an ultra-convenient format. An unparalleled and comprehensive resource, this architecture travel guide is the best way to find and enjoy contemporary built culture — whether at home or on the road.

The global perspective provided by this portable book makes it the ideal companion for all travellers who love architecture. It includes works from countries as culturally, geographically, climatically and economically diverse as Argentina, Senegal, Denmark, the Philippines, Israel, Egypt, Lithuania and the USA. The building types represented range from super-scale towers to tiny places of worship, high-tech cultural centres to regional rest stops.

Organized geographically and illustrated with 26 maps, *Destination Architecture* features a single image per building and a short descriptive text. Each project entry includes the name of the building, its architect and completion date, as well as the address. An icon-based system indicates which projects are open to the public.

This book is an essential travel companion for anyone interested in gaining an understanding of contemporary architecture around the world.

Notes
Destination Architecture divides the world into eight regions — Australasia, Asia, Europe, Africa, Middle East, North America, Central America and South America. The featured buildings are presented in a geographical sequence throughout the book, so that buildings in the same location are grouped together. Regions are indicated in the tab on the side of each page, and countries are indicated at the bottom of the page. Country maps are interspersed throughout each region, indicating the location of individual projects.

Key to Symbols
For each building, it is specified how and when it can be visited. The following symbols indicate this.

○ Open to the public 24 hours/day

◑ Exterior and interior can be viewed subject to opening hours. A web address and/or telephone number has been provided at the back of the book

● Exterior can be viewed. Interior cannot be viewed

Opening times are subject to change and access may be limited. While every care has been taken to ensure accuracy throughout this book, it is advisable to check the times and dates of opening prior to visiting or making travel arrangements.

Place, Project and Practice Names
English-language conventional place names have been used throughout this book. Local forms for project names have been given priority, and are recognized by the country concerned. For projects in languages that do not use the Roman alphabet, transliteration or transcription has been used. Practice names have been simplified throughout, but are displayed fully in the Index of Architects.

Place Name Abbreviations

The abbreviations listed below are those used in the building addresses and maps.

AB	Alberta	NH	New Hampshire
ACT	Australian Capital Territory	NJ	New Jersey
AK	Alaska	NM	New Mexico
AL	Alabama	NS	Nova Scotia
AR	Arkansas	NSW	New South Wales
AZ	Arizona	NT	Northern Territory (Australia)
BC	British Columbia		Northwest Territories (Canada)
CA	California	NV	Nevada
CO	Colorado	NY	New York
CT	Connecticut	OH	Ohio
DC	District of Columbia	OK	Oklahoma
DE	Delaware	ON	Ontario
FL	Florida	OR	Oregon
GA	Georgia	PA	Pennsylvania
IA	Iowa	QC	Québec
IL	Illinois	QLD	Queensland
IN	Indiana	SA	South Australia
KS	Kansas	SC	South Carolina
KY	Kentucky	SD	South Dakota
LA	Louisiana	TAS	Tasmania
MA	Massachusetts	TN	Tennessee
MB	Manitoba	TX	Texas
MD	Maryland	UK	United Kingdom
ME	Maine	USA	United States of America
MI	Michigan	UT	Utah
MN	Minnesota	VA	Virginia
MO	Missouri	VIC	Victoria
MS	Mississippi	VT	Vermont
MT	Montana	WA	Washington (USA)
NB	New Brunswick		Western Australia (Australia)
NC	North Carolina	WI	Wisconsin
ND	North Dakota	WV	West Virginia
NE	Nebraska	WY	Wyoming

World Map
Regions and Project Distribution

777-936

North America

959-1000

Central America

South America

937-958

237-738

37-236

Europe

Middle East

Asia

Africa

Australasia

1-36

755-776

739-754

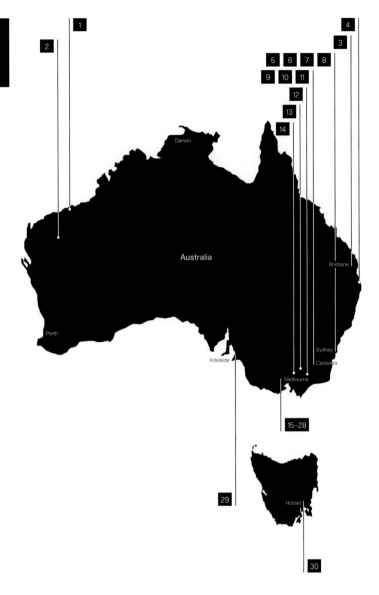

1

2

4

3

5 6 7 8

9 10 11

12

13

14

Darwin

Australia

Brisbane

Perth

Sydney

Adelaide

Canberra

Melbourne

15–28

29

Hobart

30

Wanangkura Stadium, 2012   **ARM**
Hamilton Road, South Hedland, WA 6722 ◑
This stadium provides a recreational hub designed to withstand extreme weather conditions. The exterior features a pattern modelled on cyclonic isobars rendered in waterproof vitreous enamel panels. Its galvanized-steel inner facade protects against downpours and creates a thermal cavity to mitigate the heat.

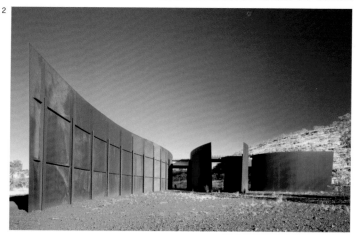

Karijini National Park Visitor Centre, 2001   **Woodhead**
Banjima Drive, Karijini, WA 6751 ◑
Inspired by the 'Kurrumanthu', or monitor lizard, the curved walls of richly weathered steel dominate the scheme of this centre; low roofs and frameless glazing enhance the effect of a building emerging from the ground. The darkened interior re-presents the impressive landscape to visitors.

Gallery of Modern Art, 2006   **Architectus Sydney**
Stanley Place, South Brisbane, QLD 4101 ◑
Sited perpendicular to the Brisbane River, Australia's largest contemporary art space contains galleries and two cinemas under a large, thin cantilevered roof. Pierced by skylights and voids, the central atrium is awash with light and animated by timber screens, balconies and walkways.

4

Abedian School of Architecture, 2013   **CRAB**
Bond University, 14 University Drive, Robina, QLD 4226 ●
A new architecture faculty for Bond University, this building features a glazed south face and solid north wall, encouraging passive climate control, while its triple-height corridor gradually rises along the building's length. Studios, offices and laboratories are arranged off this internal 'street', marked by curved cast concrete 'scoops'.

Museum of Contemporary Art (MCA), 2012   **Sam Marshall**
140 George Street, The Rocks, Sydney, NSW 2000 ◐
An addition to the pre-existing Museum of Contemporary Art, this gallery wing is comprised of a series of concrete-clad blocks in black, white, grey and brown, which are stacked irregularly and, at certain points, even cantilever over the street. The upper levels, meanwhile, reveal views over the harbour and Opera House.

Andrew 'Boy' Charlton Swimming Pool, 2002   **Lippmann Partnership**
1C Mrs Macquaries Road, Sydney, NSW 2000 ◐
A replacement for a 35-year-old Sydney Harbour icon, the new facility takes advantage of its spectacular site with two pools arranged on one level, allowing views across the bay. Visitor entry is through a progression of low, gravel- or pool-topped spaces, tucked away on the upper level.

8 Chifley, 2013   **Rogers Stirk Harbour + Partners**
8 Chifley Square, Sydney, NSW 2000 ●
This 34-storey building features a soaring ground-level atrium, and, above, is divided
into 'blocks' of three or four floors, creating interlinked vertical 'villages'. The structural
gymnastics that make this possible — four perimeter super-columns and red criss-
cross braces — have been cleverly turned into design features.

Horizon Apartments, 1998   **Harry Seidler**
184 Forbes Street, Darlinghurst, Sydney, NSW 2010 ●
Neighbours were incensed by this 43-storey, 144m tall structure's shadow, and
heritage advocates argued that the design was at odds with the rest of the suburb.
It is notable for its scalloped facade, a result of the changing aspect of the balconies. The 586 sq m penthouse has 360-degree vistas.

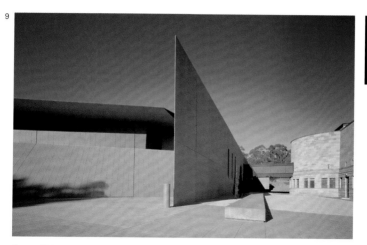

Anzac Hall, 2001   **Denton Corker Marshall**
Treloar Crescent, Campbell, ACT 2612 ◑
Embedded into rolling ground next to the existing domed Australian War Memorial, this memorial hall — beneath its low, double-curved roof — has walls that are radial to the dome in plan, creating a dramatic fan-shaped space. It also anchors a major axis in the national capital.

National Museum of Australia, 2001   **ARM**
Lawson Crescent, Acton, ACT 2601 ◑
The design of this building is based on the metaphor of a Boolean string, manifest in the form of its ribbon canopies, pathways and landscape elements. A crescent-shaped floor plan holds the permanent galleries while the Gallery of the First Australians is shaped like a broken five-pointed Star of David.

11

Ilmarinen, Finnish Embassy in Canberra, 2002   **Hirvonen-Huttunen**
12 Darwin Avenue, Yarralumla, ACT 2600 ◑
This building, designed by Hirvonen-Huttunen with MGT Architects, houses a glass-atrium three-storey secretariat, an office wing clad inside and out with stainless steel, a timber-decked residence and a wooden sauna. The result is a building that is Nordic in roots, yet fundamentally Australian.

12

Huski Hotel, 2005   **Elenberg Fraser**
3 Sitzmark Street, Falls Creek, VIC 3699 ◑
The most prominent feature of this hotel is its faceted eucalyptus facade. From the front, the wide, stacked array of timber boxes has an immediate impact. The guest apartments vary in size, from studios to two-storey penthouses. Each one has a sunny north-facing view and a balcony with built-in spa.

High Country Visitor Information Centre, 2006   **Gregory Burgess**
175 High Street, Mansfield, VIC 3722 ◑
Sinuous, curved walls of rammed earth flank tree trunks of Southern Blue Gum to form the distinctive entrance of this visitor centre, which is constructed predominantly from local materials. The floor inside features local Victorian ash timber and recycled red gum.

14

Australian Wildlife Health Centre, 2006   **MvS**
Badger Creek Road, Healesville, VIC 3777 ●
This veterinary facility treats zoo animals and wildlife rescued and brought in by the public. With a doughnut-shaped space as its focus, a transparent gallery allows visitors to observe procedures. The roof is designed to function as a 'solar chimney' and provides passive ventilation.

Heide Museum of Modern Art, 2006   O'Connor + Houle
7 Templestowe Road, Bulleen, VIC 3105 ◑
This cultural complex in Bulleen consists of four buildings: the original weather-board farmhouse; Heide II, a 1965 modernist masterpiece by David McGlashan; the Sidney Myer Education Centre, which functions as a café; and this addition, Heide III, which houses a permanent art collection and is clad in black titanium zinc.

Melbourne Museum, 2000   Denton Corker Marshall
11 Nicholson Street, Carlton, VIC 3053 ◑
Set alongside the existing nineteenth-century city museum, this facility groups research and Aboriginal centres, an IMAX cinema, and a children's area as volumes arranged around a light-filled atrium — itself containing an aviary and indoor garden, sheltered beneath soaring roof planes.

Pixel Building, 2010 **Studio 505**
205 Queensberry Street, Carlton, VIC 3053 ●
Clad in recycled coloured panels, which have been likened to a jester's cloak, this carbon-neutral office building features a facade that allows 100 per cent daylight penetration while protecting workers from direct sun and glare. On top of the four storeys is a rooftop garden with wind turbines and solar panels.

18

RMIT Design Hub, 2012 **Sean Godsell**
Victoria Street/Swanston Street, Carlton, VIC 3053 ◑
An urban research laboratory with exhibition spaces and facilities for interdisciplinary study, this energy-efficient structure is clad in more than 16,000 sand-blasted photovoltaic glass discs, set within galvanised-steel frames that provide automated sun-shading, with the potential to generate electricity for the building.

Australasia

Swanston Academic Building, 2012   **Lyons**
445 Swanston Street, Melbourne, VIC 3000 ●
Part of RMIT University's ebullient city campus, the exterior of this building looks like large-scale pixels, the scaly walls carrying a distorted image that mirrors its neighbours. Inside, the architects designed a 'vertical campus' of ten storeys with double-height lobbies intended to encourage student and staff interaction.

QV Pod H Crèche, Car Park and Office, 2005   **Kerstin Thompson**
Russell Street, Melbourne, VIC 3000 ●
A red facade, composed of brick, corrugated steel on precast concrete panels, and steel louvres, contrasts with the surrounding glass-clad towers. Gaps of varying sizes form windows and openings, with louvres ventilating the parking levels and folded panels forming the roof and pergola of the crèche.

Federation Square, 2002   **LAB**
Swanston Street/Flinders Street, Melbourne, VIC 3000 ◐
Occupying an entire urban block, this development houses national exhibition and broadcasting facilities, restaurants, shops and commercial spaces within its complex geometry. A glazed atrium, constructed from a metal frame, creates performance space; an open-air amphitheatre for 15,000 people completes this project.

Southern Cross Station, 2007   **Grimshaw**
Collins Street, Docklands, VIC 3008 ◐
This major transport interchange is essentially an open plaza sheltered by an undulating roof. Transparent facades enable passengers on the station's platforms to engage visually with the city, while elevated yellow pods connected by walkways accommodate administration offices and define retail spaces below.

Webb Bridge, 2003   **Denton Corker Marshall**
Capital City Trail, Docklands, VIC 3008 ○
A public art project spanning the Yarra River, the Webb Bridge joins an existing
structure to a new curved ramp. This leads pedestrians and cyclists through a progression of widely spaced steel hoops. The compressed, cocoon-like conclusion at
the south bank resembles a traditional eel trap or fishing net.

Niagara Galleries, 2002   **Edmond and Corrigan**
245 Punt Road, Richmond, VIC 3121 ◑
Clad in black-and-white striped painted steel with a red underside and yellow fenestration, this striking addition extends out over the rear of the Victorian terrace that
houses the original gallery. Ideal light conditions for viewing and storing artworks
are created via angled south-facing openings and a private courtyard.

Hamer Hall, 2012   **ARM**
100 St Kilda Road, Melbourne, VIC 3004 ◐
Connecting the building with the riverside walkway and refurbishing original interiors by John Truscott, this upgrade of Melbourne's premier concert hall is marked by a double-height off-form concrete podium along the lower promenade. Inside the drum-shaped venue, acoustics have been improved and the foyer enlarged.

Australian Centre for Contemporary Art, 2002   **Wood Marsh**
111 Sturt Street, Southbank, VIC 3006 ◐
This is a very urban building situated between a tangle of roads, train lines and warehouses, yet it resembles the large, rusting agricultural sheds seen in the bush. The abstract steel exterior is in stark contrast to the four white-walled gallery spaces as well as the glass foyer, which is accessed by the structure's only obvious opening.

Advanced Technologies Centre, 2011   **H2o**
Swinburne University, Burwood Road, Hawthorn, VIC 3122 ●
Housing teaching, lecture and research facilities for the university's Advanced Technologies Centre, this campus is organized as a pair of 10-storey buildings, set behind a street-facing podium. Raised dots and circular cut-outs in the concrete facade panels highlight the non-commercial nature of the towers.

Moonah Links Hotel Lodges, 2006   **Hayball Leonard Stent**
55 Peter Thomson Drive, Fingal, VIC 3939 ◐
Sited in a verdant coastal landscape, these weathered timber structures have minimal visual impact. Each lodge is arranged in an L-shaped plan, with private guest accommodation on the long side, and communal spaces at the base of the L. Vertical fins provide sun shading and a dramatic effect.

Marion Cultural Centre, 2001   **ARM**
287 Diagonal Road, Oaklands Park, SA 5046 ◑
The centre transcribes itself onto the landscape in the form of a massive built version of the word 'Marion', within which a library, art gallery, performance space and café are linked yet independently accessible. In the process, it seeks to address the the role of art and architecture in suburbia.

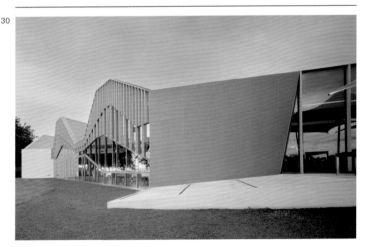

Peppermint Bay Visitor Centre, 2003   **Terroir**
3435 Channel Highway, Woodbridge, TAS 7162 ◑
The plan of this building is based on a Z-shaped line that traces a labyrinthine route both inside and along an external promenade. An internal spine wall of Tasmanian oak separates the public and service spaces. An undulating roof echoes the rolling hills, and gives a distinct identity to the building.

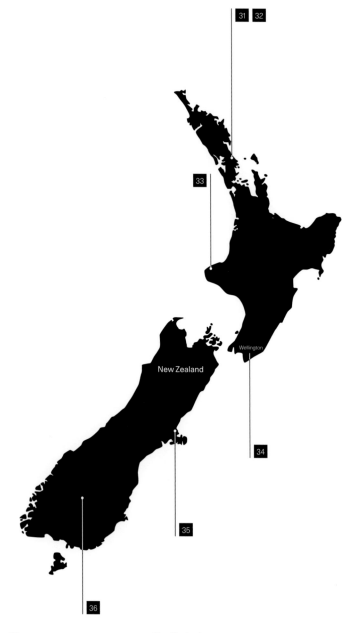

31 32

33

New Zealand

Wellington

34

35

36

New Zealand

Auckland Art Gallery, 2011   **FJMT and Archimedia**
Wellesley Street East, Auckland 1010 ◑
Echoing established trees in the adjacent park, this contemporary extension to the
city's eighteenth-century art gallery is announced by vaulted timber canopies that
sail above the forecourt, atrium and exhibition spaces. Visitors enter through a triple-
height glazed lobby. A smaller, stone-clad volume houses a restaurant and shop.

Point Resolution Bridge, 2013   **Warren and Mahoney**
Point Resolution, Auckland ○
This pedestrian bridge is comprised of three steel arches that support the concrete deck. The walkway is shaped like the hull of a boat, with extensive views,
made possible by the glass balustrade that cantilevers out over the harbour. Local
artist Henriata Nicholas's water ripple pattern decorates the glass and concrete.

Len Lye Centre, 2015   **Patterson Associates**
Queen Street, New Plymouth, Taranaki 4310 ◑
The concertina-like stainless steel curtain that enfolds this gallery is imbued with
the kinetic spirit of artist Len Lye, whose work is housed within. Inside, curved
cast-concrete walls link two large exhibition spaces, a cinema, a research archive,
an education suite, lounge areas, and various other facilities.

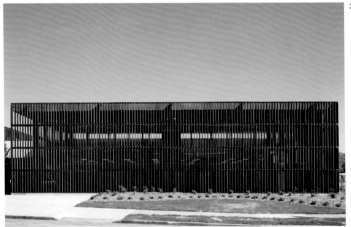

Pataka Museum of Arts and Cultures, 2001   **Architecture +**
17 Parumoana Street, Porirua, Wellington 5022 ◑
Taking its title from a Maori term that encapsulates the concepts of 'enclosure, repository and storehouse', this 1970s warehouse now provides extensive museum
accommodation and gallery space, arranged around a 'spine' block. The building is
clad in an irregular gridwork screen of steel louvres.

Christchurch Bus Interchange, 2015   **Architectus**
Lichfield Street, Christchurch Central, Christchurch 8011 ◐
Built to replace its previous incarnation, which was badly damaged in the 2011 earthquake, this bus exchange is centred around an L-shaped concourse. Its striking folded roof was influenced by the city's neo-gothic architecture, while skylights provide a sense of spaciousness and natural light.

Peregrine Winery, 2003   **Architecture Workshop**
2127 Gibbston Highway, Queenstown 9371 ◐
Located in Central Otago, the most southerly wine region in the world, this long building is sheltered from heat and snow by a wing-shaped roof made of corrugated composite fibreglass sheeting. Inside, a public tasting room, a barrel store and fermentation areas are partially dug into the Gibbston Valley.

37 38

39

40

Azerbaijan

Baku

New Delhi

India

Mumbai

41 42

Heydar Aliyev Center, 2013   **Zaha Hadid**
1 Heydar Aliyev Avenue, Baku ◑
This library, museum and concert venue is cloaked in a shell of smooth glass-reinforced concrete panels. Referencing the region's traditional ornamentation along floors, up walls and across domes, the design blurs the distinction between indoors and out, as well as public and private spaces.

Baku Crystal Hall, 2012   **gmp**
Sabail District, Bayil Settlement, National Flag Square, Baku ◑
Conceived as a modular, crystalline structure, this 25,000-seat indoor sports stadium and concert hall was designed and built in only eight months, in order to host the 2012 Eurovision Song Contest. The hall is clad in a semi-transparent membrane. At night, its angular form is illuminated by hundreds of embedded LED lights.

JRE Educomp, 2012   **Morphogenesis**
Knowledge Park IV, Greater Noida, Uttar Pradesh ●
Imagined as a miniature urban settlement, this university campus is connected by a network of streets for pedestrians and cyclists. The Academic Block is the first phase and incorporates landscaped courtyards, evaporative cooling and louvred screens allowing for passive environmental control during the extreme summers.

72 Screens, 2013   **Sanjay Puri**
JLN Marg, opposite Rajasthan University, Jaipur ●
Abstract folded screens supported by a steel framework envelop this six-storey corporate headquarters. Creating a modern reinterpretation of traditional 'jaali' — a double skin that reduces direct heat gain — the perforated glass-reinforced concrete panels are separated from the glazed facade behind.

Bombay Arts Centre, 2013   **Sanjay Puri**
KC Marg, Bandra Reclamation, Mumbai ◑
This organic, sculpted structure is dominated by a huge tinted-glass trapezoid window that resembles a TV screen, supported by a vaguely cylindrical white concrete tower pockmarked with bean-shaped openings. Inside are an auditorium, galleries and studios. It aims to provide a casual meeting point for the creative community.

GMS Grande Palladium, 2010   **Malik**
CST Road, Kalina, Mumbai ●
This wildly cantilevered office building clad in ridged aluminium is deliberately disconnected from the past. There's maybe an allusion to the corrugated-roof shacks of the nearby slums, perhaps because much of this area is earmarked for redevelopment; the architects hope that this structure creates 'a framework for the future'.

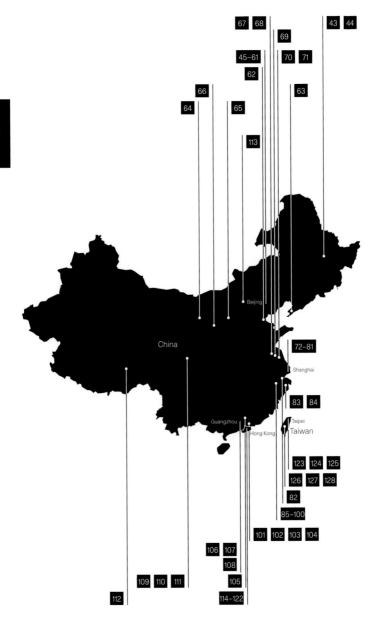

67 68
43 44
69
45–61
70 71
62
63
66
64 65
113

China

Beijing

China

72–81

Shanghai

83 84

Guangzhou
Taipei
Taiwan

Hong Kong

123 124 125
126 127 128
82
85–100
101 102 103 104
106 107
108
109 110 111
105
112
114–122

Harbin Cultural Center, 2014   **MAD**
Daoli City, Harbin, Heilongjiang ❶
Referencing the region's wintry landscape of snow dunes, this cultural centre is cloaked in undulating aluminium panels. Situated across a three-petalled floorplan, the main spaces include a 400-seat theatre, a large public plaza for outdoor performances and the grand theatre, which is clad in sinuous bands of Manchurian ash.

China Wood Sculpture Museum, 2013   **MAD**
King River Road, Harbin, Heilongjiang ❶
Characterized by its twisting reflective form wrapped in polished-steel plates, this museum showcases a collection of traditional wooden artworks. Shaped by the narrow site and by Harbin's icy conditions, the elongated floorplan maximizes display space, while rooflights overhead let natural light into the gallery interiors.

Distorted Courtyard House, Commune by the Great Wall, 2002   Rocco Design
The Great Wall, Exit 53, Shuiguan, G6 Jingzang Highway, Beijing ❶
Fortress-like white walls contrast with the dark grey steel frame of the upper storeys in this modern interpretation of a traditional Chinese courtyard home. The form is distorted by skewing the square courtyard to fit the site. A louvre-like bamboo screen hangs over the glass curtain wall.

Airport House, Commune by the Great Wall, 2002   Chien Hsueh-Yi
The Great Wall, Exit 53, Shuiguan, G6 Jingzang Highway, Beijing ❶
Echoing the appearance of modern airports, this house is organized around a central corridor with glass on one side and two stone walls on the other side. Raised on stilts, living rooms jut out over the treetops in different directions, offering views of the surrounding foothills.

Suitcase House, Commune by the Great Wall, 2002   **EDGE Design Institute**
The Great Wall, Exit 53, Shuiguan, G6 Jingzang Highway, Beijing ❶
This house, whose roof terrace offers views of the Great Wall, can be transformed
from an open space into a sequence of rooms with sliding doors, folding dividers
and pneumatically assisted floor panels. Facilities include a music chamber, library,
meditation chamber and sauna.

Bamboo Wall House, Commune by the Great Wall, 2002   **Kengo Kuma**
The Great Wall, Exit 53, Shuiguan, G6 Jingzang Highway, Beijing ❶
This house, inspired by the Great Wall in the way its horizontal structure adapts to
the site's topography, is constructed principally out of glass and bamboo. A system
of bamboo slats forms a screen behind the glass facade, creating interplay between
the exterior and interior.

Beijing Capital International Airport, 2008 **Foster + Partners**
Airport Road, Chaoyang District, Beijing ◑
Incorporating several sustainable features, this terminal building combines references to Chinese culture — including the use of traditional colours and symbols — with vast, aerodynamic curves. The public transport system is fully integrated into the design for ease of navigation.

104 Caochangdi Gallery, 2005 **FAKE Design**
104 Caochangdi, Chaoyang District, Beijing ◑
This grey-brick art gallery building is part of a larger labyrinthine complex of galleries and studios. Its courtyard layout references local tradition, but with a twist. It eschews rectilinear form for a dynamic, angular floorplan. Porches clad in geometric patterns interrupt the evenness of the facades.

National Stadium, 2008   **Herzog & de Meuron**
1 National Stadium South Road, Chaoyang District, Beijing ◑
This stadium is commonly referred to as 'The Bird's Nest', because of the 110,000 tons and 26km of interlaced and twisted steel beams that comprise its outer frame. Designed for the 2008 Olympic Games, it incorporates a red concrete seating bowl with a capacity of 91,000.

Beijing Greenland Center, 2016   **SOM**
36 Hongtai East Road, Dawangjing Business District, Beijing ●
Clad with hundreds of isosceles trapezoidal glass modules, this 260m linear skyscraper provides office, residential and retail spaces arranged around a central core. The prisms of the curtain wall give alternate light and shade, creating a woven effect, and low-emission glass panels are also self-shading.

Asia

Linked Hybrid, 2009   **Steven Holl**
Qigan Hutong, Dongcheng District, Beijing ●
Designed as a porous 'city within a city', this mixed-use project features a central garden and reflecting pool. Though each of the prefabricated concrete towers is separate, they are connected at ground level by open passages, and by glazed sky bridges, which house facilities including a gallery and a swimming pool.

77 Theatre, 2014   **Origin**
77 Houjie Street, Dongcheng District, Beijing ◑
Situated in a former printing factory, this theatre features a huge folding Corten wall that lifts up to reveal the contents of a weathered steel auditorium. A series of existing smaller buildings were removed to create the large fronting courtyard, while adjacent structures are connected via new bridges and pathways.

CCTV Headquarters, 2012   **OMA**
Guanghua East Road, Dongcheng District, Beijing ●
There is perhaps no better symbol of the ambition of twenty-first-century Beijing than this $1.2bn glass-and-steel loop, popularly nicknamed the 'big underpants'. The structure has two leaning towers — one used for broadcasting, the other for offices — bending at right angles to meet on the ground, and, giddily, at the top.

Conrad Hotel, 2013   **MAD**
29 East 3rd Ring Road North, Chaoyang District, Beijing ◐
Marked by an expressive facade that gently falls away towards the base, this hotel is designed to contrast with the orthogonal buildings around it. Its glazed curtain wall sits behind white aluminium cladding that is intentionally skewed. Windows vary in size and form, creating an irregular pattern.

Jian Wai SOHO Complex, 2005   **Riken Yamamoto and Field Shop**
39 East 3rd Ring Road, Chaoyang District, Beijing ◑
This project comprises 20 towers incorporating apartments of various sizes and layouts, offices, shops and restaurants. The two office towers are grouped along the eastern side of the site and the remaining buildings are aligned at a 25-degree angle from their north–south axis.

Water Cube National Aquatics Center, 2007   **PTW**
11 Tianchen East Road, Chaoyang District, Beijing ◑
Inspired by soap bubbles, the design of the plastic, repetitive, pillow-like shell of this building is derived from its function as a swimming pool. The shell hangs on a steel frame mostly hidden from sight, and its translucency allows nearly 90 per cent of the solar energy entering the building to be stored and re-used.

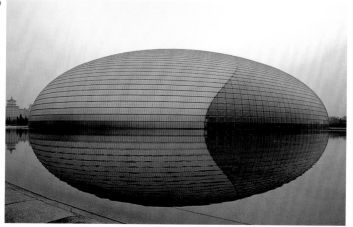

National Grand Theater of China, 2008   **Paul Andreu**
2 West Chang'an Avenue, Xicheng District, Beijing ◑
This concert hall, with its 'floating' bubble of titanium — broken by a swooping glass section reminiscent of a stage curtain — has been compared to everything from a duck egg to a dung pile. Its defenders, however, argue that there is an element of Chinese geometry in its circle-in-a-square arrangement.

Hong Luo Club House, 2003   **MAD**
Hong Luo Road, Miyun District, Beijing ●
This club house provides a social space on Hong Luo Lake. The plinth appears to float on the lake's surface, while the irregular X-shaped concrete roof creates a fluid canopy that sails over the interior. The pool is set flush with the lake level and, like the building itself, is intended to blur artificial and natural boundaries.

Tongxian Gatehouse, 2003   **NADAAA**
Xiaopu Village, Songzhuang Town, Tong District, Beijing ◐
Located within an art centre on a site abutting an industrial zone, the Tongxian Gate-house was constructed using local brick and timber. The building, which sits at the entrance to the art centre's main courtyard, is a low-rise grey brick structure that is partly raised off the ground, with a cantilevered section.

Tianjin Grand Theater, 2009   **gmp**
58-1 Pingjiang Road, Hexi Qu, Tianjin Shi ◐
This project includes an opera house, concert hall and multi-use hall, organised as three freestanding volumes on an elevated stone base. Enveloped by glass walls, the complex is united by a glazed half-circular roof that projects beyond the perim-eter. It tapers to the west, providing shelter to the terraced lakeside plaza below.

Dalian International Conference Center, 2012   **Wolf D Prix**
Zhongshan, Dalian, Liaoning ◑
This building is shaped by the functions within, namely a grand opera theatre flanked
by conference halls. Its panelled aluminium cladding is assembled in an undulating
skin that wraps a hybrid structure. Inside, a glazed skin mimics the external shape of
the shell and acts as a brise-soleil, controlling light and air.

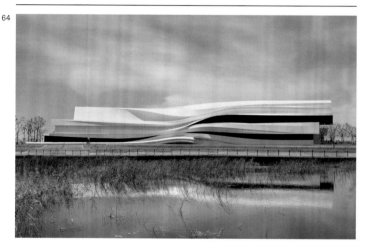

MOCA Yinchuan , 2015   **waa (we architech anonymous)**
12 HeLe Road, Xingqing District,Yinchuan ◑
Part of the Yellow River Arts Centre, this museum's ribbon-like facade draws on the
site's geology and layers of sediment left by the receding river. Constructed from
unique interlocking panels of glass fibre reinforced concrete, the rippling exterior
encloses four levels of exhibition and auditorium spaces.

Asia

Asia

Taiyuan Museum of Art, 2010   **Preston Scott Cohen**
Huandao Road, Jinyuan, Taiyuan District, Shanxi ◑
Situated within landscaped gardens, this riverside art museum houses gallery space, an auditorium, a restaurant and a library. It's clad in honeycomb panels, which are highly reflective, despite being finished with a stone veneer. Inside, adaptable display rooms encourage visitors to experience the museum in a non-linear fashion.

Well Hall Hotel, 2005   **MADA s.p.a.m.**
Lantian, Xi'an, Shaanxi ◑
This is an intimate lodge set on a small grassy bluff. A collaboration between the architect and local residents, it is built from local materials including: grey and red brick, wood and clay roof tiles. Traditional elements were newly crafted using a contemporary pattern of trapezium shapes. Within the building are two courtyards.

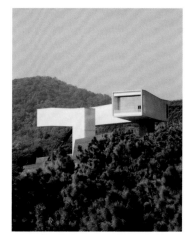

Asia

Sifang Art Museum, 2001   **Steven Holl**
9 Zhenqi Road, Pukou District, Nanjing ◑
This art museum peers out from the canopy of Laoshan Forest, at the entrance to a cultural complex. From ground-level galleries in bamboo-formed concrete that has been stained black, you ascend 30m via stairs or a lift to the 'floating' upper floor, wrapped in a polycarbonate film that allows light to permeate.

Nanjing Keyne Center, 2013   **SOM**
33 Jiangdong Middle Road, Jianye District, Nanjing ●
Broad triangular facets characterize the curtain facade of this tower. Providing increased thermal insulation, its double skin encloses diagonal steel braces that reduce structural weight. Inside, offices and hotel floors are arranged around a dramatic 27-storey atrium that admits daylight to the centre of the building.

Nanjing Wanjing Garden Chapel, 2014   **AZL**
Donghong Line, Lishui District, Nanjing ◑
A butterfly roof sits atop this riverside chapel, creating a pleasingly simple silhouette. The exterior, formed by thin pillars of wood, is semi-transparent, allowing light to flood inside. Every single element of the interior, from the pews to the ceiling, is a luminous white.

Suzhou Chapel, 2016   **Neri & Hu**
199 Yangchenghuan Road, Yangcheng Lake, Suzhou ◑
Latticed brick walls of varying heights define the meandering entranceway to this chapel. Its double-height sanctuary is naturally lit by square apertures and sliding doors to outer courtyards, with a mezzanine delineated by vertical timber battens. At night, the ethereal skin filters internal light, emitting a diffuse glow.

Suzhou Museum, 2006   **IM Pei**
204 Dongbei Street, Gusu District, Suzhou ◑
This gallery evokes contemporary aesthetics while drawing on Suzhou's heritage
as an artistic and literary powerhouse. The whitewashed walls and tiled roofs of traditional vernacular architecture are reinterpreted as white facades framed in black
granite. Polygonal shapes inspired by historic gardens also feature.

Kindergarten of Jiading New Town, 2012   **Atelier Deshaus**
Hongde Road, Jiading District, Shanghai ●
This inward-facing kindergarten is formed of a pair of long buildings connected via
an internal atrium. Each wing is clad to reflect different functions: the solid north
facade of cast concrete contrasts with the south volume, which is covered by polycarbonate panels, animated by clusters of small windows.

Poly Grand Theatre, 2014   **Tadao Ando Architect & Associates**
159 Baiyin Road, Jiading District, Shanghai ◑
Situated on an artificial lake northwest of central Shanghai, this theatre is notable for its five steel cylinders that dissect a concrete box encased in aluminium and glass. Arranged horizontally, vertically and diagonally, the cylinders create elliptical openings that function as terraces and semi-outdoor amphitheatres.

Green Pine Garden Club, 2005   **Scenic Architecture Office**
53 Qing Song Road, Qing District, Shanghai ◑
A sculptural facade of thin pine planks, in the form of a Japanese screen, is constructed over an existing concrete building, to conceal the air conditioning while ensuring privacy for the club and restaurant inside. A second building is also behind the screen, giving the appearance of a single unified structure.

Long Museum West Bund, 2014   **Atelier Deshaus**
3398 Longteng Avenue, Xuhui District, Shanghai ◑
This museum, which exhibits both antiquities and contemporary art, is a landmark
of the newly regenerated West Bund. In a nod to the area's industrial past, a 1950s
coal-unloading bridge sits untouched in the courtyard. On either side of the bridge,
two concrete columns curve towards each other, creating the illusion of an arch.

New Shanghai Theatre, 2016   **Neri & Hu**
1186 Fuxing Zhong Road, Shanghai ◑
Located on the site of a 1930s theatre, this extension offers theatregoers a series of
dramatic atriums, each of them different in configuration and lighting, owing partly
to the carefully placed apertures throughout. Built largely of stone, it also features
fluted bronze walls, suggestive of theatre curtains.

Natural History Museum, 2015   **Perkins+Will**
510 Beijing West Road, Jingan District, Shanghai ◑
Inspired by a nautilus shell, this eco-friendly museum spirals down six levels from the parkland roof of its living facade to enclose a 30m-high glass lobby. An interior cell-like structure of white lattice encircles a central pond, while its cascading terraces are reminiscent of a Chinese water garden.

Tomorrow Square, 2005   **John Portman & Associates**
399 Nanjing West Road, Huangpu District, Shanghai ●
Looming 285m above Nanjing, this glass and aluminium skyscraper rotates 45 degrees at the 37th floor, creating its distinctive form and reflecting the change of function between the apartments below and the hotel in the upper part. Culminating in a pincer-like apex, the four pointed corners encase a giant sphere.

Shanghai Tower, 2015   **Gensler**
479 Lujiazui Ring Road, Shanghai ⊙
It took just six years to top out the 632m of Gensler's twisting superstructure, which is distinctive for its double facade. The exterior layer rotates 120 degrees as it rises, while the spaces in-between form sky gardens, reached by lifts that cruise its 121 storeys at a speedy 65km per hour.

Oriental Sports Center, 2011   **gmp**
300 Yiyao Road, Pudong New Area, Shanghai ⊙
Perching on a man-made lake in former industrial brownfield land, this sports complex consists of three structures: a multi-use stadium hall, a natatorium with four pools, and a media centre. The structure makes use of 3,000 tons of steel and features broad arches, as well as triangular elements evocative of sails.

Asia

Zhujiajiao Museum, 2008　　　　　　　　　**Scenic Architecture Office**
36 Meizhou Road, Zhiuyiajiao, Shanghai ◑
At the entrance to an ancient canal town, this two-storey museum exhibits artworks relating to local history. Arranged around a central atrium, galleries on lower levels are hermetic and larger in scale. The upper level is organized as a series of small, individual 'houses' connected by stone paths, tiled courtyards and a reflecting pool.

Hangzhou Gateway, 2016　　　　　　　　　　　　　　　**JDS**
7 Yongfuqiao Road, Hangzhou, Zhejiang ◑
This 15-storey tower features offices, restaurants, a post office, a stepped roof garden recalling terraced rice-paddy fields, and a sunken passage that leads through a shopping centre. The rooftop terraces offer generous views to distant nature, while the stone louvres provide a sustainable alternative to office air conditioning.

Tea House Art Gallery, 2005 **Amateur Architecture Studio**
Shounanzhonglu, Yinzhou Park, Ningbo, Zhejiang ◑
One of five pavilions located in the Yinzhou Park, each serving a particular function,
this structure — housing a gallery — looks like a tent from a distance. The curved concrete roof blends with surroundings, while a traditional building method designed
to withstand local typhoons inspired the mud-brick and tile walls.

Tiantai Museum, 2003 **in+of**
Tiantai, Taizhou, Zhejiang ◑
The Tiantai Museum is an addition to a collection of mountain buildings dedicated
to the Tiantai Mountain sect of Buddhism. Arcade-like corridors connect three low,
horizontal structures, incorporating three interior courtyards. The design is spare
and simple, using local stone and echoing the natural surroundings.

Asia

Internet Café, Jinhua Architecture Park, 2007   **Ding Yi and Chen Shu Yu**
Qingzhao Road, Jindong District, Jinhua, Zhejiang ●
This pavilion is one of 17 set along a 2km-long ribbon of public parkland, commissioned and curated by Ai Weiwei. Created in honour of his father, the poet Ai Qing, the pavilions were designed by local and international architects in an effort to integrate ideas about the built environment from a foreign and national perspective.

Multifunctional Space, Jinhua Architecture Park, 2006   **Yung Ho Chang**
Qingzhao Road, Jindong District, Jinhua, Zhejiang ●
Clad with large-scale white paving tiles decorated with patterns drawn from historic Chinese gardens, this group of micro-pavilions ranges from a two-storey tower to a T-shaped shelter. Each structure acts as a small venue in its own right while also framing the central outdoor space, which is paved in black bricks.

Manager's Pavilion, Jinhua Architecture Park, 2007   **Buchner Bründler**
Qingzhao Road, Jindong District, Jinhua, Zhejiang ●
This pavilion serves as a home and office for the architecture park's on-site facilities manager, and also as an information centre for visitors. West and east wings contain the manager's private apartment and offices lead off from a central yard area lined with gravel and bamboo.

Museum of Neolithic Pottery, Jinhua Architecture Park, 2007   **FAKE Design**
Qingzhao Road, Jindong District, Jinhua, Zhejiang ●
Intended as a museum of ancient Chinese pottery, this windowless structure bridges a recessed ditch. Enveloped in austere poured concrete, the textured walls mimic woven bamboo. Within, an antechamber opens completely to the outside, with a small door leading into an exposed space.

Asia

Bridging Teahouse, Jinhua Architecture Park, 2003 **FR-EE**
Qingzhao Road, Jindong District, Jinhua, Zhejiang ●
This small building combines two staples of the traditional Chinese garden — a tea-house and a bridge — across an existing pond within the architecture park. Irregularly placed support columns provide the skeleton for interconnected spaces and shapes within the bridge's interior that act as separate rooms.

Reading Space, Jinhua Architecture Park, 2006 **Herzog & de Meuron**
Qingzhao Road, Jindong District, Jinhua, Zhejiang ●
The asymmetrical form of this pavilion is derived from a series of geometric shapes. Cast entirely in coloured concrete, the pavilion features a series of interlocking areas that recall archetypal spaces, such as benches, caves or tree houses, and form ideal places to explore or read.

Baby Dragon, Jinhua Architecture Park, 2006   **HHF**
Qingzhao Road, Jindong District, Jinhua, Zhejiang ●
Built from red concrete, this pavilion is composed of three volumes. Forming a permeable boundary between the open lawn and grove of trees behind, the walls are
punctured on both sides by irregular geometric shapes. These apertures create
spaces to look out from, shelves to sit on, or tunnels to climb through.

Tea House, Jinhua Architecture Park, 2006   **Jiakun**
Qingzhao Road, Jindong District, Jinhua, Zhejiang ●
Accessed by steel ladders, these elevated, glazed rooms reinvent the ancient tradition of Chinese tea houses and ceremonies. Scattered across the site, the translucent buildings have hinged wall panels that allow visitors to either sit in a protected
enclosed space, or to open the pavilion up to the elements.

Restaurant 13, Jinhua Architecture Park, 2007   Johan de Wachter
Qingzhao Road, Jindong District, Jinhua, Zhejiang ●
This multi-level restaurant pavilion is composed of platforms of various sizes and heights, suitable for different functions. The materials echo those of traditional Chinese hutongs, from stone dining tables and benches at ground level to rooms elevated on steel stilts and clad with bamboo and stone.

Multimedia Pavilion, Jinhua Architecture Park, 2007   Erhard An-He Kinzelbach
Qingzhao Road, Jindong District, Jinhua, Zhejiang ●
This small theatre is clad with small metallic tiles on its exterior and bamboo ply-wood inside. Its single continuous surface is sculpted using parametric modelling to form both external staircase seating that leads to a viewing terrace, and a viewing booth inside.

BookBar, Jinhua Architecture Park, 2007   **Michael Maltzan**
Qingzhao Road, Jindong District, Jinhua, Zhejiang ●
This structure was conceived as a space for reading, eating and contemplation, as well as housing a bookshop. The building, which is inspired by the relationship between books and architecture in Chinese history, is formed by a central wall that splits into two unequal, cantilevered wings.

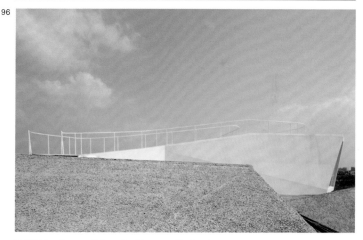

Exhibition Space, Jinhua Architecture Park, 2006   **Tatiana Bilbao**
Qingzhao Road, Jindong District, Jinhua, Zhejiang ●
Organized as a series of intersecting volumes, this space is designed to host conferences, lectures, exhibitions and small receptions. Contained in rugged, simple stone cladding, different zones are situated around a sunken plaza and straddled by a cantilevered concrete room with transparent glazing to each end.

Asia

Welcome Centre, Jinhua Architecture Park, 2005   **Till Schweizer**
Qingzhao Road, Jindong District, Jinhua, Zhejiang ●
An angular facade of wooden lattices distinguish this pavilion, which features a pair
of chunky concrete staircases. Intended as the entrance to the park, visitors can
ascend to a timber roof deck, which offers an elevated viewpoint to observe the low-
lying parkland and other pavilions beyond.

Newspaper Café, Jinhua Architecture Park, 2007   **Toshiko Mori**
Qingzhao Road, Jindong District, Jinhua, Zhejiang ●
This elongated structure comprises two levels: an enclosed ground floor and an
al fresco rooftop deck. The building's northern facade serves as a multifunctional
display case for newspapers, which, legible when standing up close, create a decorative pattern from a distance.

Asia

The Ceramic House, Jinhua Architecture Park, 2006   **Wang Shu**
Qingzhao Road, Jindong District, Jinhua, Zhejiang ●
Clad in hundreds of bands of colourful ceramic tiles, this rectangular structure is partially sunken into the site, and references a Song Dynasty inkstone. A café space is cantilevered above a small decorative pool. The building also has roof access, allowing for extensive views across the park.

Toilet, Jinhua Architecture Park, 2006   **Wang Xing Wei and Xu Tian Tian**
Qingzhao Road, Jindong District, Jinhua, Zhejiang ●
Maximizing privacy while minimising land use, these three cranked, extruded concrete structures form the toilet pavilion for the park. Simply constructed, each is punctuated by a single door, while its unglazed, exposed window is open to the elements, admitting ventilation and daylight, as well as framing views of the sky.

Mangrove West Coast, 2006 **Arquitectonica**
1 Shen Wan Yi Road, Shenzhen ●
Arranged around a large lagoon close to the China-Hong Kong border, an elbow-bend feature prevents these towers from blocking views. Two buildings jut into the water, a third emerges from the lagoon itself and bridged islands house recreational facilities.

Dafen Art Museum, 2007 **Urbanus**
Dafen Village, Longgang District, Shenzhen ◑
This three-level building is also a point of access to a school campus. Level one is an open space for local artisans to sell and promote their work. A grand staircase leads from a public plaza to gallery space on level two, while the building's flat roof provides open spaces for community use.

Shenzhen Software Industry Base, 2015   **gmp**
Xuefu Road, Nanshan District, Shenzhen ●
Comprising a total of 18 towers, this dense development consists of research, administration and service buildings for the growing local IT industry. Each building shares a uniform facade — grids of expressed metal mullions and transoms — and are connected by a series of elevated walkways, forming urban squares below.

Terminal 3, Shenzhen Bao'an International Airport, 2013   **Fuksas**
Bao'an District, Shenzhen ◑
Based on the form of a manta ray in plan, this airport terminal is enveloped by a curving steel-and-glass roof canopy, pierced by thousands of hexagonal skylights that filter daylight into the structure. Inside, distinctive conical white columns rise through the triple-storey building and support the arching roof.

Asia

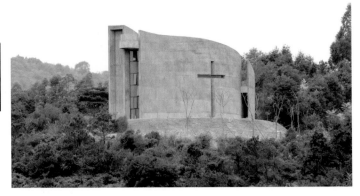

Church of Seed, 2011   **O Studio**
Luofu Mountain, Huizhou, Guangdong ◑
Situated atop sacred Mount Luofu, this Christian place of worship is also a recrea-
tion hub for locals. Wrapped with three curved concrete walls cast in-situ, the plan
emulates an abstract seed husk and forms a central hall flanked by basic amenities.
Its terraced roof rises from 3 to 12m, and includes a viewing platform.

Guangzhou International Finance Centre, 2010   **WilkinsonEyre**
5 Zhujiang West Road, Zhujiang New Town, Guangzhou ●
Standing 103 storeys high, this centre's tapered crystalline form is one of China's tallest buildings and contains offices, a luxury hotel, bars and restaurants. The triangular
plan reflects efficient internal layouts with central circulation cores that give way to
a dramatic atrium rising from the 70th-floor sky lobby.

Guangzhou Opera House, 2010   **Zaha Hadid**
1 Zhujiang West Road, Tianhe District, Guangzhou ◑
These two boulder-like structures — shaped to resemble two pebbles on the bank of
the Pearl River — are clad in glass and granite and house an 1,800-seat theatre plus
a 400-seat multifunctional hall, rehearsal rooms and entrance hall. Inside, the multi-
faceted skin provides a dramatic visual backdrop to ravine-like walkways.

Canton Tower, 2010   **Information Based Architecture**
Yiyuan Road, Haizhu District, Guangzhou ●
Soaring 600m, this multi-purpose observation tower is currently the tallest structure in China. As complex as it is tall, the twisting steel lattice seems to turn around
on itself, with columns starting on one side and finishing on another, while the overall shape narrows into a tight waist before opening up once more at the top.

Luyeyuan Stone Sculpture Museum, 2004   **Jiakun**
Yunqiao, Pidu District, Chengdu, Sichuan ◑
Surrounded by fields and groves of wild bamboo, this two-storey museum of Buddhist artefacts is reached via a winding sculpture trail. Visitors enter at the upper level from a footbridge above a lotus pond. Rooflights, narrow windows and daylight reflecting off outdoor ponds are all carefully calibrated to highlight the collection.

Qingcheng Mountain Teahouse, 2007   **Standardarchitecture**
Qingcheng Xinlijiang, Daguan, Dujiangyan District, Chengdu, Sichuan ◑
Sitting alongside a small pond at the foot of Qingcheng Mountain in Sichuan province, this teahouse is planned as five separate courtyard buildings that are huddled tightly together and separated by narrow, alley-like spaces passing through the building from north to south.

Asia

Museum of Cultural Revolution, 2008 Jiakun
Anren, Dayi, Chengdu, Sichuan ◑
Constructed over the historic town of Anren, and forming part of the Jianchuan Museum Cluster, these three brick-clad buildings are connected by a bridge corridor that spans existing streets. They house a collection of objects from recent Chinese history in circular or square rooms, spacious halls and an amphitheatre.

Lhasa Railway Station, 2006 CAG
Liu Wu Village, Stod Lung Bde, Chen Rdzong County, Lhasa, Tibet ◑
The Qinghai-Tibet railway line terminates at this palace-like structure, which is characterized by heavy walls that appear to lean in towards the grand, central entrance. Five passenger trains stop at this station each day. Thin air at such a high altitude mean walking distances must be kept short.

Ordos Museum, 2011   **MAD**
Minzu Road, Ejin Horo, Ordos, Inner Mongolia ◐
This museum is designed to recall the dunes of the Gobi Desert nearby. Clad in polished metal panels — a defensive strategy against the harsh climate — it is arranged over four storeys. The interior is organized around a lofty atrium that links the two entrances, and galleries are connected across this void by glazed sky bridges.

Jockey Club Innovation Tower, 2014   **Zaha Hadid**
Hung Hom, Hong Kong ●
At 15 storeys high, Hong Kong Polytechnic's design school is the tallest structure on campus, its fluid lines converging in a jutting crest that evokes a beacon. The building also comprises a large entry foyer with room for exhibitions, and a near-porous exterior that layers glass-and-aluminium 'fins' to usher in natural light.

115

Kennedy Town Swimming Pool, 2017   **Farrells**
2 Sai Cheung Street North, Kennedy Town, Hong Kong ◑
The distinctive triangle shape of this swimming pool complex is a result of the limitations of its site — a former car park constrained by historic tramlines. There is a large opening in its zinc-clad roof that affords swimmers panoramic views of Victoria Harbour. The complex is complemented by a landscaped outdoor garden.

116

Bank of China Tower, 1990   **IM Pei**
1 Garden Road, Central, Hong Kong ●
Despite its famously bad feng shui, having been built on a steep, sloping plot, this 72-storey tower stands out among the district's forest of skyscrapers. Given Hong Kong's position in a typhoon zone, it is designed to resist high-velocity winds via an ingenious composite structure system.

HKSAR Government Headquarters, 2011 **Rocco Design**
2 Tim Mei Avenue, Admiralty, Hong Kong ●
The HKSAR Government Headquarters is composed of two wings of offices joined at the top, creating a visual doorway that symbolizes the openness of the city. Running through this curtain-walled structure, and flanked by offices on either side, is the public Civic Park or 'Green Carpet' that connects the city to the waterfront.

Pacific Place, 2011 **Heatherwick Studio**
88 Queensway, Admiralty, Hong Kong ◑
Upgrading an ageing mall and office complex, this refurbishment includes updates of varied scales: from cast bronze lift buttons to sculptural timber bathroom doors. The greatest change occurs at podium level, where pyramidal skylights are replaced with patterned glass, creating a walkable surface that admits light to the mall below.

Tai Yip Office Building, 2002   **Denton Corker Marshall**
141–149 Thomson Road, Wan Chai, Hong Kong ●
From street level this skyscraper appears to consist of two needle towers of equal height supported by a Kahnian 'servant' core. In fact, the two eight sq m towers are different in height. The helix-like fenestration pattern is another surprise, its slenderness seeming almost organic.

HighCliff, 2003   **Dennis Lau and Ng Chun Man**
41d Stubbs Road, Hong Kong ●
Located on a slope in Happy Valley, this 73-storey apartment block is one of the tallest residential buildings in Hong Kong. It is 252m high and exceptionally narrow, with a slenderness ratio of 1:20. The self-proclaimed luxury accommodation features cherrywood flooring, Italian marble and German bathroom fittings.

Cyberport Retail and Office Building, 2003 **Arquitectonica**
100 Cyberport Road, Telegraph Bay, Hong Kong ●
This 25-hectare complex contains meeting rooms, multimedia laboratories, a cyber library, a fitness centre, cafés, lounges, bars and a retail-and-entertainment 'Cyber Centre'. The tonally varied, sharply angled dark-glass facades soften to timber flooring and sinuous bold red walls inside the building.

Hong Kong Design Institute, 2011 **CAAU**
3 King Ling Road, Tseung Kwan, Hong Kong ●
Built from concrete, glass and steel, this design institute features a massive 'sky city' platform that appears to float on four inner towers, wrapped in crisscrossing white latticework. A grass-covered podium underneath serves as an urban park, from which a 60m escalator provides access to the upper levels.

Water-Moon Monastery, 2012   **Artech**
112 Taipei City, Beitou District, Taipei ◐
Located on a tranquil site, this religious complex uses concrete and glass, as well as carefully placed natural elements like limestone and teak that reference Zen principles. Set in a lotus pond, the Grand Hall comprises a wooden box on a glazed base that appears to hover below a flat roof supported by 22 columns.

College of Social Sciences, 2013   **Toyo Ito & Associates**
National Taiwan University, 111 Taipei City, Shilin District, Taipei ●
This university faculty is a mammoth block that might feel claustrophobic were it not for irregular openings and a central void, which lends it a certain lightness. So too does the lotus-leaf design of the plaza and library's green roof, which blooms from 88 concrete 'roots'.

New Horizon, 2013 **Toyo Ito & Associates**
88 Yanchang Road, Xinyi District, Taipei ●
This centrepiece of Songshan Cultural and Creative Park accommodates shops, restaurants, a concert venue, cinemas and a hotel. Its curved, asymmetrically tiered form has a concrete grid facade with green, orange and red accents. The building's convex shape blocks out noise from the busy freeway behind.

Yuwen Library, 2012 **MAYU**
237 Yuxin Road, East District, Tainan ◑
This four-storey, mainly concrete construction is notable for its series of vertical wood louvres, which are representative of a row of books (the library itself can store 110,000 volumes). Inside, the combination of louvres and expansive glazing mean spaces are flooded with diffused natural light.

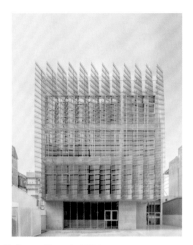

Tainan Tung-Men Holiness Church, 2015   **MAYU**
Deguang Street, East District, Tainan ◐
This church is mainly composed of cast concrete, balanced with the warm wood and copper colours used for the curved sanctuary ceiling, oak staircase and feather-like, perforated-aluminium screens of the main facade. A café and bookshop are at ground level, with a chapel and prayer rooms above.

Dadong Art Centre, 2012   **de Architekten Cie**
161 Guangyuan Road, Fengshan District, Kaohsiung ◐
This cultural centre includes a theatre, library and exhibition spaces, and is characterized by 11 huge funnels that weave through outdoor public areas. Offering protection from extreme cyclonic weather conditions, the tensile forms channel excess rain into concealed springs, or draw hot air up and away from the plaza.

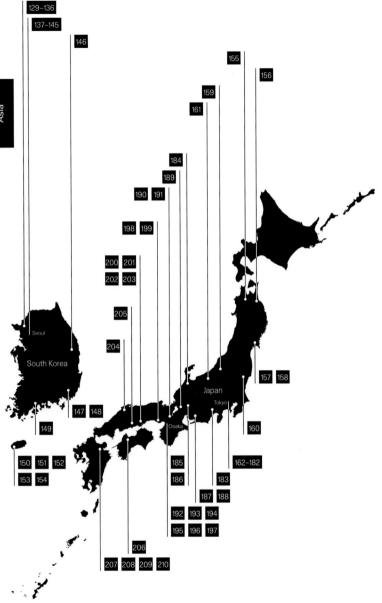

129–136

137–145

146

155

156

159

161

184

189

190 191

198 199

200 201

202 203

205

204

Seoul

South Korea

157 158

Japan

Tokyo

160

147 148

149

Osaka

150 151 152

153 154

162–182

185

186

183

187 188

192 193 194

195 196 197

206

207 208 209 210

White Block Gallery, 2012   **SsD**
Heyri Art Valley, Beopheung-ri, Tanhyeon-myeon ❶
Composed of opaque and transparent glazed boxes overlaid with a fog-like frit, this
cultural space and contemporary art gallery is the largest in the Heyri Art Valley.
The interior is divided into three volumes, with slender structural columns lining the
periphery. A central void contains stairs and bridges linking different spaces.

Jazz Hall and PoDjaGi Gallery, 2004   **Architecture Research Unit**
G39-2 Heyri Art Valley, Beopheung-ri, Tanhyeon-myeon ❶
Located near the demilitarized zone between North and South Korea, this building
contains a residence, a small jazz performance hall and art gallery space. A flat, box-
like concrete structure provides the base for two luminous pavilions, inspired by
tents and clad in translucent polycarbonate panels.

Dalki Theme Park, 2004 Ga.A
1652.69 Heyri Art Valley, Beopheung-ri, Tanhyeon-myeon ◐
As imaginative as the children's character it represents, the bulk of this building rests on concrete columns, appearing to float above the playground beaneath. Moss-like panels on the building's side enable it to merge it with the landscape, while a sloping hill leads to the roof.

Munhakdongne Publishers Office Building, 2003 KYWC
513-8 Paju Book City, Munbai-ri, Gyoha-eup, Paju ●
This five-storey building appears as a combination of stacked volumes containing a conference room in a glass box on one corner, and offices and common areas on middle and upper floors. The building's exterior is clad in rust-red Corten steel and reflective, copper panels.

Open Books Publishing Company, 2005 **Himma Studio**
521-2 Paju Book City, Munbai-ri, Gyoha-eup, Paju ➊
One of the landmark buildings in Paju Book City, the building's shape, with long continuous horizontal bands of windows, and the sloping angles of its concrete planes, gives this three-storey structure an animated energy. Concrete walls, formed of folded surfaces, enclose staircases.

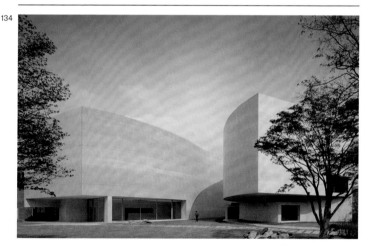

Mimesis Museum, 2009 **Álvaro Siza Vieira**
521-2 Paju Book City, Munbai-ri, Gyoha-eup, Paju ➊
This museum, based on a sketch of a cat drawn by the architect on a site visit, is an undulating, pale-grey concrete three-storey structure. Inside, its L-shaped form incorporates a café, staff area and gallery spaces, and uses a palette of marble and timber floors with whitewashed walls and ceilings.

Dul-Nyouk Publishers, 2005   **Alejandro Zaera-Polo**
513-9 Paju Book City, Munbai-ri, Gyoha-eup, Paju ●
This building is designed as a folded concrete screen that alternately defines the wall and floor plates. Timber lines these folded spaces, and is expressed as floors inside the building and a richly textured angular timber cladding on the south facade, which gives the structure a striking silhouette.

Two Moon, 2015   **Moon Hoon**
47 Jungsan-dong, Ilsandong-gu, Goyang-si, Gyeonggi-do ●
Reacting to the client's commission for two buildings — one for him, and the other for his brother — these buildings were conceived as a pair. Their cast-concrete facades are imprinted with a huge sphere, creating two crescent-moon shapes. The first structure contains a gallery and office spaces, while its twin includes a café.

Trutec Office Building, 2006   **Barkow Leibinger**
Digital Media City, Sangam-dong, Mapo-gu, Seoul ●
Modelling software was used to create this building's unique mirrored-glass skin
that is comprised of modular panels, many of which are indented while others protrude. Some panels are transparent, while others are translucent or inverted. The
collective effect is of a kaleidoscopic reflection of the surrounding city.

Kukje Gallery—K3, 2012   **SO–IL**
54 Samcheong-ro, Samcheong-dong, Jongno-gu, Seoul ◑
Responding to the historic urban fabric, the architects created a modest, rectilinear gallery and public plaza with an underground auditorium, storage and offices.
A strong yet pliable stainless-steel mesh is draped over the entire building like
chainmail, revealing its contours while providing protection.

Asia

Papertainer Museum, 2006   **Shigeru Ban**
62-35 Jangchung-dong, Jung-gu, Seoul ◑
This building takes the shape of the letter D in plan view. Divided into two parts, the museum accommodates a Container Gallery (the front part of the pavilion), offices, and a sculpture and café courtyard. Each wall is made in a chequerboard composition using shipping containers.

Ann Demeulemeester Retail Store, 2007   **Mass Studies**
650-14 Sinsa-dong, Gangnam-gu, Seoul ◑
The ground-floor entrance leads to the Ann Demeulemeester shop, with a second-floor restaurant and basement-level retail space accessed from across a concrete courtyard, via street-level stairs. The entire building is clad in sod, this living green carpet neatly framing flowing panes of glass.

House of Dior, 2015   **Christian de Portzamparc**
464 Apgujeong-ro, Cheongdam-dong, Gangnam-gu, Seoul ◑
Inspired by the couture garments of this luxury fashion house, the architects created a boutique, gallery and café draped in moulded fibreglass panels. Rising 20m, the shells billow in irregular shapes as they curl around the corner site. A narrow split marks the arched entry, shaped by perforated aluminium.

Chungha Building, 2013   **MVRDV**
Cheongdam-dong, Gangnam-gu, Seoul ◑
This refurbishment of an existing store creates over-scaled 'shop windows' for the tenants. Each of the storey-height glass apertures is delineated by curvaceous concrete frames, tiled with white mosaics. The character of individual tenants is reflected on the facade — from luxury goods to plastic surgery.

Dogok Maximum, 2016   **Moon Hoon**
Dogok-dong, Gangnam-gu, Seoul ●
Occupying a narrow urban site, this combined studio and private residence for a
photographer and his mother makes maximum use of its small footprint. Culminating in a five-storey-high peak, its concrete facade is incised with diagonal patterns,
interrupted by angular windows that admit light without compromising privacy.

Seoul National University Museum, 2005   **OMA**
1 Gwanak-ro, Gwanak-gu, Seoul ◑
A large glass-and-steel box balances dramatically over the central concrete core of
this three-level contemporary art museum. At opposite ends of the building, auditoriums have gently sloped floors, and a staircase inside the core leads to ground and
basement-level offices.

Transportation Centre, Incheon International Airport, 2002   **Terry Farrell**
272 Gonghang-ro, Jung-gu, Incheon ◑
Symbolizing native culture and flight, the steel-portal-truss roof structure of this three-rail-network interchange is designed to resemble a flying crane — a sacred bird to the Korean people. Built on a reclaimed island, it is a point of orientation for the New Seoul International Airport complex.

Moon Hoon, 2010   **Moon Hoon**
2188 Punggok-gil, Hwaam-myeon, Jeongseon, Gangwon-do ●
Providing accommodation for an amateur rock band leader, this playful collection of six small holiday units draws on various references: from cars and aeroplanes to Spanish bulls. Set atop a dry riverbed, the individual theme of each guesthouse continues in the interiors, which are equally non-conformist.

Asia

Busan Cinema Centre, 2011   **Coop Himmelb(l)au**
1467 U-1 Dong Haeundae-gu, Busan ◑
Serving as the site for the Busan International Film Festival, this cinema complex features a 'red carpet' zone and a 4,000-capacity outdoor cinema, alongside a range of indoor cinemas and production studios. An enormous cantilevered roof, decorated with LED lighting, hangs above a series of connected public plazas.

Xi Gallery, 2007   **Mass Studies**
1123-1 Yonsan-dong, Busan ◑
A chipped corner — derived from floors gradually merging inside — appears to cantilever the entrance of this showcase for model homes, which also incorporates a gallery and performance space. The building is clad with mostly translucent materials and, at night, coloured lights illuminate this skin from within.

Bae Bien-u Photography Studio, 2001   **The System Lab**
38 Yeong-dong, Suncheon-si, Jeollanam-do ●
A partly external staircase wraps itself up this four-storey building, allowing access to the art gallery, residential floor and rooftop. The textured concrete (a rare sight in the local area) encompassing the building resembles planks of wood, chosen to be in tune with the use of pine throughout the interior.

Water Museum, 2005   **Itami Jun**
108b Sangcheon-ri, Andeok-myeon, Namjeju-gun, Cheju ◑
Constructed out of local Jeju stone and concrete, this oval building with a large eliptical opening above, encloses a shallow, sky-reflecting pool for contemplating the fluid qualities of water. Sculptural rough-stone objects sit around the pool, serving as benches for visitors.

Podo Hotel, 2001   Itami Jun
San 62-3 Sangcheon-ri, Andeok-myeon, Namjeju-gun, Cheju ☽
This resort complex, inspired by its mountainous surrounds, is a low-lying, single-storey structure. A rippling bubble-like roof complements the distinctive outline of volcanic hills, while a central passageway winds its way through the restaurant, karaoke and guest rooms inside.

Duson Museum, 2006   Itami Jun
815-8 Sangcheon-ri, Andeok-myeon, Namjeju-gun, Cheju ☽
The museum's combination of smooth, shiny bands of glazing and angular form creates a dramatic contrast to its natural surroundings. Inside, a black-coated steel shell encloses the main exhibition hall, which sits underground, creating a cavernous, cathedral-like effect.

Stone Museum, 2005   **Itami Jun**
123b Sangcheon-ri, Andeok-myeon, Namjeju-gun, Cheju ◑
This simple rectangular box, made from Corten steel, houses stone sculptures of
varying sizes. Strategically placed windows filter light to the dark, polished-steel-
floored interior. A floor-level window lights low-lying stone pieces and a cylindrical
opening focuses a beam of sunlight into the heart of the building.

Wind Museum, 2005   **Itami Jun**
123b Sangcheon-ri, Andeok-myeon, Namjeju-gun, Cheju ◑
This long, pitch-roofed, timber building with overhanging eaves blends seamlessly
into this museum's surroundings. One arching wall has specially designed gaps between the wooden planks, allowing the wind to pass through and produce a variety
of sounds. Sound and light filtering into the interior create myriad sensations.

Asia

Aomori Contemporary Art Centre, 2001   Tadao Ando Architect & Associates
152-6 Goshizawa, Yamazaki, Aomori ◑
The rectangular Creativity and Accommodation blocks and the horseshoe-shaped
Display building, with its gallery and outdoor rooftop stage, sit below steel-framed
reinforced concrete flat roofs, designed to render the low-lying centre invisible in
the densely wooded landscape.

Towada Art Center, 2008   Ryue Nishizawa
10-9 Nishi-Nibancho, Towada-shi, Aomori ◑
This contemporary art museum and cultural complex was designed to revitalize the
city of Towada. Gallery spaces have been divided into separate entities and distributed throughout the site, and are connected by curving transparent passageways.
Large glazed facades present the artwork to passersby.

Kanno Museum of Art, 2005 **Atelier Hitoshi Abe**
3-4-15 Tamagawa Shogama Miyagi, Shiogama, Sendai, Miyagi ❶
Perched high on a grassy plateau, this art museum's vantage point affords views towards the Pacific Ocean. Corten steel plates, embossed with a regular dimpled pattern, clad its boxy form. Inside, steel steps descend through a spiralling cluster of faceted, irregularly shaped galleries, which hold the museums collections.

Sendai Multimedia Centre, 2000 **Toyo Ito & Associates**
2-1 Kasuga-machi, Sendai, Miyagi ❶
This public facility combines a library with seminar, exhibition and meeting spaces. Groups of tilting steel columns arranged around reinforced circular openings provide structural tubes that organize the building and allow light to enter from above. Larger tubes accommodate lift shafts and staircases.

Asia

Matsudai Small Tower, 2003   **Marin + Trottin and Peripheriques**
Matsudai, Niigata ○
Erected for the Tsumari Art Triennale, this three-storey galvanized-steel lattice
structure has an open base to allow people and animals to wander through freely,
and two enclosed middle levels accessed by a switchback staircase. An additional
roof terrace may be used by campers.

Museum of Hiroshige Ando, 2000   **Kengo Kuma & Associates**
116-9 Bato, Nasu, Tochigi ◑
Referencing the Hiroshige woodblock print *Travellers Surprised by Sudden Rain*, in
which a cloudburst is portrayed as a series of very fine lines, the architect has at-
tempted to create this entire museum from individual sticks of cedarwood. Its long
slatted walls reinforce the importance of nature in Hiroshige's artwork.

Triad, 2002　　　　　　　　　　　　　　　**Maki & Associates**
1856-1 Maki, Hotaka-machi, Minamiazumi-gun, Matsumoto, Nagano ◐
This gallery is composed of three buildings for the Harmonic Drive Company. Each structure reflects its function, including the exhibition space, which is scaled specifically to fit the owner's artworks. The stainless-steel shell of the research centre provides a double-height space to develop the company's precision instruments.

Saitama Shin-Toshin Station, 2000　　　　**Edward Suzuki Associates**
57-3, 4-chome Kishiki-cho, Ohmiya-ku, Saitama ◐
The main part of the station sits under a skewed, barrel-vaulted space with cross-ventilation and natural sunlight. The most distinctive feature of the station is its roof, which is made from corrugated metal sheets that extend along the full length of the platforms, undulating in a singular gesture.

Tomihiro Art Museum, 2004   **AAT+Makoto Yokomizo**
Kusaki, Azuma-Cho, Midori, Gunma ◑
This museum's plan was designed to promote freedom of movement, with 33 circular rooms contained within a single-storey square box. With no sequential routes through the building, visitors move randomly through the linked circular spaces, their progress drawing parallels with the way that soap bubbles collide.

Yokohama International Port Terminal, 2002   **FOA**
1-1-4 Kaigan-dori, Yokohama, Kanagawa ◑
This structure appears like an extension of the land behind it. With its uninterrupted timber decking and ramps stitching the upper and lower levels together, the transition from inside to outside is gradual. Folded steel grids provide structural integrity to withstand seismic activity.

Tama Art University Library, 2007   **Toyo Ito & Associates**
Hachioji Campus, 2-1723 Yarimizu, Hachioji, Tokyo ◑
Structural arches of differing widths characterize the facades of this facility, providing large windows. The concrete-encased steel structure is arranged in a loose
grid and the arches continue throughout, supporting the floors of the library and
influencing the internal layout.

Murai Masanari Art Museum, 2004   **Kengo Kuma & Associates**
1-6-12 Naka-machi, Setagaya, Tokyo ●
This museum once exhibited the work of the late Murai Masanari, housing a gallery,
his actual studio and its contents just as he left them. The studio's original exterior
timbers were reassembled as louvres on the new facade creating a lattice-like effect, and the studio is tucked away at the back of the L-shaped exhibition hall.

Za-Koenji Public Theatre, 2009　　　　　　　　**Toyo Ito & Associates**
2-1-2 Koenji-kita, Suginami-ku, Tokyo ◑
Toyo Ito's concept of 'an enclosed tent or playhouse' as a home for performing arts is unapologetically dramatic. The meteor-like concrete construction is punctured by myriad portholes that emit an otherworldly glow at night. Three levels both above and below ground house an auditorium, civic hall, studio theatre and café.

Tokyo Senju Campus, 2012　　　　　　　　**Maki & Associates**
Tokyo Denki University, Adachi-ku Senjuasahicho 5, Tokyo ●
Commemorating the centenary of Denki University, this new campus is designed around a low-rise agora — a large public square. The materials used — timber, metal and concrete, as well as transparent and ceramic-printed glass — relate to design elements and the scale of neighbouring low-rise buildings.

Sumidai Hokusai Museum, 2017   **Kazuyo Sejima**
2-7-2 Kamezawa, Sumida-ku, Tokyo ◑
Built to honour the ukiyo-e woodblock master Katsushika Hokusai, this museum
houses more than 1,800 works. Deep cut-aways, sharp angles and a reflective
facade give the aluminium-clad museum a levity, and although it is not remotely
similar to its neighbours, it harmonizes surprisingly well.

Mikimoto Ginza 2, 2005   **Toyo Ito & Associates**
2-4-12 Ginza, Chuo-ku, Tokyo ◑
This nine-storey, light-pink building accomodates a luxury retailer. The windows,
each with curved corners, disregard the rhythm of the interior space. At times, the
windows expose the floor slab as one window stretches between floors, or wraps
around a corner — as it does on the street level, providing display case.

Dear Ginza, 2013 **Amano Design Office**
6-8 Ginza, Chuo-ku, Ginza, Tokyo ◑
Built in a difficult backstreet location, this tower nevertheless has real presence.
Nine stories tall, it stands out from its bland neighbouring buildings thanks to a double skin of an inner glazed curtain wall and punched-aluminium panels that up-close
form a floral pattern, calling to mind a giant crumpled sweet wrapper.

Tokyo Plaza Ginza, 2016 **Nikken Sekkei**
5-2-1 Ginza, Chuo-ku, Ginza, Tokyo ◑
The facade of this 13-storey mall is made of triangular panes of tinted glass, cut using
the technique 'Edo Kiriko', which gives the building a contemporary feel in this trendy
part of town. Taking up an entire block, this creates a large 3D diamond-shaped
pattern that reflects the surroundings.

Nicolas G Heyak Centre, 2007   **Shigeru Ban**
7-9-18 Ginza, Chuo-ku, Tokyo ◑
This variation on a traditional shopping arcade houses a range of luxury boutiques. Its four-storey-high retractable glazed shutters reveal an internal arcade that stretches from the main shopping street to the back street behind, and oversized glass lifts act as moving showrooms.

Dentsu Office Tower, 2002   **Atelier Jean Nouvel**
1-8-1 Higashi-shimbashi, Minato-ku, Tokyo ●
A facade of subtly graded grey glass panels and a crescent-shaped plan mean that this 50-storey skyscraper appears almost weightless, despite having a massive, earthquake-proof internal steel structure. They also give the tower an elusive presence, constantly changing depending on the angle of view.

Nezu Museum, 2009   **Kengo Kuma & Associates**
6-1 Minami-aoyama, Minato-ku, Tokyo ◑
Like the traditional tori gates that lead to a shrine, this low-slung building was designed as a symbolic gateway. This is clearly evident in the live bamboo wall that
encompasses the museum, while the traditional pitched Japanese roof, made of
charcoal-coloured ceramic tiles, creates a large canopy over the outer walkways.

SunnyHills, 2013   **Kengo Kuma & Associates**
3-10-20 Minami-aoyama, Minato-ku, Tokyo ◑
The design for this cake shop, an intricate lattice of Japanese cypresswood, was
inspired by the notion of creating a forest in the city. The three-storey building resembles a woven bamboo basket and was assembled without using glue or nails
— any screws on show are purely for aesthetic reasons.

Miu Miu Aoyama Store, 2015   **Herzog & de Meuron**
3-17-8 Aoyama Minato-ku, Minamia-oyama, 3-17 Minami, Tokyo ◑
This two-storey boutique for luxury brand Miu Miu is distinguished by its arresting steel facade. Angled away from the storefront as if sliced by a knife, the over-scaled metal awning shades the interior. The awning's underside is clad with textural copper — a material that is repeated on wall finishes inside.

TOD'S Omotesando, 2004   **Toyo Ito & Associates**
Omotesando Boulevard, 5-1-5 Jingumae, Shibuya-ku, Tokyo ◑
The design for TOD'S Tokyo branch takes its cue from the Zelkova trees outside, by implementing an abstract tree graphic, doubling as a branch-like structure for the skin of the building. A thin wall system of concrete, inlaid with frameless glass and several opaque panels, supports the floors.

Christian Dior Building Omotesando, 2003   **SANAA**
5-9-11 Jingumae, Omotesando, Tokyo ◑
Christian Dior's flagship Tokyo store sits prominently on the fashionable Omotesando Boulevard. Layers of transparent flat glass and translucent, undulating acrylic screen compose this otherwise simple rectangular volume, allowing the interiors to be on nearly full display to the street.

hhstyle Retail Store, 2005   **Tadao Ando Architect & Associates**
14-3 Jingumae, Shibuya-ku, Tokyo ◑
A folded black steel shell hides this project's complex interior, which is defined by a series of platforms placed at intermediate floor heights. A concrete frame supports the main staircase and the steel skin of the building. The starkly minimalist entrance, a horizontal window and rooflights provide the only exterior features.

Asia

Gyre Shopping Centre Omotesando, 2007　　　　　　　**MVRDV**
5-10-1 Jingumae, Shibuya-ku, Tokyo ◑
This shopping mall combines high-profile retail space with galleries, dining and
catering facilities. Cloaked with shiny, dark tiles, the arcade's floors shift and project out at different angles from each other, providing terraces for dining. Extensive
glazed areas allow passers-by on the street to see inside.

182

Undercover Lab Studio and Showroom, 2001　　　　　　**Klein Dytham**
Jingumae Harajuku, Tokyo ●
This fashion design building occupies a compact site at the end of a narrow lane.
A long, timber-clad showroom adjoins a three-storey brick studio building before
cantilevering over the driveway below. A metal staircase rises through a glazed
circulation spine, linking warehouse, studio and showroom.

Kionji Temple, 2012   **Waro Kishi + K Associates**
2-10-6 Yamamoto-naka, Takarazuka, Hyogo ◑
Organized in a cross-shaped plan, this Zen temple unites three functions: the temple stretches west, crowned by a peaked wooden-shell roof, and the reception hall extends to the east. Perpendicular to the junction of the halls, a two-storey building houses the monks' quarters.

21st Century Museum of Contemporary Art Kanazawa, 2004   **SANAA**
1-2-1 Hirosaka, Kanazawa City, Ishikawa ◑
Linked by free-flowing circulation space with no set route, the different shaped galleries operate as independent chambers within a unifying circular form. Four fully glazed courtyards sit informally within a round glass perimeter that looks out to the surrounding urban area.

Meiso no Mori Crematorium, 2006　　　　　　　　**Toyo Ito & Associates**
Kakamigahara, Gifu ●
This two-storey crematorium is situated between a small body of water and a wood-ed slope. The thin concrete roof, a continuous plane integrating rainwater drainage, touches the ground at 12 points, where it transforms into conical columns. The funeral hall takes its name from the Japanese words for 'forest of meditation'.

Museum of Modern Ceramic Art, 2002　　　　　　**Arata Isozaki & Associates**
4-2-5 Higashi-machi, Tajimi-shi, Gifu ◑
In a nation with the largest number of ceramics museums in the world, this partly sunken building houses an exhibition and conference hall as well as displays from its extensive collection. Lakeside Japanese tea rooms, a roof plaza and an observa-tory for enjoying the mountain scenery complete the attractions.

187

Kaisho Forest 'View Tube', 2005 — **Atsushi Kitagawara**

304-1 Yoshino-machi, Seto, Aichi ◑

This watchtower explores sustainability in its construction: sections of its wooden lattice are made of forest thinnings and its small sections are light enough to be transported easily and assembled without machinery. Each joint is designed to give the tower the elasticity to withstand earthquakes.

188

Clover House, 2015 — **MAD**

5-6-6 Hishida Fukuokacho, Okazaki-shi, Aichi ●

This project transforms a traditional two-storey timber-framed Japanese dwelling into a contemporary kindergarten. The exterior has been clad in a shingled white asphalt skin. Irregular-shaped windows puncture the skin and a slide links the second floor to an outdoor playground.

Asia

Slowtecture S Cultural Centre, 2002   **Shuhei Endo**
688-10 Samegi, Maihara-cho, Shiga ⓞ
A corroding steel skin is stretched over this linear cultural centre, which houses
ground-floor shops and upper-level training facilities, and is pierced by a protruding
glass-and-steel shard at one end. This corrugated weatherproof skin is intended to
weather and rust, forming a protective coating in the process.

Sfera Building, 2003   **Claesson Koivisto Rune**
17 Benzaiten-cho, Kyoto ⓞ
Set among traditional wood buildings, this complex is cloaked in a titanium facade
perforated with a cherry-blossom-leaf pattern by Markus Moström — a nod to classic Japanese screens. A three-storey high atrium creates a feeling of cohesiveness
between the centre's galleries, shops, cafés and restaurants.

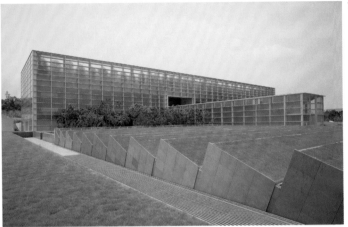

Kansai-kan National Diet Library, 2002   **Fumio Toki Associates**
8-1-3 Seikadai, Seika-cho, Soraku-gun, Kyoto ◑
The entrance to this extension to the National Diet (Parliament) Library is marked by a waterfall and path running parallel to the grass-covered, serrated rooflights that illuminate the reading room below ground. The 20 million volume collection of books and other media is housed in climate-controlled subterranean stacks.

Shiba Ryotaro Memorial Museum, 2001   **Tadao Ando Architect & Associates**
3-11-18 Shimokosaka, Higashi-osaka, Osaka ◑
Incorporating the private library of Shiba Ryotaro, a twentieth-century novelist, this museum is a crescent-shaped glazed volume around a wall of reinforced concrete. The books are stacked on floor-to-ceiling Japanese oak shelves. The panes of glass are arranged in a Mondrian-esque design.

Asahi Broadcasting Corporation, 2008   **Kengo Kuma & Associates**
1-30 Fukushima Itchome, Fukushima-ku, Osaka ◗
Housing the headquarters of the Asahi Broadcasting Corporation, this waterfront building is dramatic, accessible and sustainable. Its chequered reconstituted-timber facade evokes an old Japanese puzzle box. A grand open-air staircase guides visitors through the heart of the structure and on to a riverside deck.

Organic Building, 1993   **Gaetano Pesce**
9-3 Minamisenba, Osaka ●
This building responds to the lack of green space in densely packed Osaka. Its facade is composed of terracotta-hued steel-encased concrete panels that support a series of jumbo pot plants — altogether over 80 different types of indigenous plants and trees are featured.

Asia

Abeno Harukas, 2014　　　　　　　　　　　　　　**Pelli Clarke Pelli**
1-1-43 Abenosuji, Abeno-ku, Osaka ◐
At 300m tall, this skyscraper is currently Japan's tallest, exceeding the Landmark
Tower in Yokohama by 4m. The tiered high-rise, wrapped in glass and steel, houses
a mixed-use complex that includes a department store, a modern art museum,
a 360-room hotel and a two-level sky garden observation deck.

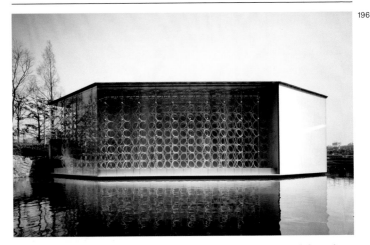

White Chapel, 2006　　　　　　　　　　　　　　**Jun Aoki & Associates**
1-13-11 Nanko-kita, Suminoe-ku, Osaka ◐
Reserved for wedding ceremonies, this white marble chapel sits within the pond of
a hotel garden. Accessed by a bridge, its perimeter is an elongated, irregular polygon. The marble-floored triangular interior has fabric screens that filter ambient
light, and a wall of connected steel rings.

Sayamaike Historical Museum, 2001 **Tadao Ando Architect & Associates**
2 Ikejirinaka, Osakasayama-shi, Osaka ◑
A historical exhibition related to the adjoining irrigation pond, this austere concrete edifice conveys the elemental power of water, introducing visitors, via a dramatic switchback ramp, to a central pool. Cascades of falling water diffuse the light entering the exhibition rooms below.

Setre Chapel, 2005 **Ryuichi Ashizawa & Associates**
11-1 Kaigandouri, Tarumiku, Kobe, Hyogo ◑
This white concrete structure emerges from the landscape to provide a wedding chapel for the adjacent hotel. An entirely glazed western facade heads a 5m cantilever — which faces the Kobe Sea — over surrounding gardens, and floods the chapel with light.

Akashi Ferry Terminal, 2003   **Waro Kishi + K Associates**
2-10-1 Hon-machi, Akashi-shi, Hyogo ◑
Clad in dark metal, this low, box-like terminal building connects to the departure gate by a narrow glazed passageway. A cross-shaped rooflight centred on a shallow dome provides the waiting lounge's focal point and acts as a sundial, casting crisp beams of light onto the floor.

Teshima Art Museum, 2010   **Ryue Nishizawa**
607 Karato, Teshima, Tonosho-cho, Shozu-gun, Kagawa ◑
This musuem stands on a hill overlooking the Seto Inland Sea, and is located in the corner of a rice terrace that was restored in collaboration with local residents. The building consists of a simple concrete shell, devoid of pillars. Two oval openings in the shell allow wind, sounds and daylight into this organic space.

Teshima Yokoo House, 2013 **Yuko Nagayama & Associates**
2359 Ieura, Teshima, Tonosho-cho, Shozu-gun, Kagawa ●
A collaboration with the artist Tadanori Yokoo, this art museum is housed in a series of remodelled single-storey timber houses. Composed of three galleries and a waterfall tower installation, all linked by a colourful stone garden, the complex's use of coloured glass and mirrors alter the visitor's spatial and chromatic perceptions.

Chichu Art Museum, 2004 **Tadao Ando Architect & Associates**
3449-1 Naoshima, Kagawa ◑
Carved into the scrubby coastal terrain, each subterranean gallery focuses on one of three artists: Claude Monet, James Turrell or Walter De Maria, with anterooms and corridors tying them together. Some halls are open-air, such as the entrance forecourt and the prismatic core of the building.

Inujima Seirensho Art Museum, 2008   **Sambuichi**
327 Inujima, Higashi-ku, Okayama-shi, Okayama ◑
On the island of Inujima, this art museum was converted from a copper refinery dating
from the early twentieth century. Much of the original structure has remained intact,
with discarded local granite and bricks being re-used to construct the interior. Solar
and geothermal energies power the building.

Shimane Museum of Ancient Izumo, 2006   **Maki & Associates**
99-4 Kizuki-higashi, Taisha-cho, Izumo, Shimane ◑
This museum houses workshops, galleries and exhibition space. Symbolizing the
passage from new to old, a large angular-roofed building displaying archaeological
artefacts is reached via a passageway running alongside a Corten steel wall, sepa-
rating it from the three-storey glass entrance hall.

Island City Central Park, 2005　　　　　　　　**Toyo Ito & Associates**
4-chome, Kashiiteriha, Higashi-ku, Fukuoka ⦿
This environmental research facility is located on an island of reclaimed land. Reinforced concrete shell-like structures, covered in landscaping, offer environments for different vegetation. Timber boardwalks wend their way across the roofs and lead to lush greenhouse areas beneath.

206

Komyo-ji Temple, 2000　　　　　　　　**Tadao Ando Architect & Associates**
550 Omachi, Saijo-shi, Ehime ⦿
Consisting of a large space with three layers of interlocking beams, this reconstruction of a 250-year-old shrine appears to float. Its laminated timber framework is a conscious effort to re-examine the origins of wooden building techniques, without slavishly copying the original structure.

Tenjin Minami Subway Station, 2005   **Shoei Yoh**
Fukuoka City Subway Nanakuma Line, Fukuoka 810 ◑
At street level, two groups of white cylindrical columns support a long tensegrity canopy via a system of cables. Folded planes of a self-cleaning laminated glass hang from the canopy that marks this subway station's entrance. Inside, clean lines and dramatic lighting lend a cool, contemporary flair.

Oita Prefectural Art Museum, 2010   **Shigeru Ban**
2-1 Kotobuki-machi, Oita ◑
This museum and cultural centre follows a simple, rectangular plan and is designed to welcome passers-by as well as art enthusiasts. The double-height atrium's street facade is clad in large-scale glass doors that fold up, opening the entire ground floor to the adjacent plaza. A bamboo grid shell wraps the upper level.

Oita Stadium, 2001   **Kisho Kurokawa & Associates**
1351 Yokoo, Oita ◑
One of many venues for the 2002 FIFA World Cup, this gently curving structure
houses a football pitch and athletics track with removable seating. The roof shell
is retractable, but its transparent Teflon membrane allows sufficient light through
during the day, to deviate the need for artificial lighting.

Soda Pop Spa, 2005   **Terunobu Fujimori**
7676-2 Nagayu, Naoiri-machi, Takeda City, Nagayu, Oita ◑
Located near the warm, carbonated spring that attracts visitors to the site, this
building is divided into three main sections: an art museum, male and female baths
and baths used solely by families. Exterior walls are clad in carbonized cedarwood
beams and plaster, while hand-bent copper tiles clad the roof.

Asia

211

212 213

214 215 216

219 220 221

Hanoi

Thailand

Bangkok

Vietnam

Manila

Philippines

Ho Chi Minh City

217 218

Singapore

Indonesia

222–232

233 234 235 236

Asia

Panyaden School, 2010   **24H**
Chiang Mai ●
Housing a bilingual private school, this building emphasizes sustainability through the use of local earth and bamboo, while a water recycling system further reduces its carbon footprint. The design, too, is inspired by nature: its sequence of undulating pavilions are arranged to resemble a tropical fern.

Elephant Tower, 1997   **Ong-ard**
369/38 Thanon Phahon Yothin 26, Bangkok ●
A testament to the local affinity for all that's eye-popping, the Elephant Tower, brainchild of real estate and engineering mogul Arun Chaiseri and the architect, would not have worked in any other capital. Its leg-like pillars, pinkish-grey facade and cut-out eye might be gaudy, but somehow, in a Thai context, have a camp, quirky appeal.

Central Embassy, 2017   AL_A
1031 Thanon Ploenchit, Bangkok ◑
Consisting of a luxury mall and upscale hotel, this building marks the eastern end of
a row of shops. The ribbon glass and aluminium shingles facade, inspired by classic
Thai patterns, which envelops both the six- level retail podium and the 27-storey hotel
tower above, gives it a shimmer that glints in the sun.

MahaNakhon Tower, 2016   OMA
114 Thanon Narathiwat, Bangkok ●
At 314m high, this tower is currently the tallest in Thailand, although it is set to lose
this title in 2018. More striking than its height is the design: a wave of 'pixels' —
stepped boxy recesses that house terraces and balconies — which twist around the
facade, counteracting its immense scale.

215

The Met, 2005   **WOHA**
123 Thanon Sathorn Tai, Bangkok ◑
This building was designed for high-density living in the tropics, expanding the low-rise model into a 228m-high tower. Units are connected every five storeys by sky terraces, allowing natural ventilation, while recessed balconies act like traditional timber houses, reducing heat levels. The cladding riffs on Thai ceramic tiles.

216

Museum of Hanoi, 2010   **gmp**
Pham Hung Road, Me Tri, Tu Liem, Hanoi ◑
The three levels of the Museum of Hanoi tier outwards from bottom to top, forming an inverted pyramid that appears almost to defy gravity. This feature, as well as being visually striking, has an energy-saving benefit: each level provides shade for the one below. Inside, visitors ascend the building via a white spiral ramp.

Apartment Building, 2016   **Sanuki Daisuke**
Binh Thanh District, Ho Chi Minh City ●
This block of seven small apartments is organized across two low towers, set
around an open courtyard. All of the homes are orientated towards the court, which
provides communal green space and admits natural light and ventilation. A screen
made of terracotta blocks faces the street.

UAH Campus, 2015   **Truong An and UAH Department of Architecture**
48 Dang Van Bi, Phuoc Long, Thu Duc, Ho Chi Minh City ●
Divided into two parts, this building rises eight floors on one side and four floors on
the other, to conform with the surrounding neighbourhood. The design of the facade
is a combination of varied rectangles. All classrooms face either north or south,
to avoid direct solar gain.

Church of the Gesù, 2002
Quezon City, Manila ◑   **Recio+Casas**

The tetrahedral form of this modern Jesuit church symbolizes the Holy Trinity, as well as the distinctive triangular eaves of the nipa hut. The building is light and airy, with space for 1,000 worshippers. It features slanting walls with open louvres, and is topped with a glass prism, illuminated like a beacon at night.

Zuellig Building, 2012   **SOM**
Paseo de Roxas, Makati, Manila ●

This building's form was inspired by the intersection at its site. With 33 floors, and standing at 160m tall, the fan-shaped floorplan opens the office fronts to the east and west, allowing for views of the village and park. A distinctive ceramic frit pattern is used on the glass curtain wall.

City Center Tower, 2017 **CAZA**
7th Avenue/30th Street, Fort Bonifacio, Manila ●
This mixed-use building comprises 30 storeys, its rectangular floorplans compressed by a broad elliptical pattern above the retail podium, as if impacted by a planet. The concentric circle 'displaces' the floor's volume, forming balconies and bulging metal mullions, creating a rippled effect across the curtain wall.

Learning Hub, 2015 **Heatherwick Studio**
Nanyang Technological University, 52 Nanyang Avenue, Singapore ●
Nicknamed 'The Dim Sum' for its likeness to a stack of steamer baskets, this structure features 12 towers, each with eight stories, comprising 56 rough-hewn concrete pods. There are almost no straight edges — from the undulating walls, cast with Aztec-like motifs, to the slanted load-bearing pillars that resemble tree trunks.

Church of St Mary of the Angels, 2003 **WOHA**
5 Bukit Batok East Avenue 2, Singapore ⓞ
On the wooded slopes of Bukit Batok, this spacious church manages to maintain privacy. The vaulted eyrie of the main prayer hall is lined with white-oak benches and lit by giant candelabras, with a light-drenched columbarium. There are also 12 reflection pools, a friary, offices and an apartment block for priests of the parish.

Singapore University of Technology and Design, 2015 **UNStudio**
8 Somapah Road, Singapore ●
This building is oriented around two main axes: one used for residential purposes, and the other for teaching. Overlapping laterally and vertically, the campus is a non-linear network, comprising five buildings with a white concrete facade, which include red, green, and purple lining along the corridors to help navigate departments.

Expo Transport Station, 2001   **Foster + Partners**
21 Changi South Avenue 1, Singapore ◑
Serving a new exhibition centre, this interchange features two dramatic roof structures: a stainless-steel, 38m disc over the ticket hall; and a 200m ellipse sheltering
passengers. The titanium cladding on the latter deflects the sun's rays, creating
a microclimate several degrees cooler than outside.

ION Orchard, 2009   **Benoy**
2 Orchard Turn, Singapore ◑
Resembling an upside-down tropical flower, this 218m steel-and-glass frame encompasses boutiques over eight levels, four of which are underground. A curtain of
coloured lights sheaths the facade's 'petals', while the 'stem' consists of 46 storeys
of apartments towering over the retail strip.

Skyline @ Orchard, 2014   **Maki & Associates**
23 Angullia Park, Singapore ●
Comprising luxury apartments, this 33-storey tower is elevated on cast-concrete columns, raising it 20m above ground level to maximize views. Set around a central circulation core, and with shared recreational facilities at ground level, all units include glazed balconies, intended to connect residents to green spaces.

ArtScience Museum, 2011   **Moshe Safdie**
6 Bayfront Avenue, Singapore ◐
This flower-like building is comprised of ten spheroid petals that rise as high as 60m. The top of each petal contains a rooflight that floods the three-floored galleries below with natural light, while a rainwater drain cascades through the middle of the building into an internal pond.

The Star Performing Arts Centre, 2013   **Aedas**
1 Vista Exchange Green, Singapore ◑
Funded in part by a Singaporean megachurch, the Star Performing Arts Centre features a shopping mall and a 5,000-capacity auditorium — which plays host to both pop concerts and a regular Sunday service. Built from steel and concrete, the auditorium is propped up by large, white columns that rise up through the mall below.

SkyTerrace@Dawson, 2015   **SCDA**
90 Dawson Road, Singapore ●
This high-density public housing consists of five towers, boasting sky gardens and yoga pavilions. There are double-height ceilings in many of the 758 units to allow compartmentalization for multi-generational communal living. Vegetated bridges connect the blocks, creating shared recreational areas.

Asia

The Interlace, 2013   **OMA and Ole Scheeren**
180-226 Depot Road, Singapore ●
This inspired architectural jigsaw is framed by the green Southern Ridges. A series of six-storey blocks, 31 in total, is angled, cantilevered and interlocked in a rough hexagonal plan, enabling a surfeit of leisure space across various levels. It easily encompasses over 1,000 condo units, with no sense of over-crowding.

Reflections at Keppel Bay, 2011   **Studio Libeskind**
Keppel Bay View, Singapore ●
This family of residences at the entrance to Keppel Harbour is comprised of six curving high-rises to the rear and eleven low-rise villas along the waterfront. Constructed of glass, anodized aluminium and stainless-steel mesh — the towers appear to bow to each other. A reflecting pool skirts the towers.

Menara Karya Tower, 2005   **Arquitectonica**
Jalan HR Rasuna Said Block X-1, Kavling 1-2, Jakarta ●
This 26-storey commercial tower in Jakarta's business district stands out for its immense crystalline form; the facade is designed to be reminicent of the glinting facets of a diamond. The only break in form occurs on levels 24 and 25, where the cantilevered wedge of a business centre interrupts the smooth glassy planes.

Arrayyan Mosque, 2003   **Djuhara+Djuhara**
Galaxia Bumi Permai Block, N7-20, Surabaya ◑
Situated in a dense urban neighbourhood in Surabaya, this mosque breaks from the traditional, onion-domed mould. The worship area is defined by a ceiling that arcs down from a full-height space at the front facade to half the volume's height at the back, and serves to focus attention on the Imam.

Ize Hotel, 2012   **Studio TonTon**
Jalan Kayu Aya 68, Seminyak, Bali ◑
Characterized by triangular turquoise panels that line the entrance canopy, this hotel is arranged along its narrow site to furnish increasing levels of privacy: dining areas face the street, while reception and guest access is at the rear. To maximize natural ventilation and light, rooms open off wide corridors clad with perforated screens.

236

Infinity Wedding Chapel, 2006   **Studio TonTon**
Jalan Pratama 168, Conrad Beach, Benoa, Kabupaten Badung, Bali ◑
This chapel, surrounded by pristine beach, is raised off the ground on a blackstone-clad base. A marble path leading to the building appears to float over shallow reflecting pools, which cover the stone's surface and lead towards an altar and beautifully framed sea views.

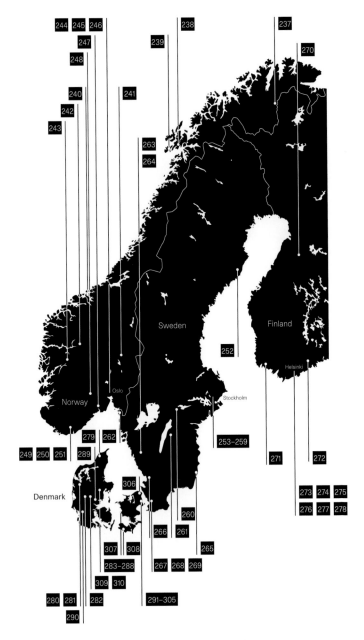

Europe

244 245 246

247

248

240

242

243

241

238

239

237

270

263

264

Sweden

Finland

252

Helsinki

Oslo

Stockholm

Norway

279 262

249 250 251 289

253–259

271 272

306

Denmark

273 274 275

276 277 278

260

266 261

307 308

265

283–288

267 268 269

309 310

280 281 282

291–305

290

Sámi Parliament Building, 2000   Stein Halvorsen and Christian Sundby
Kautokeinoveien 50, 9730 Karasjok ●
This complex is rampart-like from the outside, modulating its concrete with timber
shades against the low sun, but it opens up within to encircle a conical debating
chamber. This timber-clad form has been built to resemble the traditional Sami tent,
the lavvo.

National Tourist Routes, 2005   70°N
Torvdalshalsen, 8360 Bøstad ◑
This rest area and bike shed comprises a steel-frame structure clad in plywood
panels. The lower level is for bicycle storage, while the upper level offers a space
for viewing the natural surroundings. The rest area, in the form of a long terraced
platform with a wall defining one of its edges, provides shelter.

National Tourist Routes, 2005   **70°N**
Lofoten Islands, 8300 Vestvågøy ➊
Part of a large-scale programme to fund small architecture projects, these two observation towers for birdwatching have sturdy frames that minimize vibrations. They are clad in vertical planks of untreated wood, with three carefully planned openings, and a hidden door leading into a weather-protected room.

Romsdal Folk Museum, 2016   **Reiulf Ramstad**
Per Amdams Veg 4, 6413 Molde ➊
The pinewood used to build this folk museum reflects the local region's history and topography, while its spiky, zigzagged roof is designed to mirror Romsdal's traditional pitch-roofed architecture. Natural interior lighting is provided by a series of vertical strip windows and recessed glazing.

Lillehammer Art Museum Extension, 2016   **Snøhetta**
Stortorget 2, Lillehammer, 2609 Oppland ◐
Alongside the 1960s art museum and cinema complex designed by Erling Viksjø, this
addition connects the existing buildings with a new exhibition hall. A cantilevered
volume of polished stainless steel marks the eastern volume, set above a full-height
glazed children's workshop. The extension also includes extra cinema screens.

Borgund Stave Church Visitor Centre, 2005   **Askim/Lantto**
Riksveg 630 80, Borgund, 6888 Sogn og Fjordane ◐
The building is clad externally with untreated heartwood pine, designed to weather
in a similar fashion to the medieval church itself. The visitor centre houses a café,
toilets and an exhibition area, while large windows and an outdoor seating area encourage visitors to view the church from a distance.

Aurland Lookout, 2006   **Saunders**
Bjørgavegen, Aurland, 5745 Sogn og Fjordane ○
This pine-clad viewing platform offers a bridge-like path, leading visitors out onto a perch overlooking the Aurlandsfjord. The steel structure doubles back on itself like a sideways V and, resting on concrete foundations, its sweeping form makes minimal contact with the ground.

The National Museum — Architecture, 2008   **Sverre Fehn**
Bankplassen 3, 0102 Oslo ◑
This addition to a classicist 1830s bank building is a glass pavilion set within its own walled enclosure. The square exhibition space has four pillars supporting a concrete roof that tapers upwards to meet a facade of structural glass walls. The shuttering's geometric pattern is echoed in the timber flooring.

Norwegian National Opera and Ballet, 2008   **Snøhetta**
Kirsten Flagstads Plass 1, 0150 Oslo ◑
Extending into the harbour, Oslo's opera house precinct provides three theatres and
rehearsal spaces, and a large public lobby. Clad with white marble slabs and aluminium panels, its low-slung profile is cut through by a 15m glazed facade above the
foyer. The plan puts public and stage areas west, and production areas east.

Mortensrud Church, 2002   **Jensen & Skodvin**
Helga Vaneks Vei 15, 1281 Oslo ◑
This natrualistic worship space incorporates rocks and pine trees within its steel-
and-glass shed, rubble walling, raw timber belltower, glass gallery and non-orthog-
onal steel girders. Its looseness of form and use of diverse materials is a deliberate
attempt to disrupt the view of churches as reverential spaces.

Porsgrunn Maritime Museum, 2013   **COBE and Transform**
Tollbu gate 23, 3921 Porsgrunn ◑
This aluminium-clad museum of maritime history is organized into 11 interlinked blocks with asymmetric roofs, which form a zigzagged profile. Scaled in relation to gabled historic buildings nearby, the museum's principal exhibition space is on the upper level, accessed from a grand central staircase.

Seljord Watchtower, 2011   **Rintala Eggertsson**
Bjørgeøyane, Seljord, 3840 Telemark ◑
One of several lookouts around Seljord Lake, this five-storey construction is clad with vertical wooden louvres that frame the expanding views as visitors ascend the timber staircase. Landings at first and second floor levels reveal views to a nesting area and mature trees. At the top, a cantilevered room offers panoramic lake views.

Europe

Vennesla Library and Cultural Center, 2011   **Siv Helene Stangeland**
Venneslamoen 19, Vennesla, 4700 Vest-Agder ◑
One generous space houses all major public functions of this library, which includes a café, meeting rooms and administrative areas. Its form is supported by 27 pre-fabricated timber column beams that gradually alter in size. As well as supporting the structure, the ribs house reading niches, bookshelves and mechanical services.

Kilden Performing Arts Centre, 2012   **ALA**
Sjølystveien 2, Kristiansand, 4610 Vest-Agder ◑
Announced by an enormous undulating oak underbelly that cantilevers towards the harbour, this concert hall's plan is organized longitudinally into three bands. Visitors enter via the lofty lobby, which spans the building's length, then move into the second zone of auditoriums and theatre. The production zone is arranged to the rear.

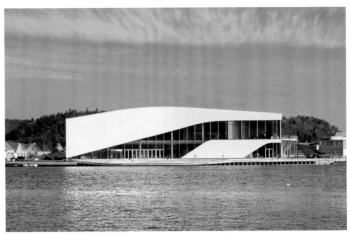

The Arch Cultural Center, 2012   **3XN**
Havnegata 2, Mandal, 4515 Vest-Agder ◑
This curving two-storey structure houses a cinema, concert hall and library, as well as social spaces. Its concrete facade wraps the upper levels and meets at an oblique angle on the quay. Panoramic windows to the river and city pierce the white exterior, which references the town's characteristic white houses.

Väven, 2014   **Snøhetta**
Storgatan 46a, 903 26 Umeå ◑
This riverside cultural centre combines various functions, including a library, theatre, museum conference centre and a hotel tower. The whole complex is wrapped in tapered bands of transparent and opaque glazing, designed to recall the white and black striations of local birch trees.

Europe

Arlanda Airport, 2002   **KHR**
190 45 Stockholm ◑
This building was designed to rationalize baggage handling and passenger flow.
Double-glazed facades act as both acoustic buffer and temperature regulator. Five
levels of accommodation hang from a steel 'tree' construction serving 12 gates.
Light wells enhance the overall feeling of openness.

Victoria Tower, 2011   **Wingårdhs**
Arne Beurlings Torg 3, 164 40 Kista ◑
Cloaked in eight variations of triangular metal oxidised glazing, this 34-storey tower
rises from a rectilinear podium, which accommodates a restaurant and conference
facilities. Crowned with a cubic volume projecting beyond the shaft below, the tower
is mostly occupied by a hotel, with offices on the remaining floors.

Quality Hotel Friends, 2013   **Wingårdhs and Karolina Keyzer**
Råsta Strandväg 1, 169 56 Solna ◑
Accommodating a hotel and conference facilities, this tall and narrow rectangular building is notable for its optically playful facade. Clad with square panels punctuated by three differently sized holes, the apertures are arranged to create the illusion of waves rippling across the exterior.

Aula Medica, 2013   **Wingårdhs**
Nobelsväg 6, 171 65 Solna ●
This lecture hall and office complex is built of laminated timber and clad in 6,000 triangular glass panes in shades of blue, yellow and brown. Each of its seven floors is slightly larger than the one below, resulting in a soft, rounded form. At its apex, the angle of incline is 33 degrees.

KTH School of Architecture, 2015   **Tham & Videgård**
Osquars Backe 5, 114 28 Stockholm ◑
A Corten steel facade wraps the elliptical plan of this six-storey architecture faculty, which was conceived in concert with surrounding brick buildings. The project occupies a former courtyard, its curved exterior forming continuous external pathways. Broad, recessed windows frame the facilities inside.

Sven-Harrys Konstmuseum, 2011   **Wingårdhs and Anna Höglund**
Eastmansvägen 10, 113 61 Stockholm ◑
The building, financed by real-estate mogul Sven-Harry Karlsson, houses a contemporary art museum and luxury flats. Clad in a golden alloy similar to that used for coins, and interspersed with tinted windows, the resulting solid mass resembles a bank vault. It consists of exhibition spaces, a restaurant and a rooftop sculpture park.

Sånga-Säby Conference Centre, 2006　　　　　　　　　**Tovatt**
Sånga-Säbyvägen 187, 179 96 Svartsjö ●
Located on the island of Färingsö, just to the west of Stockholm, this building is an extension to an established complex. Clad in black timber, its stepped facade corresponds to the theatre-style space within, where four large windows frame elevated views over Lake Mälaren.

Örsta Gallery, 2010　　　　　　　　　**Claesson Koivisto Rune**
Örsta 511, 692 72 Kumla ◐
Sitting atop an artificial hill, this gallery's curved base follows the hill's topology, which is also mirrored in its bowed roof profile, creating the illusion of concave walls. Square in plan, its facades are incised with full-height windows that blur its sense of scale, while bold external coloured lights give it a chameleon-like presence.

New Svinesund Bridge, 2005   **Lund+Slaatto**
Idefjorden, Svingenskogen, Nordby ○
This road bridge spans the Idefjord — a narrow body of water between Sweden and
Norway. A reinforced-concrete arch carries a superstructure of two steel box-gird-
er bridge decks on either side, and suspends a series of traverse beams from above.
When illuminated, the bridge's silhouette frames the the fjord.

Facts Tåkern Visitor Centre, 2008   **Wingårdhs**
Glänås Besöksområde, 590 22 Väderstad ◑
Set in a nature reserve beside annual nesting grounds on Lake Tåkern, this centre
is clad in reed thatching, camouflaged like a birdwatcher's hide. Arranged in a U-
shaped plan, its pitched interior features timber elements, while a rooflight replaces
the more typical thatched ridge.

Europe

Nötkärnan, 2016   **Wingårdhs**
Rymdtorget 8B, 415 19 Göteborg ●
Floating on pillars above an existing car park, this private health clinic alleviates its concrete surrounds with a glazed envelope of offset, overlaid patterns that colour the building and give the illusion of movement. Inside, four lush garden walls arranged perpendicular to each other screen patients from the consulting rooms.

Kuggen, 2011   **Wingårdhs**
Lindholmsplatsen, 417 56 Göteborg ●
A cylindrical tower in the town square, this *kuggen* ('cog') is formed of progressively larger floors offset to the south, providing solar shading to offices within. Clad with glazed terracotta panels and glass, the triangular windows admit light deep into the structure. First-floor sky bridges connect to adjacent buildings.

Europe

Kalmar Konstmuseum, 2008   **Tham & Videgård**
Stadsparken, 392 33 Kalmar ⟳
This black cube-like gallery sits in a city park alongside a sheltered sea inlet. A spiral staircase connects the gallery's four floors, while a glazed link accesses a restaurant pavilion that was built in the 1930s. Glazing provides the first-floor exhibition space with sea views, while saw-tooth rooflights illuminate the top floor.

Halmstad Library, 2006   **Schmidt Hammer Lassen**
Axel Olsons street 1, 302 27 Halmstad ⟳
This library projects out over the Nissan River, supported by a series of slender pillars. A green roof integrates the building into its landscape, reducing drainage needs and regulating the internal climate. Double-height glazed concave facades afford ground and mezzanine floors panoramic views of the park and river.

Turning Torso Office and Apartment Tower, 2005   **Santiago Calatrava**
Lilla Varvsgatan 14, 211 15 Malmö ●
This high-rise building is derived from a sculpture bearing the same name, itself a
geometric abstraction of a twisted torso. Turning through 90 degrees from ground
level to rooftop, nine cubic volumes (each of five floors) interlink through a central
core. The facade comprises over 5,000 curved aluminium and flat glass panels.

Bo01 Restaurant, 2001   **Sandell Sandberg**
Amiralsgatan 35, Folkets Park, 214 37 Malmö ◑
This single-storey kidney-shaped pavilion was originally intended to be a temporary
contribution to a housing exhibition but proved so popular that the city of Malmö
decided to keep it. The polished metal frame is clad entirely in striated polyurethane,
lending it a hazy transparency amid a grove of orange trees.

Emporia Shopping Centre, 2013   **Wingårdhs**
Hyllie Boulevard 19, 215 32 Malmö ◑
This shopping mall has two gaping entrances made out of brightly coloured curved glass, one amber and one blue. Inside, three storeys of retail are organized in a figure-of-eight plan, with coloured atria distinguishing different zones. A rooftop park features sedum, prairie grass and trees, as well as wind-sheltered patios.

Kärsämäki Church, 2004   **OOPEAA**
Pappilankuja 24, Kärsämäki ◑
This modern design employed materials and construction techniques from the eighteenth century, when the original church had been built. A square box with a gabled roof utilizes concepts of core and cloak. The cloak is made of tar-dipped aspen shingles and a crowning lantern directs natural light inside.

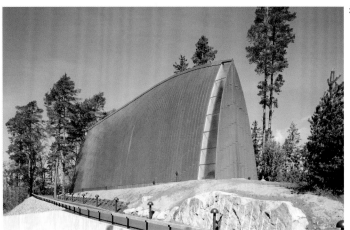

St Henry's Ecumenical Art Chapel, 2005   **Sanaksenaho**
Seiskarinkatu 32, 20900 Turku ◑
This art gallery and chapel references the biblical story of Jonah, with structural ribs of laminated pine inside and in external profile resembling an upturned ship's hull. The exterior copper shingles will acquire a green patina and blend in with the landscape.

Sibelius Congress and Concert Centre, 2001   **Artto Palo Rossi Tikka Oy**
Ankkurikatu 7, 15140 Lahti ◑
Part of a conversion of old waterside industrial buildings, this concert hall abuts the laminated-timber structure of the Forest Hall — a glazed banqueting chamber. The largest public wooden structure built in Finland in a hundred years, its interior materials combine the timber structural elements with birch plywood wall finishes.

Lohja Main Library, 2005   **Lahdelma & Mahlamäki**
Karstuntie 3, 08100 Lohja ◑
The city block's angled lines determined this library's shape and its elongated front facade. The redbrick exterior references Finnish architect Alvar Aalto's work, as well as the surrounding civic buildings. Cone-shaped rooflights illuminate the main reading room and a window provides views to the nearby medieval church.

Suvela Chapel, 2016   **OOPEAA**
Kirstintie 24, Espoo ◑
Clad in a shimmering copper carapace and constructed with a hybrid system of timber, concrete and steel, this religious and community events venue has a U-shaped plan, with an open courtyard at its centre. All interiors face inwards, including the main chapel, which features a steeply pitched roof with wooden beams.

AV Media, 2003   **ARK-house**
City College of Technology, Muotoilijankatu 3, 00560 Helsinki ●
Coloured metal sheets clad the south-facing facade of this nine-storey school of film and media. Their colour-block pattern is reminiscent of shipping containers, a reference to the area's past. The northern exterior of the building is made from glass, while the interiors feature galvanized steel, colourful plywood and raw concrete.

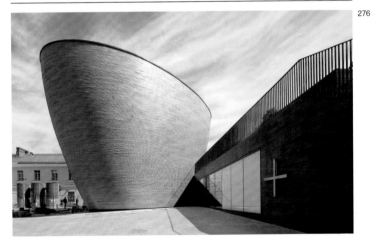

Kamppi Chapel of Silence, 2012   **Kimmo Lintula**
Simonkatu 7, 00100 Helsinki ◐
Standing in a bustling square in central Helsinki, this chapel offers visitors a site for peaceful contemplation, regardless of their religious beliefs. Its curved facade is constructed from horizontal strips of spruce. With no exterior windows, the only source of daylight is a circular aperture that loops the ceiling.

Laajasalo Church, 2003   Kari Järvinen ja Merja Nieminen
Reposalmentie 13, 00840 Helsinki ◑
An intimate, timber-clad parish building painted with Finnish red ochre opens into
a courtyard facing the adjacent park. A larger structure, containing the church
hall, bellfry and stone-clad sacristy of this Helsinki church complex, is wrapped in
green-patinated copper sheets.

Vuotalo Cultural Centre, 2000   Heikkinen–Komonen
Mosaiikkitori 2, 00980 Helsinki ◑
This arts centre is arranged in a semi-circle and includes a library, music facilities
and a wedge-shaped theatre for arts performances. The curving, windowless rear
is cloaked in industrial stainless-steel mesh. In contrast, the wide double-height
entrance is glazed, highlighting the activities inside.

Europe

Vendsyssel Theatre, 2017 **Schmidt Hammer Lassen**
Banegårdspladsen 4, 9800 Hjørring ◑
A series of Corten steel cubes arranged around an open-plan, double-height glazed lobby and café forms this complex, along with music and rehearsal halls, a theatre and workshop. Its weathered-steel finish is left raw, or cloaked behind a layer of glass panels, backed with colour-changing LED lights that glow in the evening.

Krabbesholm Højskole, 2012 **MOS**
Krabbesholm Allé 15, 7800 Skive ●
In this series of studios for art, architecture, graphic design and photography at a Danish school, the architects sought to simulate a campus rather than separate buildings. Sharing a common palette of cement-panelled structures with deep, pitched roofs, the four studios are arranged around a triangular courtyard.

UDK Holstebro, 2012   **CEBRA**
Hostrupsvej 8, 7500 Holstebro ●
A triangle in plan, this three-storey office building is shaped to allow the optimum daylight levels to reach each workstation. Orientated to the north, the structure allows views out — and light in — through ribbon windows. The southwestern entrance opens to a large hexagonal roof-lit atrium.

Herning Museum of Contemporary Art, 2009   **Steven Holl**
Birk Centerpark 8, 7400 Herning ➊
Uniting three different cultural institutions, this complex accommodates galleries, a 150-seat auditorium, a restaurant and rehearsal rooms. A series of turf roofs conceal the parking and service areas, and the concrete exterior has a fabric-like texture — a nod to Herning's history of textile manufacturing.

Salling Tower, 2015
Basin 7, between Piers 3 and 4, Aarhus ◑
Dorte Mandrup

Anchored on the edge of Aarhus's Docklands, this arrow-shaped tower is composed of steel sheet pierced with holes and folded to encompass a two-level viewing platform. Rendered in white marine paint, the tower is accessed from a staircase to the first platform; a second staircase leads to the panoramic lookout.

Isbjerget, 2013
Mariane Thomsens Gade 43, 8000 Aarhus ●
JDS

This block is arranged in four jagged L-shaped wings orientated towards Aarhus Bay. The architects designed the peaked-steel roof profiles to maximize sunlight and sea views for every apartment. The development also includes recessed roof courtyards and balconies for a greater sense of connection with the outdoors.

Light*House, 2013 UNStudio
Aarhus Harbour, Aarhus ●
This complex ranges terraced apartments along the Aarhus harbour promenade.
Buildings are set around shared gardens and designed to capture views of the sea
from north elevations, and sunlight from the south. A motif of cast concrete 'waves'
undulate along the perimeter, defining the balconies between homes.

Your Rainbow Panorama, 2011 Studio Olafur Eliasson
Aros Allé 2, 8000 Aarhus ◑
Situated on the roof of the ARoS Aarhus Art Museum, this 150m circular walkway of
glazing includes all the colours of the spectrum. Mounted on slender columns, the
raised promenade spans 3m and allows visitors to pass inside the ring, looking out
at the city panorama through rainbow-tinted panels.

Europe

Aarhus Library, 2015   **Schmidt Hammer Lassen**
Hack Kampmanns Pladsen 2, 8000 Aarhus ◑
Set above a new train station, this building's angled planes obscure hierarchies
between its front and back. Four large staircases rise past the podium to a glazed
double-height library. Library floors have 360-degree views and link via large voids.
Overhead, offices in an irregular polygonal volume are clad in expanded metal.

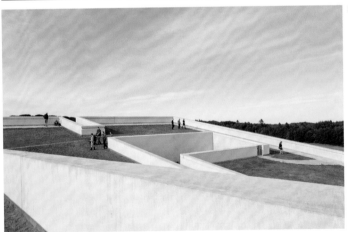

Moesgaard Museum, 2015   **Henning Larsen**
Moesgård Allé 15, 8270 Højbjerg ◑
A turf roof sits atop this museum, allowing the building to blend in with the country-
side. The roof, on which flowers, grass and moss grow, functions as a site for picnics
and lectures. The many terraces within the interior are inspired by the process of archaeological excavation, reflecting the museum's main area of interest.

Kongernes Jelling, National Museum of Denmark, 2000   **Wohlert**
Gormsgade 23, 7300 Jelling ◑
Two white-painted, rectangular brick buildings are placed parallel to each other, the area in-between containing the foyer, café and main staircase of this Viking muse-um. The larger of the two wings, housing permanent exhibitions, lines up with an ex-isting church, while a roof terrace provides views over the surrounding landscape.

Gas-insulated Switchgear Stations, 2013   **CF Møller**
Vandmøllevej 10, Revsing, 6600 Vejen ●
The serrated profile of this building encloses a station for transporting energy, wrapped by modular panels of zinc. Arranged along the rectilinear plan in a series of fins, the sloping roof and sides create a formidable triangulated structure. Like gills, the envelope admits air, and allows glimpses of the switchgear within.

Finance for Danish Industry, 2002 **3XN**
Langelinie Allé 43, 2100 Copenhagen ●
Adjoining a listed warehouse, this office block adopts the scale of its neighbour while asserting its own identity: its considerable plan-depth is improved by recessed gardens and entrances. A system of adjustable aluminium shutters is controlled by photocells.

UN City, 2013 **3XN**
Marmorvej 51, 2100 Copenhagen ◑
This complex accommodates the Scandinavian head office for the United Nations, which has gathered its employees on an artificial island. The burnished steel base emulates rusting piers, while the white main body is a salute to passing cruiseships. Pierced aluminium shutters provide shade without blocking light.

Opera House, 2004 Henning Larsen
Ekvipagemestervej 1, 1438 Copenhagen ❶
Set in an area called Doköen (meaning Dock Island) and surrounded by canals, this opera house's high, cantilevered roof provides the unifying concept for its design. Panelled in stained maple to evoke a violin, the shell-like auditorium is visible through the facade from all over Copenhagen's inner harbour.

Tivoli Concert Hall, 2005 3XN
Vesterbrogade 3, 1620 Copenhagen ❶
This project renovated and extended an original 1956 concert hall in the Tivoli gardens in the centre of Copenhagen, providing a café and new entrance, as well as a new lobby, cloakrooms and bathrooms beneath the main concert hall. Stage space was also updated and a new rehearsal hall was created.

Europe

Black Diamond, 1999 **Schmidt Hammer Lassen**
Søren Kierkegaards Plasdsen, 11221 Copenhagen ◑
An extension to the Royal Library of Denmark, the Black Diamond divided opinion upon completion, with some viewing it as a thing of sleek beauty and others as an aggressive shard of glass. Clad in black granite, the building is visually split in two by a wide, glazed crevasse.

Cirkelbroen, 2015 **Studio Olafur Eliasson**
Christianshavns Kanal, Copenhagen ○
Spanning Christianshavns Kanal, this bridge is formed of five interconnecting circular platforms, each pierced by a narrow steel mast linked by a cone of fine steel cables to the perimeter railings. Varying in diameter, the circular platforms include a rotating section that allows boats to access the canal.

Gemini Residence, 2005   **MVRDV**
Islands Brygge, 2300 Copenhagen ●
Part of Copenhagen's old harbour, this pair of apartment blocks get their circular footprint from the reuse of two concrete silos at its heart. Lit by rooflights, the central cores contain lobby and circulation spaces, with all apartments arranged around the perimeter. Rising eight storeys, it's clad with floor-to-ceiling glazing.

DR Koncerthuset, 2009   **Ateliers Jean Nouvel**
Ørestads Boulevard 13, 2300 Copenhagen ◑
A 45m-tall rectangular box, this concert hall changes appearance depending on the weather and time of day. Its distinctive, translucent blue exterior doubles as a screen onto which images can be projected, while the golden colours of the interior are inspired by the sunset in Edward Munch's *The Scream*.

AC Hotel Bella Sky, 2011   **3XN**
Center Boulevard 5, 2300 Copenhagen ◑
This hotel, the largest in Scandinavia, is arranged over two towers that shoot up while tilting 15 degrees in opposite directions. The facade is covered in a graphic skin of triangular glass and aluminium panels, creating a pixelated effect, while a sky bridge connects the towers on the 23rd floor.

Mountain Dwellings, 2008   **BIG and JDS**
Ørestads Boulevard 55, 2300 Copenhagen ●
Submerging a car park below a terraced cluster of housing, this residential complex combines urban density with suburban living. Cascading in steps from the eleventh to the ground floor, all 80 apartments include a roof garden orientated to the south, which connects to timber-clad living spaces through glazed sliding doors.

VM Houses, 2005 **BIG + JDS**
Ørestads Boulevard 57-59, 2300 Copenhagen ●
Placed diagonally across their site, these buildings comprise the first residential project building Copenhagen's new Ørestad district. V-Building apartments have triangular balconies and fully-glazed external walls, while apartments in M-Building have south-facing terraces.

The Blue Planet, 2013 **3XN**
Jacob Fortlingsvej 1, 2770 Kastrup ◐
Inspired by waves, the organic shape of this aquarium mimics a whirlpool from above. A swirling path leads you into the building, an almost seamless transition from the surrounding landscape of water and fields. The facade is fashioned from more than 30,000 diamond-shaped shingles that look and feel like scales.

8 House, 2010   **BIG**
Richard Mortensens Vej, 2300 Copenhagen ●
Planned as a figure of eight tilted around two interior courtyards, this mixed-use complex organizes functions horizontally. The 'three-dimensional' neighbourhood means houses step up and around the structure, animated by shops, individual gardens and two over-sized green roofs.

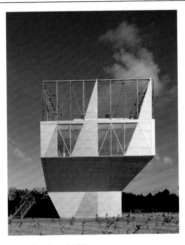

Herstedlund Community Centre, 2009   **Dorte Mandrup**
Herstedhus, Robinievej, 2620 Albertslund ❶
Catering to a variety of uses, each level of this three-storey structure has a dedicated function, rising from a kitchen, performance space and multi-purpose room, through to a rooftop sports court enveloped by mesh. Its facade of perforated or solid aluminium panels reveals or conceals interiors, depending on their function.

Europe

ARKEN Museum of Modern Art, 1996   Søren Robert Lund
Skovvej 100, 2635 Ishøj ◑
Surrounded by a manmade beachscape just south of Copenhagen, the ARKEN Museum of Modern Art resembles a giant beached ship, and is 18m tall at its highest point. The huge indoor gallery axis is shaped like a hull with tall, heavy doors of iron, exposed rivet-like bolts and metal staircases.

Danish National Maritime Museum, 2013   BIG
Ny Kronborgvej 1, 3000 Helsingør ◑
The solid concrete mass of an aged dry dock embeds the centre of this underground maritime museum. Three double-height glazed bridges zigzag between its walls, forming an extension of the harbour promenade. Museum exhibits are arranged in a continuous loop around the dock.

Musholm Bay Vacation and Recreation Centre, 2001 **Arkos**
Musholmvej 100, 4220 Korsør ◐
In this turf-roofed residential centre for people with muscular dystrophy, wheel-chair-accessible single villas and duplex units are grouped between high, thuja-wood party walls, which resemble the breakwaters found along this coastline. Conical bathrooms were individually designed by 16 different artists.

Fuglsang Art Museum, 2008 **Tony Fretton**
Nystedvej 71, 4891 Toreby ◐
Located within Lolland's flat landscape, this art museum's austere exterior adopts the materials of nearby utility buildings. A facade of white-painted brick is surmounted by three diagonally placed, grey-brick roof volumes. A wide corridor guides visitors to roof-lit exhibition spaces.

309

Danfoss Universe Exhibition Centre, 2007   **J Mayer H**
Mads Patent Vej 1, 6430 Nordborg ◑
These two buildings belong to a science park, and provide winter accommodation
for exhibitions and science demonstrations. Each volume is created by horizontally
extruding a flat elevation with a scalloped outline. Curved openings in the facades
correspond with interior spaces.

310

Concert Hall and Science Park, 2007   **3XN**
Alsion University, Alsion 2, 6400 Sønderborg ◑
This project combines university laboratories and study space, offices for private
companies, and a concert hall for the local symphony orchestra. Interspersed
granite-clad steel atria and precast concrete offices look out over the water, with
the box-within-a-box concert hall located halfway along.

Europe

311
312
313
314
315 316 317
318
319

371
Northern
Ireland
323 324 325
329 330
Edinburgh
Scotland
320 321
322
327
328
331
335
369 370
Republic
of Ireland
332
333
Dublin
371

Wales
England
London
326
334
372
373
374
375
376
365
359
360
361
362
336–358
363 364
377
378 379 380
366
367
368

New Library, 2005   **Schmidt Hammer Lassen**
University of Aberdeen, Bedford Road, Aberdeen AB24 3AA ◑
A new academic library for the university's science and research departments, this building rises from a plinth of Caithness stone. Its double-height ground floor holds exhibition space, a café and a rare book collection, while upper levels include study areas and 13km of stacks. It's all linked by a curved, off-centre atrium.

An Turas, 2003   **Sutherland Hussey**
Scarinish, Tiree, Inner Hebrides PA77 6TN ○
A waiting area for the ferry on the westernmost island of the Inner Hebrides chain, the whitewashed entrance corridor and glass box of this shelter draw a line in the landscape. Protected from the weather, but open to the beach through a slatted floor, the two volumes are connected by a traditionally felt-roofed bridge.

The Lookout, 2014   **Angus Ritchie and Daniel Tyler**
Balquhidder, Lochearnhead, Perthshire FK19 8PQ ○
This lookout point, situated within the Loch Lomond and Trossachs National Park, both frames and reflects views of the surrounding lochs and glens. It features a wood-framed pavilion, clad in mirrored stainless steel, with benches built into its different elevations to frame various vistas of the landscape.

Falkirk Wheel, 2002   **RMJM and Tony Gee & Partners**
Lime Road, Tamfourhill, Falkirk FK1 4RS ●
The first ever rotating boat lift, this wheel connects the Grand Union Canal with the Forth and Clyde Canal, by means of two giant steel arms — each containing lock-gated boat 'containers' — that revolve around a central hub.The design is derived from fish-skeleton and Ferris-wheel forms.

The Seona Reid Building, 2014 **Steven Holl**
Glasgow School of Art, 167 Renfrew Street, Glasgow G3 6RQ ⦿
Wrapped with a double skin of recycled glass, this five-storey structure contrasts with the decorative sandstone of Charles Rennie Mackintosh's 1909 building opposite. It houses studios, galleries and seminar rooms, with a rectangular floorplan pierced by three full-height cylindrical light shafts.

Riverside Museum, 2011 **Zaha Hadid**
100 Pointhouse Road, Glasgow G3 8RS ⦿
This museum of transport houses more than 3,000 exhibits and is enveloped by an extruded zigzagging section clad in patinated zinc. Almost Z-shaped in plan, its ends are enclosed by 36m-high glazed walls. The broad spans of the pitched roof create tall, open-plan galleries that accommodate large-scale displays.

BBC Scotland, 2007   **David Chipperfield**
40 Pacific Quay, Glasgow G51 1DA ●
Situated by the River Clyde, this digital broadcasting centre features a central atrium with a tiered sequence of red sandstone steps and terraces, emphasizing collective work areas and public spaces. Its transparent double-glazed facade contains a natural ventilation system, as well as maximizing light and views over the river.

Edinburgh Sculpture Workshop, 2014   **Sutherland Hussey Harris**
21 Hawthornvale, Edinburgh EH6 4JT ◑
An addition to the Sculpture Workshop, the Creative Laboratories is a low-slung building with a cloistered courtyard, which is lined with panels of steel grating. Inspired by traditional Italian campaniles, the 22.5m brick-clad tower emits a soft glow at night, ambiently illuminated from a large, angled aperture at its apex.

Europe

Scottish Parliament, 2004   **Miralles Tagliabue EMBT**
1 Horse Wynd, Edinburgh EH99 1SP ◑
Some regard the Scottish Parliament building as a disaster — energy-inefficient and
poorly constructed, despite coming in three years late and ten times over budget.
Yet those who love it praise a tour de force in local granite, concrete and decorative
wood detailing that reflects the drama of the surrounding landscape.

Gateshead Millennium Bridge, 2001   **WilkinsonEyre**
South Shore Road, Gateshead NE8 ○
This bridge for pedestrians and cyclists links the new arts and cultural quarter on
the Gateshead Quays with Newcastle's North Bank. Composed of two steel curves,
one forming the deck and the other supporting it, the bridge rotates upwards when
shipping requires access. Its form echoes the nearby iconic Tyne Bridge.

Ogden Centre for Fundamental Physics, 2017   **Studio Libeskind**
Durham University, South Road, Durham DH1 3LE ●
The form of this centre for cosmology and astronomy follows a spiraling plan. Offices are placed along the exterior, and central communal areas are lit by a large glazed atrium. The Scottish larch facade is incised by ribbon windows along the flanks, and huge picture windows at the building's north and south elevation.

Hepworth Wakefield, 2011   **David Chipperfield**
Gallery Walk, Wakefield WF1 5AW ◑
Named after the Wakefield-born artist Barbara Hepworth, this purpose-built art gallery is composed of irregular pigmented-in-situ concrete trapezoidal volumes grouped around a central staircase. Adjacent to the River Calder, the building can be accessed via a new footbridge.

Beetham Tower, 2006   **Ian Simpson**
301 Deansgate, Manchester M3 4LQ ●
The tallest building in the UK outside of London, Beetham Tower, which houses a hotel and apartments, is also one of the world's thinnest skyscrapers. On the 23rd floor, roughly halfway up the building, a 4m-long cantilever projects outwards, providing the building with its distinctive silhouette.

Manchester Civil Justice Centre, 2007   **Denton Corker Marshall**
1 Bridge Street West, Manchester M60 9DJ ●
The central block of this building's spine contains its serves and circulation system. Courtrooms and offices sit on one side of this spine, and on the other side is a tall glazed atrium with balconies and coloured pods suspended above. Irregularly stacked, cantilevered floors add formal interest.

Imperial War Museum North, 2002　　　　　　　　**Studio Libeskind**
Trafford Wharf Road, Stretford, Manchester M17 1TZ ◑
This building beside the Manchester Ship Canal is formed of three intersecting
curved volumes. These represent battles fought in the air, at sea and on land. The
concrete and steel construction, with slash-hole apertures and aluminium cladding,
references the technology of modern warfare.

Museum of Liverpool, 2011　　　　　　**3XN and Kim Herforth Nielsen**
Pier Head, Liverpool L3 1DG ◑
Organized in two angular wings that rise in opposite directions, the new museum for
Liverpool showcases the region's social and cultural history. Clad in textured lime-
stone and set atop a podium, the wings culminate in broad projecting window bays
facing the city and the River Mersey.

Winter Gardens and Millennium Galleries, 2001   **Pringle Richards Sharratt**
90 Surrey Street, Sheffield S1 2LH ◑
The vast temperate glasshouses of the Winter Gardens rise from either end of a T-shaped, enclosed public route, their glazed elliptical timber arches rippling towards the surrounding streets. The light-filled, airy complex contains the adjacent Millennium Galleries, an arcade and public spaces.

Nottingham Contemporary, 2009   **Caruso St John**
Weekday Cross, Nottingham NG1 2GB ◑
Inspired by the facades of the city's nineteenth-century Lace Market, this building's lace-patterned panels sit on a base of shiny, black concrete. Gold-coloured, anodized aluminium clad the building's two towers. Inside, galleries are modelled after warehouse spaces.

New Art Gallery Walsall, 2000   **Caruso St John**
Gallery Square, Walsall WS2 8LG ◑
Set in a 30m-high tower clad in terracotta tiles that diminish in size towards the top, this art gallery features spaces for conferences, teaching and dining at lower levels. Timber-floored rooms house the permanent Garman Ryan collection, and top-lit spaces exhibit temporary works on the upper two floors.

Selfridges Birmingham Department Store, 2003   **Future Systems**
Bullring Stairway, Birmingham B5 4BP ◑
This bulbous development in Birmingham's historic Bull Ring area accommodates four storeys of retail, an underground loading area and rooftop terrace. Clad with anodized aluminium discs, a sprayed concrete mesh encloses the steel frame. The space-age footbridge connects to a multi-storey car park.

Cowan Court, 2016   **6a**
Churchill College, University of Cambridge, Storey's Way, Cambridge CS3 0DS ●
A new hall of residence for Churchill College, this 68-room building references the
materiality and proportions of its neighbouring 1960s accommodation. Its facades
of untreated, reclaimed oak-board echo existing masonry cladding and rise to three
storeys, all arranged around a central courtyard.

Balancing Barn, 2010   **MVRDV**
Thorington, Halesworth IP19 9JG ❶
Inland from the Suffolk coast, this holiday house — clad in reflective metal panels and
shaped like a barn — capitalizes on its natural landscape, cantilevering off a small hill.
To maximize the sense of connection with the surrounding reserve, windows pierce
all sides of the volume, even the floor in the furthest cantilever.

The Dune House, 2011   **Jarmund/Vigsnæs**
Suffolk Coast and Heaths, Thorpeness, Leiston IP16 4NR ◑
Crowned with a black, faceted upper storey, this seafront holiday house references the local vernacular of gabled barns. To maximize views out, the ground floor is clad entirely in glass. The upper level, clad in dark-stained timber, is organized as four triangular rooms beneath a steeply pitched, zigzagging mansard roof.

Blavatnik School of Government, 2016   **Herzog & de Meuron**
University of Oxford, 120 Walton Street, Oxford OX2 6GG ●
Within the University of Oxford's renowned campus, this department for governance unfolds around an open forum at its centre, ringed by concrete walkways. Intended to encourage student interaction, the atrium rises through all seven floors and is expressed externally in upper tiers of glazed discs.

Henry Moore Studios and Gardens, 2017   **Hugh Broughton**
Perry Green, Hertfordshire SG10 6EE ◑
The Henry Moore Foundation was founded by the artist and his family in 1977 to encourage public appreciation of the visual arts. This extension includes a visitor centre, an archive and new sculpture stores. A former dwelling has been fully refurbished. The extension features a new monopitch wing clad in oxidised steel panels.

Velodrome, 2010   **Hopkins**
Queen Elizabeth Olympic Park, Abercrombie Road, London E20 3AB ●
Inspired by the design and efficiency of a bicycle, the hyperbolic paraboloid shape of this velodrome results from a deceptively simple cable-net roof structure. The building's lightweight skin is clad in cedar laths, with narrow openings for natural ventilation, which meet the 360-degree glazed concourse below.

London Aquatics Centre, 2004   **Zaha Hadid**
Queen Elizabeth Olympic Park, London E20 2ZQ ◑
Designed for the 2012 Olympic Games, the aquatics centre is distinguished by a large sinuous roof that sweeps up from the ground on a pivotal axis, with the competition and diving pools inside. Its billowing shape is formed from a concrete parabolic arch structure set on three main supporting columns.

Rivington Place, 2007   **Adjaye Associates**
Rivington Place, London EC2A 3BA ◑
This sculptural, simple building is clad in charcoal concrete and reflective black aluminium panels, with eight rows of windows spread over just five floors, topped off with raked rooflights. Galleries and auxiliary spaces are housed within the five-storey block, with public areas at street level and private areas above.

Idea Store Whitechapel, 2005   **Adjaye Associates**
321 Whitechapel Road, London E1 1BU ◑
This community facility combines library and educational space, and is the largest of seven Idea Stores planned to replace traditional libraries in the area. Located on a busy high street, striped, glazed facades mimic and amplify the striped awnings of market stalls below.

30 St Mary Axe Office Building, 2004   **Foster + Partners**
30 St Mary Axe, London EC3A 8BF ●
Located in London's financial district, this landmark building is created from a stack of concentric circles of varying diameters, set within a self-supporting steel dia-grid. Broadening from its base to its widest point at level 17 before tapering to fit a private dining room at the top, diamond-shaped glazing defines the exterior.

The Leadenhall Building, 2014   **Rogers Stirk Harbour + Partners**
122 Leadenhall Street, London EC3V 4AB ●
This office tower's 18,000-ton steel frame is revealed through its glass skin. To protect views to St Paul's, the principal facade leans back by 10 degrees, which earned the building its 'Cheesegrater' nickname. Hoisted 28m on giant struts, it hovers over a public plaza, a device intended to give some space back to the dense City.

20 Fenchurch Street, 2014   **Rafael Viñoly**
20 Fenchurch Street, London EC3M 8AF ◑
Nicknamed 'The Walkie Talkie' due to its curving shape, this skyscraper, with a top-floor 'sky garden', managed to produce a reflection intense enough to melt a parked car. As a result, horizontal aluminium louvres were added to the glass facade from the 3rd to the 34th floors to deal with the reflective issue.

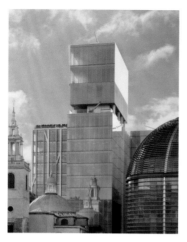

New Court, 2011   OMA
New Court, St Swithin's Lane, London EC4N 8AL ●
Housing the headquarters of the Rothschild group, this glazed 10-storey cube
is topped by a sky pavilion. Given that the entrance is on a narrow medieval cut-
through, the facade is partially hidden at street level, giving way to views of the
marble forecourt and St Stephen Walbrook church.

344

The Shard, 2012   **Renzo Piano Building Workshop**
32 London Bridge Street, London SE1 9SG ◐
Inspired by ship masts and London spires, this mixed-use skyscraper is formed of
eight glass facades that incline towards each other without ever meeting. Its glass
is particularly white and reflective, allowing the facade to respond to the climate and
time of day, subtly changing its appearance.

Guy's Hospital, 2007   **Heatherwick Studio**
Great Maze Pond, London SE1 9RT ●
Reviving what had become a 'back-door' hospital entrance, this project required the
re-routing of traffic and pedestrian flows, as well as the creation of a new identity.
Based on a tessellated metal-framed panel of woven steel tape, rotated to create an
undulating effect, its arresting modular wall wraps the west entrance.

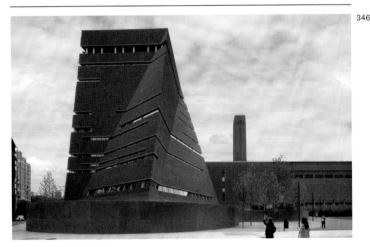

Switch House, 2016   **Herzog & de Meuron**
Tate Modern, Hopton Street, London SE1 9TG ◑
This latticed brick ziggurat extends the Tate Modern art gallery. Set above three
subterranean tanks for performance art, the extension unfolds around a central
core, providing three new gallery levels of exhibition space. Indoor bridges at first
and fourth floors link the Switch House to the existing turbine hall.

Europe

347

Palestra Office Building, 2006 **Will Alsop**
197 Blackfriars Road, London SE1 8JZ ●
Located opposite London's Southwark underground station, the Palestra building provides tenants with large, flexible floor plates. The glazed facade is decorated with an abstract pattern, and photovoltaic panels and wind turbines on the roof generate a proportion of the building's energy needs.

348

City Hall, Greater London authority HQ, 2002 **Foster + Partners**
The Queen's Walk, London SE1 2AA ●
Housing the chamber for the London Assembly, the offices of the Mayor of London and 500 staff, this highly public building is situated in a relatively undeveloped section of the Thames's South Bank. Energy consumption is minimized by using a form based on a modified sphere.

Europe

33433333333333333333333England   193

Great Court, 2000   **Foster + Partners**
The British Museum, Great Russell Street, Bloomsbury, London WC1B 3DG ◐
Covering an area of 6,100 sq m and containing information points, a bookshop and café, the Great Court is the largest enclosed public space in Europe. Two broad staircases encircle the Round Reading Room and a glazed roof-canopy spans the irregular gap between its dome and the galleries.

Saw Swee Hock Student Centre, 2014   **O'Donnell + Tuomey**
London School of Economics, 1 Portugal Street, London WC2A 2AP ●
The perforated redbrick facade here allows natural light and ventilation into the building, which slopes outwards and skywards at varying angles. Jatoba-wood window frames temper the geometry's sharpness. Beyond the canopied entrance, the interior features a wide staircase that spirals through the central space.

The Photographers' Gallery, 2012   **O'Donnell + Tuomey**
16-18 Ramillies Street, London W1F 7LW ◑
This Central London gallery has extended its redbrick Victorian warehouse with a
two-storey extension, contained in black steel-framed walls with a double-height
north window. At ground level, part of the facade is cut away to reveal the open-
planned lobby and café, and a stairway leads to the basement bookshop.

Serpentine Galleries, 2013   **Zaha Hadid**
West Carriage Drive, London W2 2AR ◑
The two galleries are located on either side of the Serpentine lake. The original venue
occupies a 1930s tea room, and the newer one, the Sackler, is a former gunpowder
store. The architect converted its vaulted brick interior to create exhibition space
and an extension to house a restaurant, featuring a distinctive white undulating roof.

Europe

62 Buckingham Gate, 2013   **Pelli Clarke Pelli and Swanke Hayden Connell**
62 Buckingham Gate, London SW1 ●
Accommodating retail and office space, this building features an elegant facade composed of folding glass planes, the surface of which reflects light differently depending on the time of day. At street level, a series of bays, sheltered by a multicoloured glass canopy, are used for outdoor restaurant seating.

Newport Street Gallery, 2015   **Caruso St John**
Newport Street, Lambeth, London SE11 6AJ ◑
Built to house the private collection of Damien Hirst, this gallery repurposes a series of Victorian scenery painting workshops, as well as adding two extensions. The conversion is harmonious, extending the industrial aesthetic of the original buildings by using a similarly pale redbrick. A zigzagging, saw-tooth roof adds a touch of drama.

Greenwich Peninsula Low Carbon Energy Centre, 2006   **CF Møller**
Greenwich, London SE10 ●
Rising 49m beside a prominent motorway, this faceted tower of perforated-steel panels, by artist Conrad Shawcross, signals the heat energy centre beside it, which contains boilers and CHP (Combined Heat and Power) systems for the developing Greenwich Peninsula region.

Olympic and Paralympic Shooting Arenas, 2012   **Magma**
Repository Road, Woolwich, London SE18 4BH ●
Enclosing the spectators' areas for the 2012 Olympic Games shooting ranges, these white double-curved PVC membrane skins dotted with coloured nodes provide an eye-catching exterior. The dots act as tensioning points for the membrane, and allow natural ventilation, while lower nodes also provide entry points.

Europe

Chiswick House Café, 2010   **Caruso St John**
Burlington Lane, Chiswick, London W4 2QN ◑
Part of a masterplan for Chiswick Gardens, this café is situated where stables once
stood close to Chiswick House. Drawing on references to the arcaded facades of
Venetian country villas, its stone colonnade provides covered seating alongside the
café interior, framing views across the historic landscape.

Sackler Crossing, 2006   **John Pawson**
Royal Botanic Gardens, Richmond TW9 3AE ◑
This footbridge crosses a lake within Kew Gardens, located near the River Thames.
The bridge's gently curved S-shape provides different vantage points as it is
crossed. The curved steel superstructure is set in piles within the shallow lake, and
water is visible through polished black granite treads.

Bombay Sapphire Distillery, 2014 **Heatherwick Studio**
Laverstoke Mill, London Road, Whitchurch RG28 7NR ◑
Occupying a converted eighteenth-century paper mill, this production headquarters for a gin distillery features two cloche-like glasshouses, which support tropical climates. The metal-ribbed structures appear to spill from an existing brick building, and sustain the botanicals used in Bombay Sapphire's recipe.

Turner Contemporary, 2011 **David Chipperfield**
Rendezvous, Margate CT9 1HG ◑
This seaside gallery is housed in six identical, two-storey pitched volumes clad with acid-etched glazing fixed between aluminium T-sections. An arts studio occupies the west wing with offices in the east. The central section houses the foyer and café at ground floor, with galleries above illuminated by skylights.

The Shingle House, 2010 **NORD**
Dungeness National Nature Reserve, Romney Marsh TN29 9NE ◑
Situated directly on a beach and nature reserve, this holiday home nods to the simple fishing huts nearby. Tarred black shingles outline its gabled form, which is organized in two halves: the larger northern wing contains reception, bedroom and bathing areas, while the lower levels house a kitchen, dining room and courtyard.

Bandstand, 2000 **Niall McLaughlin**
Marina, Bexhill-on-Sea, East Sussex TN33 9BN ○
A contemporary bandstand for the De La Warr Pavilion which was originally designed by Mendelsohn and Chemayeff in 1935, this innovative and playful design reflects the involvement of local children and a craftsman. The wings of the plywood and fibreglass canopy help to project the sound forward.

Downland Gridshell, 2001   **Cullinan Studio**
Singleton, Chichester, West Sussex PO18 0EU ◑
The latest addition to this museum houses a store for an archive of construction artefacts and, above it, a workshop for timber repairs. The double-layer gridshell is formed from a complex weave of curving green oak sections and is clad with red cedar and polycarbonate.

East Beach Café, 2007   **Heatherwick Studio**
Littlehampton, West Sussex BN17 5GB ◑
Located on a seafront promenade, this café's glazed southern facade offers sea views, while its northern side shelters occupants in inclement weather. Comprised of irregularly curved graduated steel plates, a protective, oil-based treatment produces its distinctive patina. Retractable shutters protect the windows at night.

SeaCity Museum, 2004   **WilkinsonEyre**
Havelock Road, Southampton SO14 7FY ◑
This maritime museum is situated in a converted 1930s courthouse, to which a new
pavilion wing has been added. Composed of three interlocking triangular bays, the
pavilion suggests the sails of a ship, while, at the entrance, a red oxide wall references the anti-foul paint used on the *Titanic*.

The Eden Project, 2005   **Grimshaw**
Bodelva, Par PL24 2SG ◑
This facility dedicated to the exhibition and conservation of plants occupies a former china clay pit. Featuring eight geodesic domes, an ETFE skin allows maximum
daylight to reach over a million plants. In 2003 a Foundation Building helped meet
growing administrative needs, and in 2005 an education building was added.

National Assembly for Wales, 2005   **Richard Rogers**
Cardiff Bay, Cardiff CF99 1NA ◑
Symbolising transparency between the elected and the electorate, the Welsh National Assembly building is enclosed by a large glazed envelope. Set upon a slate-clad plinth stepping down to Cardiff Bay, the dominant timber roof extends beyond the glass perimeter, providing a sheltered plaza.

Great Glasshouse, 2000   **Foster + Partners**
National Botanical Garden of Wales, Llanarthne SA32 8HN ◑
Embedded into the hills of Carmarthenshire, within the National Botanic Garden of Wales, the world's largest single-span glasshouse rests its elliptical curved-glass roof on a retaining wall that contains public and educational facilities. The structure comprises 24 tubular-steel arches springing from a concrete ring beam.

The Skainos Centre, 2012 **Donnelly O Neill**
241 Newtownards Road, Belfast BT4 1AF ◑
This 'urban village' is an exemplar cross-community project. The centrepiece of the 2012 scheme is a main building of brick and exposed concrete: a cool, calm space for local support groups. Standout eco features include green walls, solar panels and bird boxes, while its enamel panels were painted by local artist Jonny McEwen.

Lyric Theatre Belfast, 2012 **O'Donnell + Tuomey**
55 Ridgeway Street, Belfast BT9 5FB ◑
Featuring a butterfly roof, this theatre is built in similar redbrick to the residential area that surrounds it. The same material is used to great effect in the interior of the studio, while its 389-seat auditorium is comprised of dramatically faceted iroko-wood surfaces.

Model Arts and Niland Gallery, 2000   **McCullough Mulvin**
The Model, The Mall, Rathquarter, Sligo ◑
Incorporating the former Model School, this refurbishment provides additional galleries, performance spaces and a new pavilion to house the Niland collection of Jack Butler Yeats paintings. A courtyard gives the arts complex a revitalized heart and links the simple cedar-clad box to the existing stone-built gallery.

Solstice Arts Centre, 2006   **Grafton**
Railway Street, Dillonsland, Navan, County Meath ◑
Set on a limestone plinth, this arts centre is imagined as a 'manmade rock outcrop'. Its glazed theatre, foyer and green rooms are set beneath a black marble mosaic slab cantilevered above, which contains gallery spaces and offices. The project capitalizes on the sloping site: a natural fit for the raked seating within.

Civic Offices, 2001 **Grafton**
16 Drumree Road, Grangend, County Meath ●
This modest building serves the housing estates that surround it. The projecting council chamber and two existing cedar trees frame a slender space above which floats a cantilevered canopy. The building's skeleton of exposed concrete is combined with timber and glass screens.

Sean O'Casey Community Centre, 2008 **O'Donnell + Tuomey**
Saint Mary's Road, East Wall, Dublin ◐
This complex houses a five-storey classroom-office tower, and facilities for the community, including a nursery, daycare centre for the elderly, a theatre and a sports hall. Cast corrugated concrete, punched with three sizes of circular windows, is used throughout, with different spaces separated by iroko-lined internal courtyards.

Republic of Ireland

Department of Mechanical & Manufacturing Enginering, 2002 **Grafton**
Parsons Building, Trinity College, Dublin ●
Slotted between a nineteenth-century stone building and later brick-faced additions, this extension features facilities for research and teaching. The building is
clad in coarse granite and set on a podium containing laboratories. Multiple landings
in the circulation connect this building to its older neighbours.

Urban Institute of Ireland, 2002 **Grafton**
University College Dublin, Clonskeagh Road, Farranboley, Dublin ●
An institute for cross-disciplinary research, this two-storey building connects to
the adjacent redbrick library. Its upper levels are clad in terracotta wall tiles. Inside,
staggered concrete block piers encircle the central double-height void, with quiet
or collaborative spaces delineated by plywood screens.

Offaly County Council Offices, 2002 **ABK**
Áras an Chontae, Charleville Road, Kilcruttin, Tullamore, Offaly R35 F893 ●
The modern council offices stand in sharp contrast to Tullamore's other institutional buildings. Beyond the small entrance forecourt are a roof-lit atrium and three-storey offices. A single-storey extension contains the café, archives, walled garden and crèche. A timber lattice offers shade and privacy.

Crawford Municipal Art Gallery, 2000 **Erick van Egeraat**
Emmett Place, Centre, Cork ◑
Within the wedge-shaped former courtyard of the gallery is this two-storey extension. As well as providing two large temporary exhibition spaces, the extension, which is constructed from curved planes of brick, links the old building to create a unified whole.

Europe

Cork City Council New Civic Offices, 2007   **ABK**
City Hall, Anglesea Street, Ballintemple, Cork ●
An L-shaped block engages the existing City Hall, while a rectangular block addresses the street at the opposite end of the site. A rigorous, partly random grid of glass and concrete defines the facade of the first block, and a lantern-like double-skin facade of glass clads the second.

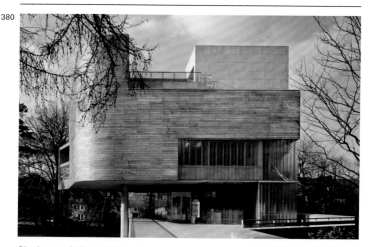

Glucksman Gallery, 2004   **O'Donnell + Tuomey**
College Road, University College, Cork ◑
This gallery provides resources for the community and art exhibitions of an international standard. A limestone-clad podium base houses a café that opens onto surrounding gardens, while concrete cores and slim columns support cantilevered gallery spaces above, wrapped by curving walls of horizontal hardwood planks.

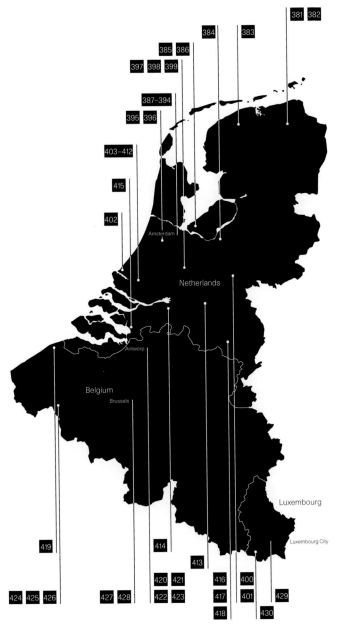

Europe

381 382

383

384

385 386

397 398 399

387–394

395 396

403–412

415

402

Amsterdam

Netherlands

Antwerp

Belgium

Brussels

Luxembourg

Luxembourg City

419

414

413

420 421

416 400

424 425 426

427 428

422 423

417 401

429

418

430

Blue Moon Hotel, 2001   **FOA**
Kleine Gang/Grote Gang, Schuiteschuiverskwartier, Groningen ◑
As part of the 2001 Blue Moon Festival, architects were invited to design dual-function live/work buildings. The four-storey, corrugated steel hotel houses a café and apartments. The front facade is a system of shutters that articulates the concepts of public or private.

La Liberté Housing and Offices, 2012   **Dominique Perrault**
16 Aprillaan, 9728 CG Groningen ●
A pair of towers designed for social housing and offices, this project encourages the preservation of green spaces. A footbridge links the towers, which rest on glazed three-storey podia containing workspaces, and rise 80 and 40m respectively. Clad in distinctive black and white they contrast pleasingly with their parkland surrounds.

Bastion Island Holiday Houses, 2000   **Dok**
De Wielendwinger 1-20, 8926 XJ Leeuwarden ●
These 20 holiday houses are arranged around a rectangular communal courtyard, projecting out on to the lake. Presenting an introspective face to the courtyard, each house points ike a boat towards the water, with alternate volumes of prow and conservatory living spaces lining the waterfront.

De Verbeelding Centre for the Arts, 2000   **René van Zuuk**
De Verbeelding 25, 3892 Zeewolde ◑
Sited in a park dedicated to the preservation of art and nature, this pavilion, its sculptural form a response to its water-based location, houses exhibition spaces. The elongated shape was influenced by American sculptor Richard Serra's *Sea Level*, which can be viewed from the end glass wall.

Apartment Tower, 2001 **Claus en Kaan**
Hengelostraat 101-158, 1324 GZ Almere ●
Located close to the centre of Almere, a town built in the 1980s beside an artificial lake, this aluminium-clad tower contains 58 apartments of varying room heights, design and layout. At lower levels, the block projects out towards a park, while at upper levels it turns towards the lake.

The Sphinxes Apartment Buildings, 2003 **Neutelings Riedijk**
Gooimeerpromenade, Huizen ●
Five apartment blocks project out into Gooimeer Lake, just east of Amsterdam, connected to the land by narrow jetties. Clad in unpolished aluminium sheets, their protruding box-like head and tapering wedge-like form have earned them the nickname 'The Sphinxes'.

Silodam Mixed-use Building, 2002
Silodam 129, 1013 Amsterdam ●

MVRDV

Containing commercial units and residential spaces, the Silodam building rises from the water on strong, angled piloti. Various apartment types and configurations are arranged in mini-neighbourhoods, the facade of each using different colours and materials, resulting in the building's variegated elevations.

EYE Film Institute, 2012
IJpromenade 1, 1031 Amsterdam ◑

Delugan Meissl

Clad in folded layers of aluminium panels, this film institute's angular exterior mimics the spatial organization inside. A sloping riverside promenade leads to the glazed podium entrance and oak-lined lobby. Three smaller theatres are grouped in the northern wing, while the large auditorium is located in the eastern volume.

De Loodsen Social Housing, 2006 **Wingender Hovenier**
Piet Heinkade 183 and 211, Veembroederhof, 1019 HC Amsterdam ●
These two towers — part of a group of six — are situated on opposite corners of a site in the eastern harbour district of Oostelijke Handelskade. The brickwork pattern between the uniformly spaced windows shifts part way up the towers, interrupting the otherwise monolithic facades.

Whale Housing, 2000 **de Architekten Cie**
Sporenburg Peninsula, Baron GA Tindalplein, 1019 Amsterdam ●
Located beside the River Ij, this ambitious project stands out within a low-rise development, aiming to combine the housing density of the inner city with a suburban feel. Despite its scale and mass, the Whale's interior and central courtyard garden create a feeling of intimacy.

Piramides Apartment Building, 2006
Jan van Galenstraat 1a-29e, 1051 KE Amsterdam ●

Soeters Van Eldonk

The form of these intertwined triangular towers is inspired by a number of sources: Christmas trees (previously sold here), the island's shape and Amsterdam's historic gables. The towers contain 82 apartments of varying sizes. Spaces for social and cultural events are located in the buildings connected base.

The New Rijksmuseum, 2013
Museumstraat 1, 1071 XX Amsterdam ◑

Cruz y Ortiz

In transforming this nineteenth-century gallery, with only minimal alterations to the building itself, the architects chose to strip away later additions. The museum's major features include a new entrance formed from two inner courtyards, glazed overhead and linked underground, as well as a new Asian Pavilion of stone and glass.

LJG Synagogue, 2012   **SeARCH**
Zuidelijke Wandelweg 41, 1079 RK Amsterdam ◑
Designed for the city's Liberal Jewish community, this canalside synagogue is set within a large rectangular volume, its long elevations cut with ornamental fenestration of an abstract menorah. The windows mirror the void within that holds the chamber, flanked by three levels of symmetrically arranged seating.

Gerrit Rietveld Academy, 2004   **Benthem Crouwel**
Fred Roeskestraat 96, 1076 ED Amsterdam ●
This building houses the fine art department of the Rietveld Academy on a site opposite the academy's original building. Black floors, white walls and staircases in primary colours reflect Gerrit Thomas Rietveld's philosophy. Semi-transparent Czech glass tiles cover most of the south, east and west facades.

Hydra Pier Exhibition Centre, 2002   **Asymptote**
Floriade, Haarlemmermeer ⦾
Originally commissioned for the 2002 Floriade exhibition, this viewing pavilion is located in the town of Haarlemmermeer, which is set on an artificial lake resulting from land reclamation. This theme is reflected in the continually flowing water that shrouds the building, gathering in pools above a laminated glass bubble.

Dutch Reformed Church, 2006   **Claus en Kaan**
Aalsmeerderweg 747, 1435 EK Rijsenhout ⦾
A tower topped by a metal staff signals the religious nature of this church, with the different purposes of each space reflected externally in the decreasing heights of the volumes. Inside, a window screen is made of pre-rusted metal cables and a ceiling is crisscrossed with bare fluorescent strip lights.

Europe

City Hall, 2000　　　　　　　　　　　　　　　**Miralles Tagliabue EMBT**
Korte Minrebroederstraat 2, 3512 GG Utrecht ●
Miralles has reworked Utrecht's confusing city hall, which had been altered and extended through the centuries, re-orientating the complex so that it opens on to a new public square. The additions have been inserted into the existing fabric, while elsewhere older fragments of the building have been exposed.

398

The Aluminium Forest, 2001　　　　　　　　　**Abbink De Haas**
Voorveste 2, 3992 DC Houten ◑
This aluminium information centre is made of the very material that it is promoting. A simple 1,000 sq m box sits lightly on 368 piloti of varying dimensions. The dense distribution of the supporting columns enables the building to defy expectations of the strength of aluminium.

City Hall and Theatre, 2000   **UNStudio**
Overtoom 1, Zenderpark, 3401 BK Lelystad ➊
Located between the new and old parts of IJsselstein, this City Hall and Theatre provides the town with a new civic focus. Built on a kite-shaped site, the building is divided into cultural facilities on one side and civic functions on the other, but unified by its cladding of recycled glass.

National Heritage Museum, 2000   **Metro**
Schelmseweg 89, 6816 SJ Arnhem ➊
This design alludes to buildings from different regions and periods that pepper the surrounding park. A long wall formed of multifarious bricks represents different regions of the country and a cobbled path leads to a sliding metal door in the wall and continues into the hall beyond.

Cultural Centre Rozet, 2013   **Neutelings Riedijk**
Kortestraat 16, 6811 EP Arnhem ❶
A cultural centre between Arnhem's railway station and the church square, this
long, triangular building is organized around a glazed central corridor. The interior
and exterior are defined by a dense pattern of concrete mullions that feature traditional decorative reliefs.

Geothermal Station, 2012   **Jan Splinter**
The Hague
The biggest geothermal station in the Netherlands, the energy this structure provides is distributed across several districts. Constructed on a concrete foundation
and built in red-coloured steel, the station has two gabled roofs, with a tower protruding from the larger of the two, giving the building a chapel-like appearance.

Saint Mary of the Angels Chapel, 2001   **Mecanoo**
Nieuwe Crooswijkseweg 123, 3034 PN Rotterdam ❶
Situated in the nineteenth-century Roman Catholic cemetery of St Lawrence, this chapel takes an irregular, curvilinear form, its exterior walls constructed of steel and timber. The inside wall, slotted between two bands of glazing, appears to be separate from floor and ceiling.

Centraal Station, 2014   **Benthem Crouwel**
Stationsplein 2, 3013 AJ Rotterdam ❶
This station is split into two distinct sections. The first, the entrance to which is in a historic neighbourhood, is modest in design. The second, meanwhile, echoes the grandeur of the city centre, with a soaring-stainless steel roof and a glass-and-wood hall.

Markthal, 2014   **MVRDV**
Dominee Jan Scharpstraat 298, 3011 GZ Rotterdam ◑
A giant grey arch announces this combined market hall and residential building, with food stalls and hospitality at the lower two levels, and apartments above. The market hall's interior is lined with a mural, punctured by residents' windows. Apartment balconies run along the curved exterior.

Boijmans-van Beuningen Museum, 2003   **Robbrecht en Daem**
Museumpark 18-20, 3015 CX Rotterdam ◑
This large-scale renovation and extension project combines contemporary insertions with a consolidated historic core. Interwoven into Van der Steur's original building are 5,000 sq m of new gallery and public areas all enveloped in sleek concrete and glass.

Unilever Nederland BV, 2007   **JHK**
Nassaukade 5, 3071 JL Rotterdam ●
The lowest floor of this glass-clad office building, which is propped up by girdles, is 25m above the quay. The structure provides a dramatic contrast to the classical nineteenth-century building next door. A series of atriums and patios allow light to enter the building.

De Rotterdam, 2013   **OMA**
Wilhelminakade 139, 3072 AP Rotterdam ◑
This project was conceived as a mixed-use vertical city of offices, flats, conference facilities, exhibition space, a hotel, shops and restaurants. The three 150m-tall glass towers are connected by a shared plinth, which houses each of the tower's lobbies, creating a public place for office workers and residents alike.

Timmerhuis, 2015   **OMA**
Meent 119, 3011 JH Rotterdam ●
This building accommodates municipal services, offices and residential units. It's conceived as a modular building with repeated units gradually set back from the street as they rise into two irregular peaks. Two large atriums store warmth in summer and cold in winter, releasing this energy as warm or cold air as required.

Scheepvaart en Transport College, 2005   **Neutelings Riedijk**
Lloydstraat 300, Rotterdam
Situated on a disused pier, the zigzag shape of this building is inspired by surrounding cranes. Classrooms sit on top of each other in the tower, linked by escalators allowing 2,000 pupils to change one floor in 10 minutes. A protruding cantilever at the top holds a 300-person auditorium.

Europe

Erasmusbrug, 1996   **UNStudio**
3011 BN Rotterdam ○
With the redevelopment of the docks in the 1990s, a bridge was needed to link this area to the city centre, resulting in this 139m-high structure. Lights strung along the cables illuminate the bridge at night, picking out the cables as strands of pure white, perfectly complementing the pylon, which locals call 'The Swan'.

Book Mountain and Library Quarter, 2012   **MVRDV**
Markt 40, 3201 Spijkenisse ◑
This 'mountain' of books is constructed by stacking the library's services and storage into a pyramidal central form, wrapped by 480m of bookshelves and reading niches. Constructed from brick and dark-stained wood, the five-storey book tower sits inside a larger structure of timber beams, clad with glazing.

Exhibition Building, 2001　　　　　　　　　　　**Claus en Kaan**
Lunettenlaan 600, 5263 NT Vught ◑
Situated in a former concentration camp, a small piece of land and remnants of a crematorium have been landscaped to accommodate this pavilion, which contains exhibition spaces, an auditorium and offices. The plain rectangular form appears blank, the only interruption being bands of tiles alternating with rows of bricks.

Popstage Mezz, 2002　　　　　　　　　　　**Erick van Egeraat**
Keizerstraat 101, 4811 HL Breda ◑
This new music hall, visible from Breda city centre, is part of the urban development scheme for an abandoned military campus. The double-skinned biomorphic form has an outer shell of steel and concrete covered with poured concrete and pre-oxidized copper panels.

Europe

Moses Bridge, 2011   **RO&AD**
Schansbaan 8, 4661 PN Halsteren ○
This bridge's 'invisibility' is a playful nod to the history of its site, which was originally a military defence line. Built entirely in wood, the bridge lies beneath the surface of the water — its appearance suggests a trench, as well as the biblical story from which it takes its name. From a distance, it is almost entirely invisible.

Student Housing Campus, 2016   **Office Winhov, Office Haratori and BDG**
Eindhoven University of Technology, 5612 AZ Eindhoven ●
Formed of two rectilinear halves staggered around a central corridor, the load-bearing facade of this student housing is made of prefabricated concrete elements that create a modular grid. The building is bookended by circulation cores, with shared south-facing outdoor patios on each floor.

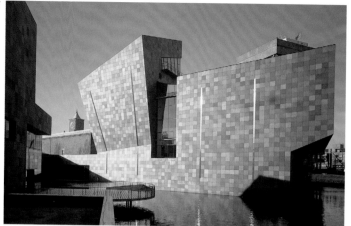

Stedelijk Van Abbemuseum, 2002   **Abel Cahen**
Bilderdijklaan 10, 5611 NH Eindhoven ◑
This extension, completed after 12 years of planning battles, has given the museum an exhibition space four times its original size. The central bevelled tower and canted geometry dominate the existing redbrick facade and bell tower that architect Abel Cahen had originally wanted to demolish.

Kennedy Business Centre, 2004   **KCAP**
John F Kennedy Plein, 5611 Eindhoven ●
This site includes offices, underground parking and a winding public thoroughfare. A diagonal walkway cuts through the development and connects Eindhoven's Central Station with the campus of the Eindhoven University of Technology. Its tiles will eventually turn the same rust colour as the Corten steel pavement outside.

Concert Hall, 2002 **Robbrecht en Daem**
Het Zand 34, 8000 Bruges ◑
Backed by a skyline full of church spires, the monolithic form of Bruges's red-tiled concert hall is dominated by its Stage Tower and Lantern Tower. A large auditorium is defined by two inclining side walls and the more intimate chamber music hall is arranged as an atrium surrounded by a spiral walkway.

The Port House, 2016 **Zaha Hadid**
Zaha Hadidplein 1, 2030 Antwerp ●
This project repurposed a derelict fire station into a new headquarters for the port of Antwerp. An extension, which 'floats' above the existing building, is shaped like the bow of a ship, and points towards the Scheldt River. The structure has a faceted glazed facade that reflects the changing tones and colours of the city's sky.

Europe

Europe

Apartment Towers Westkaai 1 + 2, 2009   **Diener & Diener**
Westkaai 41 and 51, 2170 Antwerp ●
A fraternal pair of buildings, these 56m-tall towers differ slightly in their cladding of rippled glass or aluminium sheet. Organized around a central core, the towers include 11 variations of apartments. A systematic layout of types orders the apparently random facade arrangement of recessed windows and loggias.

422

Law Courts, 2005   **Rogers Stirk Harbour + Partners**
Bolivarplaats 20, 2000 Antwerp ●
Although it has a low profile, the dramatic sail-like roofline of Antwerp's Law Courts is visible from the edge of the city centre. Each roof 'pod', formed from a steelwork frame and interconnected concrete units, houses a courtroom, while the rest of the building incorporates offices, archive space and a central public hall.

Het Huis, 2012   **Robbrecht en Daem**
Middelheimlaan 61, Antwerp ○
An addition to Antwerp's Middelheim museum, this pavilion provides exhibition space for sculptures that require a degree of protection from the elements. Its structure features exposed columns, concrete floors and untreated timber knots, while steel-lattice screens allow for ever-changing configurations of light inside.

Buda Art Centre, 2012   **51N4E**
Dam 2, 8500 Kortrijk ◑
Situated in a former textile factory, much of which has been retained, this arts centre features a pair of five-sided pavilions made from sandy bricks. The first freestanding, open-air pentagon announces the pavilion's entrance, while the second taller insertion carves through the centre of the plan, creating an open atrium.

Gavo, 2011 URA
Provinciedomein De Gavers, Kortrijk, Provincie West-Vlaanderen ●
Situated in a popular nature and recreation park on the edge of Kortrijk, this building
features an information centre, a restaurant, laboratory and educational facilities
for children. Its slatted wood facade echoes the forest around it, while large glass
windows allow for unrestricted views of the lake beyond.

Concordia Textiles Head Office, 2000 Vincent Van Duysen
Flanders Fieldweg 37, 8790 Waregem ●
This addition to an existing textiles plant includes new offices and a showroom.
Based on a 2.5m modular system, concrete, metal and glass characterize the low-
rise elevation, which is punctuated by three two-storey light monitors, while a
raised exterior walkway acts as a buffer between the offices and the street below.

MAD Brussels, 2017   **V+**
Place du Nouveau Marché aux Grains 10, 1000 Brussels ◑
Much of the existing industrial building was preserved to create new exhibition and office spaces for a Belgian fashion and design platform. A homogenous whole is shaped by the materials: predominantly brick, cast-steel columns and white-painted concrete. Public exhibitions, seminars and events are held at ground level.

Le Toison d'Or, 2016   **UNStudio**
Avenue de la Toison d'Or, 1000 Brussels ◑
Avoiding the uniform qualities common to block structures, this retail and residential complex is framed by curving bands of reinforced concrete. The exterior walls feature stone tiles, expansive shop windows and golden-hued aluminium balconies. The upper floors contain 72 apartments and an elevated city garden.

429

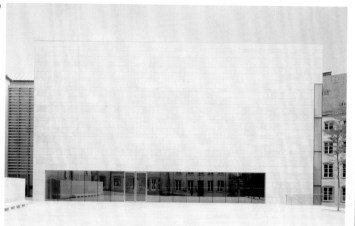

National Museum of History and Art, 2002   **Christian Bauer**
Marché-aux-Poissons, 2345 Luxembourg City ◑
Within the crowded historic heart of the city, this museum stands on one of only three public squares. The plaza has been integrated into the overall design by the use of the same light stone as the museum's expansive facade, in which a low slot signals the entrance.

430

La Maison du Savoir, 2015   **Baumschlager Eberle**
University of Luxembourg, 2 Avenue de l'Universite, 4365 Esch-sur-Alzette ●
The Maison du Savoir is located on the site of a former steelworks, and the building was designed with this in mind — the dimensions of the tower block at its centre, for example, match those of a steel furnace. The interior, meanwhile, with its numerous foyers and seating areas, emphasizes its use as a communal space.

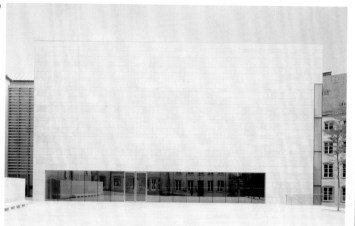

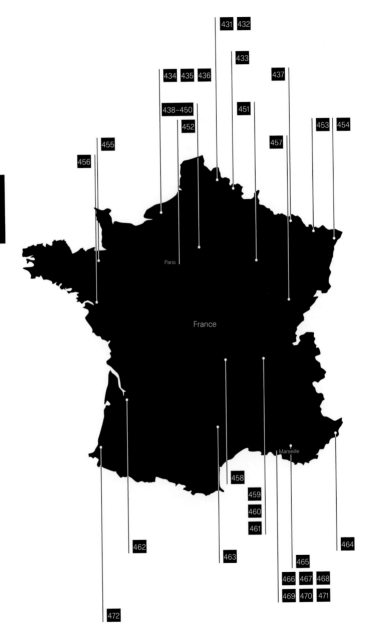

431 432
433
434 435 436
437
438–450
451
452
453 454
455
456
457

Paris

France

458
459
460
461
462
463
464
465
466 467 468
469 470 471
472

Marseille

Lille Métropole Musée Extension, 2010　　　　　　**Manuelle Gautrand**
1 allée du Musée, 59650 Villeneuve-d'Ascq ◑
This extension comprises five snaking volumes, punctured with an irregular pattern, which wrap around an existing building that was originally designed in 1983. On the north side, 'ribs' house a restaurant opening onto a central patio, before fanning out on the east to accommodate five galleries displaying Outsider art.

Louvre-Lens, 2012　　　　　　　　　　　　**SANAA**
99 rue Paul Bert, 62300 Lens ◑
No mere satellite of its progenitor, Louvre-Lens shows works from the Louvre's collection in the 3,000 sq m Grande Galerie, while exhibits in the Glass Pavilion synchronise with regional galleries across France. Low steel-and-glass structures let in light and reflect the surrounding landscaped park, built on a defunct coal mine.

Europe

Musée Matisse, 2002 **Beaudouin**
13 place du Commandant-Richez, 59360 Le Cateau-Cambrésis ◑
This development complements the existing eighteenth-century building and provides an auditorium, exhibition space and conservation studios. The pared-down volumes are faced in redbrick, matching the decorative facades of the original museum.

Sports Palace, 2012 **Dominique Perrault**
40 rue de Lillebonne, 76000 Rouen ◑
Akin to a mirrored inverse ziggurat, the terraced soffit along the southeastern edge of this sporting arena is constructed from polished stainless steel. Its attention-grabbing form is mimicked in flights of concrete steps that lead to the upper level entry. Inside, two sports halls dominate the space.

Concert Hall and Exhibition Complex, 2001　　　　　　**Bernard Tschumi**
Parc des Expositions, 76120 Rouen ◑
Visible from the motorway outside Rouen, the concert hall and the Miesian exhibition space are a bold gateway to the city. The steel skins of the concert hall wrap around each other, creating a foyer space. A restricted palette of materials allows clarity of form.

Théâtre d'Eclat, 2001　　　　　　**Jakob + Macfarlane**
Place Général de Gaulle, 27500 Pont-Audemer ◑
Based around Pont-Audemer's original theatre built by Maurice Novarina in the 1960s, this intervention encases the sandblasted skeleton of the existing structure with a skin of galvanized steel and glass panels. The interior space of the auditorium determines the folds of the continuous wall.

Centre Pompidou-Metz, 2010 **Shigeru Ban**
1 parvis des Droits de l'Homme, 57020 Metz ◑
This museum's roof, inspired by a Chinese bamboo-woven hat and punctured by a tall spire, comprises wooden hexagonal segments covered in a Teflon-coated fiberglass membrane. Inside, cantilevered galleries float above the ground and include large apertures offering views of the city beyond.

Tower Flower, 2004 **Edouard François**
23 rue Albert Roussel, 75017 Paris ●
This 10-storey tower is the vertical continuation of an adjacent park. Its giant flower pots, hanging from the balconies, were inspired by Parisian window planters. The precast concrete structure is arranged around a central glazed circulation core, which brings light into the building's centre.

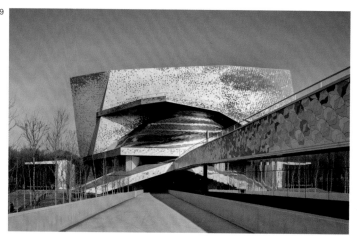

Philharmonie de Paris, 2015　　　　　　　**Ateliers Jean Nouvel**
221 avenue Jean Jaurès, 75019 Paris ◑
Although its architect has publically denounced it, there are plenty that commend
this concert hall. Its angled, folded planes are clad in an aluminium and steel mesh,
whose silver and charcoal nuances glisten in the sun, evoking a flock of birds. Inside,
the 2,400-seat auditorium features a series of voluptuous ramps and balconies.

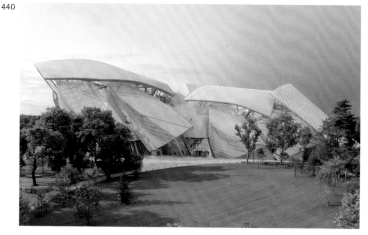

Fondation Louis Vuitton, 2014　　　　　　　**Frank Gehry**
Bois de Boulogne, 8 avenue du Mahatma Gandhi, 75116 Paris ◑
This contemporary art museum houses the collection of Louis Vuitton chairman
Bernard Arnault. The building comprises an assemblage of white blocks (known as
'The Icebergs'), clad in panels of fibre-reinforced concrete, and 12 enormous glass-
panelled sails, which are supported by wooden beams.

Department of Islamic Art, 2012   **Mario Bellini**
The Louvre, rue de Rivoli, 75001 Paris ◑
The undulating layer of 2,350 triangular panels in gold and silver aluminium mesh, that occupies Cour Visconti, shields the treasures of the Louvre's Islamic art collection. The illusion of suspension and fluidity gives the project an unexpected lightness, entirely in keeping with the museum's now-iconic glass pyramid.

Epée de Bois Nursery, 2014   **h2o**
5 rue de l'Épée de Bois, 75005 Paris ●
On a narrow courtyard site, this glazed volume, wrapped with a billowing gauze canopy, forms the extension to an existing nursery. It contains three levels, with an outdoor play space situated on the roof. A courtyard beside the entry is glazed, allowing daylight into the basement, which houses staff amenities.

Le Monde Headquarters Office Building, 2005   **Christian de Portzamparc**
80 boulevard Auguste Blanqui, 75013 Paris ●
This renovated 11-storey tower houses offices for newspaper *Le Monde*. One wing
was widened to create office space and volumes of varying height were added at the
back of the building. An outer layer of glass is etched with the newspaper's mast-
head, a passage on freedom of the press by Victor Hugo and a world map.

Jérôme Seydoux-Pathé Foundation, 2014   **Renzo Piano Building Workshop**
73 avenue des Gobelins, 75013 Paris ◑
This headquarters for the Pathé film foundation contains a screening room, exhibition space, archives and offices. Entrance is via the listed 1869 facade, originally
sculpted by Rodin. From here, bridges lead into the curvaceous carapace of glass
tiles, underpinned by timber ribs, which are linked by a spiral staircase.

School of Architecture, 2007 **Frédéric Borel**
3-15 quai Panhard et Levassor, 75013 Paris ●
Situated along the River Seine, this project comprises two parallel buildings connected by a ground-floor entrance and upper-storey walkways. A renovated factory contains exhibition space and a library, while a new building houses classrooms and auditoriums, with upper floors supported by angled piloti.

La Seine Musicale, 2017 **Shigeru Ban and Jean de Gastines**
1 cours de l'Île Seguin, 92100 Boulogne-Billancourt ◑
Situated on an island on the Seine River, this music venue extends nearly 280m along the riverbank. Its key feature — a spherical, latticed auditorium with a 'sail' of solar panels — responds to the curvature of the island. Inside, the 1,150-seat auditorium is lined with a variety of timber forms and patterns.

Arches Boulogne, 2016   **Antonini Darmon**
21 rue Marcel Bontemps, 92100 Boulogne-Billancourt ●
Formerly a Renault factory site, this six-storey residential building is part of a new urban precinct with a central shared garden. Reinterpreting the factory buildings, its white concrete facades repeat the classical language of arches, which extend around the outer perimeter of the irregular polygon.

Montreuil Coeur de Ville, 2012   **Dietmar Feichtinger**
ZAC Coeur De Ville, 5 rue Franklin, 93100 Montreuil ◑
This complex is composed of three spaces: a new retail area; a civic plaza that faces the existing town hall; and a new theatre and cinema complex. Outside, a large urban park is lined with bars and restaurants, and functions as a venue for outdoor events.

Le Château, 2014 **Bona-Lemercier**
Parc Culturel de Rentilly, 1 rue de l'Étang, Bussy-Saint-Martin ◑
Having been destroyed in WWII, this sixteenth-century château has been reborn as a contemporary art space. The entire facade is cloaked in mirror-polished stainless steel that reflects the surrounding gardens. The roof has been converted into a terrace, with expansive views of the park and nearby lakes.

Sénart Theatre, 2016 **Chaix & Morel et Associés**
8 allée de la Mixité, 77127 Lieusaint ◑
Located in a new town southeast of Paris, this theatre is dedicated to dance, drama and music, and houses two large halls, alongside rehearsal rooms and technical workshops. Clad in light-reflecting aluminium, the exterior is topped with a tall steeple, which provides a landmark silhouette for the town's skyline.

Le Signe National Centre for Graphic Design, 2016   **Moatti-Rivière**
7-9 avenue Foch, 52000 Chaumont ◑
This minimalist construction — a conversion of a former nineteenth-century bank
— takes graphic design as its inspiration, with thin stone sheets on an aluminium
beehive base representing the designer's canvas of page, poster or screen. The
architects also used the same colour natural limestone as the adjacent building.

FRAC Centre, 2013   **Jakob + Macfarlane**
88 rue du Colombier, 45000 Orléans ◑
The extruded, faceted surfaces of this contemporary museum are cloaked in steel-
framed panels of metallic woven mesh. The first and tallest extrusion contains temporary exhibitions, and the smallest houses an audiovisual gallery, while the third
encompasses a lobby with a large glazed facade.

Sarrebourg Museum, 2003   **Bernard Desmoulin**
Rue de la Paix, 57400 Sarrebourg ◑
Housed in three parallel sheds — two of which are clad in patinated copper, with the third in concrete — this museum's collections include Gallo-Roman remains and works by Marc Chagall. The two double-height sheds house temporary exhibitions, while the taller third structure comprises two floors devoted to artworks.

Park and Ride Tram Station, 2001   **Zaha Hadid**
67800 Hoenheim ◑
Part of a new initiative to reduce congestion and pollution, this tram station and car park is characterized by patterns of lines that are generated by the movement of cars, trams and pedestrians. Linearity is expressed in the ceiling strip-lights, floor markings and the lines of the parking spaces.

Frac Bretagne, 2012   **Studio Odile Decq**
19 avenue André Mussat, 35011 Rennes ◑
The site for this contemporary art centre is on a small hill overlooking Rennes. The
building sits next to an Aurelie Nemour sculpture, installed in 2005. A south-facing
facade is clad in grey-tinted glass, which reflects images of the sculpture nearby.
The interiors are defined by a central atrium and the red mass of the auditorium.

Nantes Courthouse, 2000   **Ateliers Jean Nouvel**
Quai François Mitterand, 44000 Nantes ●
Sited on the Loire's Sainte-Anne Island and part of a local regeneration scheme, this
building is essentially a black perforated box of steel and glass. The grid theme is
repeated inside, in the enormous mesh screens that separate the courtrooms from
the vast lobby.

Cite des Arts et de la Culture, 2013   **Kengo Kuma & Associates**
12 avenue Arthur Gaulard, 25000 Besançon ◑
A chequered timber facade and roof unites the Besançon Art Centre and the Cité de la Musique that comprise this complex, and spans the open terrace between the pair of three-storey buildings. Steel and glass panels are interspersed with wooden panels to define the spaces inside.

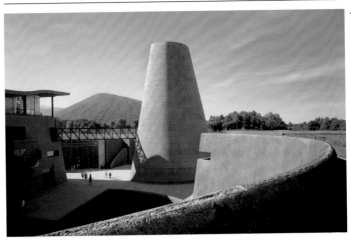

Vulcania Museum, 2002   **Hans Hollein**
Route de Mazayes, 63230 Saint-Ours-les Roches ◑
Situated within an extinct volcano, this museum's sunken plaza is dominated by a conical structure housing two amphitheatres and an exhibition hall. Additional buildings accommodate an IMAX theatre, research and conference facilities and a second conical element offers glimpses of simulated magma below the site.

The Orange Cube, 2011 **Jakob + Macfarlane**
42 quai Rambaud, 69002 Lyon ❶
In a former harbour zone of the city of Lyon, this five-storey cultural centre cuts a striking form, its orange cube carved out by an enormous conical hole. Creating a huge atrium that rises through the heart of the volume, the void interrupts the fine, mesh facade of pixelated metal.

Lucie-Aubrac Media Library, 2001 **Dominique Perrault**
2-4 avenue Marcel Houël, 69200 Vénissieux ❶
Located between a public square and a church, the library is a square glass box with all its functions on the same level. Offices are accommodated in a three-storey box on top of the space. Rooflights and the perforated metal and glass facades allow light deep into the interior.

Musée des Confluences, 2014   **Coop Himmelb(l)au and Wolf D Prix**
86 quai Perrache, 69002 Lyon ◑
Sited at the tip of a peninsula, this building is organized into three principal components: circulation in 'The Crystal', which includes a spiralling ramp and bridge pathway; 'The Cloud', clad in stainless-steel panels, which holds galleries; and 'The Plinth', composed of reinforced concrete and housing auditoria and workshops.

Bordeaux Stadium, 2015   **Herzog & de Meuron**
Cours Jules Ladoumegue, 33300 Bordeaux ◑
This stadium for sport, concerts and events is framed by 900 slim white steel columns, creating an ethereal effect that belies the structure's scale. Protected by a rectilinear roof, the tapered seating bowl is intersected by a ribbon-like structure that weaves around the perimeter and accommodates food stalls and amenities.

Millau Viaduct, 2004   **Foster + Partners**
Gorge du Tarn ○
Spanning a river valley in the south of France, this is the highest road bridge in the world. Pylons taper upwards, splitting to allow for the expansion and contraction of the roadway. Concrete masts above mirror this design, beginning as two elements that meld into one, and anchoring metal cables that support the road.

Musée Jean Cocteau, 2011   **Rudy Ricciotti**
2 quai de Monleon, 06500 Menton ◑
Dedicated to the French artist Jean Cocteau, the museum incorporates the collection of businessman and Cocteau enthusiast Séverin Wunderman. The one-storey facade is constructed from tinted glass, while the fragmented concrete shell has been likened to a fierce set of teeth.

Conservatory Darius Milhaud, 2013 **Kengo Kuma & Associates**
380 avenue Mozart, 13100 Aix-en-Provence ◑
In response to the varied levels of elevation within the site, the project uses flexible aluminium cladding for its facade, while the emphasis on light and shadow was partly inspired by the works of Aix-en-Provence artist Paul Cézanne. Inside, the concert hall features distinctive and dramatic asymmetrical angles.

CMA CGM Headquarters Tower, 2010 **Zaha Hadid**
4 quai d'Arenc, 13002 Marseille ●
The tallest building in Marseilles, this 147m tower has become an icon, thanks to its shape, which resembles a deconstructed lighthouse or sail, and its colour, which echoes the sea and sky. The expanse of glass and steel swoops gracefully down to an elongated 135m base, giving the impression of movement.

Orange Vélodrome, 2016   **SCAU**
3 boulevard Michelet, 13008 Marseille ◑
The architects refurbished and extended an existing stadium with a 25m deep windbreak around the open pitch, made from Teflon-impregnated fibreglass canvas that minimizes maintenance. Stretched over a metal framework, its undulating silhouette of translucent material becomes a beacon at night, illuminated from within.

Tour-Panorama, La Friche Belle de Mai, 2013   **Matthieu Poitevin**
41 rue Jobin, 13003 Marseille ◑
This tower is situated on an abandoned factory complex, renamed 'La Friche' (The Wasteland) by the artists who repurposed the space. Resembling a pearlescent box, the tower provides space for contemporary art, while the glass panels of its northern facade frame the surrounding terrace, permitting natural light to enter.

Europe

Villa Mediterranee, 2013 **Stefano Boeri**
Porto Torres, Marseille ●
This institution is dedicated to the history and cultures of the Mediterranean region.
Constructed from reinforced concrete and steel, the building features a subterra-
nean conference centre and a third-floor exhibition gallery that is contained within
a 36m cantilever.

Marseille Vieux Port, 2013 **Foster + Partners**
Quai de Rive Neuve, 13001 Marseille ○
This stainless-steel, open-air pavilion was built as part of a regeneration scheme for
Marseille's Old Port. Its thin canopy tapers towards the edges, minimizing its profile
and reducing the structure's visual impact. The polished underside of the roof acts
as a mirror for the surrounding port, and reflects the street scene below.

FRAC PACA, 2013   **Kengo Kuma & Associates**
20 boulevard de Dunkerque, 13002 Marseille ◑
This contemporary arts centre occupies a triangular site, and features a chequered glass facade comprised of hundreds of panels that vary in opacity and orientation to the six-storey building. A larger southern section of the building accommodates exhibition spaces and offices, while the taller northern end contains an auditorium.

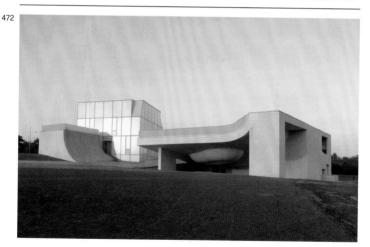

Cité de l'Océan et du Surf, 2011   **Steven Holl**
1 avenue de la Plage, 64200 Biarritz ◑
Interpreting the museum's role to raise awareness of oceanic issues, this wave-like form creates a concave roof and plaza, mirrored internally by convex exhibition spaces embedded in the site. The building's cobbled concourse slopes towards the ocean, integrating two glass 'boulders' holding a restaurant and surf kiosk.

Europe

473
474 475
476 477 478
479 480
481 482 483 484 485
486 487 488–495
519 520 527 496
497–504
505
506 509

Portugal
528 529
530 531
532 533
Lisbon

Madrid
Spain

Barcelona

507 508
510 511
512
526
534 525 536
513
537 521 522
523 524
535
514
515 516

538
517 518
Funchal Canary Islands

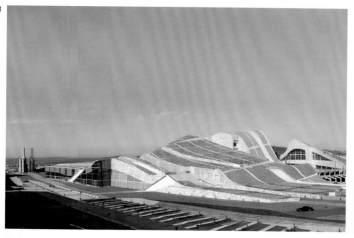

Galicia City of Culture, 2011   **Eisenman**
Santiago de Compostelas ⓞ
This scheme is based on the amalgamation of a medieval street plan, a modern Cartesian grid and the current hillside topography. It comprises six buildings whose glass, steel and stone facades emerge from the ground, while undulating rooflines create their own topography, moulding themselves around the interior's programme.

National Museum of Science & Technology, 2007   **aceboXalonso Studio**
Plaza del Museo Nacional 1, 15011 A Coruña ⓞ
This structure was conceived to house a dance conservatory and a provincial museum, each with independent entrances. At its core are concrete volumes of varied widths and heights, designed to fit the school's varied programme. Adjacent areas form the museum, enclosed by a steel mesh and panes of diffuse patterned glass.

Pilgrims' Hostel, 2000 **Jorge Meijide Tomás**
Road to Mondoñedo, 27800 Vilalba Lugo ◐
This building provides hostel accommodation for some of the many pilgrims who make the journey to Santiago de Compostela each year. It is constructed from slabs of local slate. The interior spaces are refreshingly spare and white with highly polished stone floors.

León Tanatorio, 2000 **BAAS**
Avenida de los Peregrinos, 24008 León ○
Surrounded by a large housing estate, this mortuary is sunk beneath a reflecting pool, the chapel light chutes the only aspect of the project visible above ground. Inside, the simplicity of unadorned rectilinear volumes lit by the skylights cut through the pool evokes a contemplative mood.

MUSAC Museum, 2004 **Mansilla + Tuñón**
Avenida de los Reyes Leoneses, 24, 24008 León ◗
Inspired by stained glass-windows in León Cathedral, the principal facades of this
contemporary art museum are clad in vibrantly coloured glass panels, set forward
of the walls to create a thermal barrier. Inside, cellular galleries arranged in parallel
rows, zigzag in unison, with some cells removed to create interior patios.

Concert Hall, 2002 **Mansilla + Tuñón**
Avenida de los Reyes Leoneses, 24008 León ◗
This hall's main facade highlights a series of recessed bays containing windows of
different sizes arranged in five increasingly tall levels. Inside, windows bring light
into the entrance foyer. The exhibition space beyond is accessed via a ramp with the
auditorium housed in the back wing.

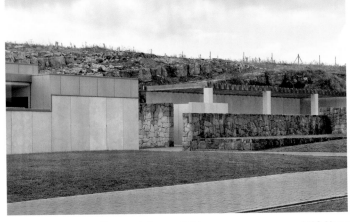

Altamira Museum and Research Centre, 2001 **SMC Alsop**
Cuevas de Altamira, 39330 Santillana del Mar ◑
As a result of having to restrict the number of visitors to the Altamira caves, this complex has been designed to house a replica cave, research centre and museum. Built into a sloping site, a series of volumes rises up from the vestibule, allowing natural light inside.

Fundación Botín, 2017 **Renzo Piano Building Workshop**
Calle Pedrueca 1, 39003 Santander ◑
Located near Santander's seafront, this arts complex is separated into two sections, joined by a walkway that cantilevers over the sea: the first block houses gallery space, while the second accommodates workshops and a lecture theatre. Its facade is clad with 360,000 ceramic discs and glazed with large glass windows.

Guggenheim Museum Bilbao, 1997   **Frank Gehry**
Avenida Abandoibarra 2, 48009 Bilbao ◐
This 1997 masterpiece — likened to everything from an artichoke to Marilyn Monroe's skirt — was the catalyst for Bilbao's metamorphosis from industrial slug to cultural butterfly. It features a titanium 'fish-scale' skin. In the sunlight, the structure seems to shape-shift like an underwater reflection depending on your viewpoint.

Sede de Osakidetza, 2008   **Coll-Barreu**
Alameda Recald 39, 48008 Bilbao ●
Housing the Basque Department of Health, this building riffs on the adjacent nineteenth-century blocks by exaggerating traditional elements, such as the tower and recessed top floor, and then wraps the whole structure in a double-glazed skin. The exterior produces a patchwork of images reflected from the street and the sky.

Ascensor de Ametzola, 2008 **Bilbao Ría 2000**
Ascensor de Irala, 48012 Bilbao ○
Part of the Bilbao regeneration scheme that launched in 1992, these slightly drunk-looking concrete and green-glass lift towers connect the Ametzola and Irala areas, which had previously been seperated by a 10m drop. The towers are approximately 22 and 15m tall, respectively, and lead down to a subterranean car park.

Parish Church of Santa María Josefa, 2008 **IMB**
Askatasuna Etorb 11, 48003 Bilbao ◑
Inside this concrete church, a white and pinewood triangular nave tapers towards the altar. One wall is inset with rectangular glass panes in religiously significant colours — purple, green and red — in an update on traditional stained glass. Similar windows run up the 24m spire, framing a staircase that leads up to the belfry.

Casa Vita, 2011 Iñaki Aspiazu Iza
Barrio Olagorta 6, 48287 Ea
This rural retreat includes five stand-alone properties; the original finca dates from the fifteenth century, making the embrace of modernity within the main building all the more surprising. A glass-and-larch box, it's one of the most eco-friendly builds in Europe. Set in an eucalypt grove, it features a floating terrace.

Hotel at Marqués de Riscal, 2007 Frank Gehry
Calle Torrea 1, 1340 Elciego ❶
This collection of boxes and terraces, lifted up on sandstone legs and topped with a canopy of titanium ribbons, forms part of a complex built around existing wine cellars. Originally conceived as the vineyard's headquarters, as the project evolved it became a luxury hotel. Public spaces are organized to allow breathtaking views.

Contemporary Art Centre of Aragon, Beulas Foundation, 2005   **Rafael Moneo**
Avenida Doctor Artero, 22004 Huesca ◑
The undulating exterior walls of this building reinterpret the local rocky mounds.
The centre exhibits the work of José Beulas in a building adjacent to the painter's
farm and studio. Inside, the exhibition space is filled with natural light filtered down
through deep beams via a glass roof.

Forum 2004 Southeast Coastal Park, 2004   **Alejandro Zaera-Polo**
Rambla de Prima, 8019 Barcelona ◑
This park occupies reclaimed land close to the sea and next to a major highway. A
simple repetition of half-moon concrete tiles forms a network of paths and zones encouraging various sports and leisure activities. Two open-air auditoria are embedded
within a dune-like landscape amid robust vegetation.

Europe

Mediapro Building, 2005   **OAB**
Audiovisual Campus, Avenida Diagonal 177, Distrito 22, 8018 Barcelona ●
This complex is organized in two volumes: a rectilinear, low podium, and an angular tower. The podium building houses production and teaching facilities with a broad glazed facade revealing inner workings to the street. Perpendicular to it, the 15-storey office tower rises with an identical facade of metal window grids.

CCCB, 1994   **Albert Viaplana and Helio Piñón**
Carrer de Montalegre, 5, 8001 Barcelona ◑
This renovation project adds a partly cantilevered glass facade, one half of which is darker than the other, to the Casa de Caritat almshouse. The centre itself functions as a hub for art and music, as well as hosting a cross-section of multi-disciplinary festivals, debates, lectures and courses.

Edifici Gas Natural Fenosa, 2006
Plaça del Gas 1, 8003 Barcelona ●

Miralles Tagliabue EMBT

The sculptural form of the Gas Natural headquarters comprises a low-rise plinth whose height corresponds to neighbouring residential buildings, a high-rise tower and mid-rise horizontal slab dramatically cantilevered over a public entrance plaza. The exterior is glazed with subtle variations in colour, transparency and reflectivity.

Torre de Comunicaciones de Montjuïc, 1992
Avenida de L'Estadi, 8021 Barcelona ●

Santiago Calatrava

Standing proud at 136m, and adorned with Gaudí-style trencadís at its base, this futuristic steel tower serves as a giant sundial that casts the time on Plaça d'Europa. Built to transmit the 1992 Olympics, its fluid form represents an athlete holding the Olympic flame, but locals have since christened it *el pirulí* — The Lollipop.

Spain

Barcelona City of Justice, 2011   David Chipperfield
Gran Via de les Corts Catalanes 111, 8075 Barcelona ●
Located on a public plaza, this scheme comprises nine buildings that vary in size
and colour. Four of these are connected by a concourse building with mesh-covered, frameless glass facades. The remaining buildings have load-bearing concrete
facades.

494

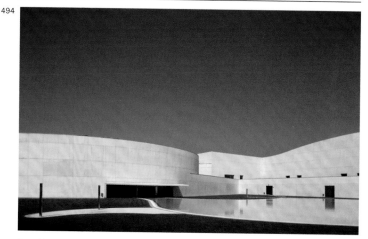

Parc Esportiu Llobregat, 2005   Álvaro Siza Vieira
Avinguda Baix Llobregat, 8940 Cornellá de Llobregat, Barcelona ◑
The plan is organized to create a modest public square in front of the main entrance.
This sport complex comprises a linear reception block containing fitness suites and
administration, a large sports hall contained in a rectangular block and an indoor
pool housed in an oval form and covered by a dome roof with circular lights.

Mercat Encants, 2013
Carrer de los Castillejos 158, 8013 Barcelona ◑
b720 Fermín Vázquez

This mirrored canopy provides shelter for Barcelona's famous flea market. A soaring 25m-high kaleidoscopic roof, its gilded steel panels, reflecting scenes of the stalls, wraps around the market. The idea of one continuous commercial area can be seen in the design of the inclined walkways that connect the different levels.

Oficinas Zamora, 2012
Plaza de la Catedral 5, 49001 Zamora ●
Alberto Campo Baeza

Nested within two-storey stone walls that wrap the site's perimeter, this office block for the Consejo Consultivo of Castilla y León is composed of full-height glass walls. The double-layered includes a cavity for thermal control, with internal columns set back from the periphery to emphasize a sense of weightlessness.

Europe

Sanchinarro Mirador Apartments, 2005 **MVRDV**
Calle de la Princesa de Éboli 13, 28050 Madrid ●
Breaking from the uniformity of surrounding blocks of flats, this landmark 22-storey building features a shared balcony, providing a community garden. Housing clusters provide a range of different accommodation, expressed externally in the modulation of window type and cladding.

Cuatro Torres, 2004-2010 **Various**
Paseo de la Castellana, 28029 Madrid ●
This ensemble of four towers consists of the Torre Bankia, a stacked-box profile by Foster + Partners; the angular Torre Cristal by Pelli Clarke Pelli; Carlos Rubio and Enrique Álvarez-Sala's Torre PwC, featuring a double skin that wraps around three fissured sections; and Henry N Cobb's twisted Torre Espacio.

Puerta de Europa, 2006　　　　　　　　　**Philip Johnson and John Burgee**
Plaza Castilla, 28020 Madrid ●
The 'Gateway of Europe' comprises the Torres KIO, two towers that are 114m high and lean towards each other at 15-degree angles, making them the first inclined sky-scrapers in the world. The glittering structures of granite, steel and glass give an almost surreal, sci-fi impression. They frame a statue of José Calvo Sotelo.

Terminal 4, Barajas Airport, 2006　　　　　**Rogers Stirk Harbour + Partners**
Avenida de la Hispanidad, 28042 Madrid ◐
Consisting of two linear structures, Terminal 4 increases the airport's annual ca-pacity. Yellow Y-shaped steel columns with concrete footings support undulating steel-framed roofs. Laminated bamboo strips clad the underside of the roof where rows of oculi filter light. Air-conditioning outlets rise from angled white pedestals.

Museo ABC, 2010 **Aranguren + Gallegos**
Calle Amaniel 29, 28015 Madrid ◑
Converted from a brewery, this museum focuses on the history of the *ABC* newspaper, in effect, tracing Spain's modern history. The snowy-white, latticed exoskeleton incorporates the museum, multifunctional areas and restoration workshops, but the design reaches its zenith in the long, light-filled space of the café.

Valle Inclán Theatre, 2005 **Paredes Pedros**
Plaza de Lavapiés, 28012 Madrid ◑
This theatre complex, which houses two performance venues, represents a focal point for the regeneration of a once-neglected area of Madrid. Arranged in geometric concrete blocks, the glazed facade, when lit up at night, provides a source of light, while inside the interior is lined with sycamore wood.

Regional Library and Archives of Madrid, 2002
Ramírez de Prado 3, 28045 Madrid ◑
New additions fill the spaces between the buildings of a former brewery to create this library and archival complex. The archives are housed in a purpose-built volume, which is encased in a translucent double skin that allows natural light to enter without damaging its fragile contents.

Mansilla + Tuñón

Public Library at Usera, 2000
Avenida Rafaela Ybarra 43, 28041 Madrid ◑
Standing next to Usera's town hall and rising from its half-buried ground floor as a self-contained block, this library proclaims its presence. Darker horizontal lines in the pale-pink concrete cladding define the levels, and the vertical windows are placed irregularly, so that daylight penetrates only discreetly or indirectly.

Ábalos & Herreros

Europe

Escaleras de La Granja, 2000 **Martínez Lapeña-Torres**
La Granja, 45001 Toledo ◑
Cut into Toledo's massive city walls, this 36m tall, six-stage external escalator links a new underground car park to the hilltop. Built on piles 30m deep, the ochre-coloured concrete planes frame the structure, forming shelter and viewing platforms, while the journey ends with the structure's belvedere.

Casar de Cáceres Bus Station, 2003 **Justo Garcia Rubio**
Egido Bajo, 10190 Casar de Cáceres ○
A reinforced concrete loop defines this new bus station in the west of Spain. Its expressive shape departs from traditional utilitarian designs, while capturing the imaginations of children at the nearby schools. Glazed walls fill the smaller loop's vertical planes, and a basement accomodates storage and a bar.

Cultural and Musical Centre, 2003 **Eduardo de Miguel Arbonés**
Plaça del Rosari 3, 46011 València ◑
Located on the site of an old musical hall, this three-storey building comprises a multipurpose hall, civic centre and ancillary spaces. The existing facade forms the entrance to the complex, in contrast to the new robust, formal facades. Inside, a double-skinned wall encloses the generous public spaces.

America's Cup Building, 2006 **David Chipperfield**
Port America's Cup, 46011 València ◑
Designed for the America's Cup, this four-storey pavilion includes a ground-floor VIP reception area and a public bar and restaurant, with a viewing deck above accessing a park. Terraces accentuate the floor slabs and horizontal planes, with the roof and top floor cantilevered over lower levels.

Chapel, 2000　　　　　　　　　　　　　　　　**Sancho-Madridejos**
Valleaceron, 13480 Almadanejos ◑
Placed among the rocky hills on a private property, this chapel is scaleless in a landscape free of human intervention. Its profile changes dramatically from each viewing angle, the glazed panels cut into the form appearing from a distance like shadows. The multi-faceted interior is unadorned.

Canopy Over a Roman Site, 2011　　　　　　　**Amann Cánovas Maruri**
Parque de El Molinete, Cartagena ◑
This lightweight canopy protects the remains of a Roman ruin, and connects to an elevated walkway along the south boundary. To minimize structural supports, the architects used a long-span structure that admits filtered light through its two-part assembly of translucent polycarbonate sheets beneath perforated-steel roof plates.

Ascensor Panorámico, 2005 **Amann Cánovas Maruri**
10 Avenida Gisbert, 30202 Cartagena ◑
This project links Cartagena to the hilltop castle of Asdrubal. Breaks in a concrete wall provide light to a series of offices built into the hillside. A steel tower containing a panoramic lift is encircled by a staircase. This leads via a footbridge to ramps that zigzag their way along angled concrete walls towards the castle.

512

Caja General Headquarters, 2001 **Alberto Campo Baeza**
Carretera de Armilla, Granada ●
This bank headquarters on the outskirts of Granada occupies a stone box atop a large podium, which accommodates parking. The box's southern facades act as a brise-soleil, filtering sunlight and illuminating the open-plan office areas. Northern facades are clad in flush horizontal strips of glass and travertine.

Centro de Arte Contemporáneo C3A, 2013
Plaza Cruz del Rastro, 14009 Córdoba ◑
                                                            Nieto Sobejano

Inspired by Córdoba's Moorish history and the geometry prevalent in Islamic architecture, this art gallery incorporates a hexagonal pattern carved into its roof and a facade perforated with polygonal openings. The use of concrete in the interior allows for flexible exhibition spaces, which blend with the artists' studios below.

Metropol Parasol, 2011
Plaça de la Encarnación, 41003 Seville ○
                                                            J Mayer H

A series of six connected timber parasols, the appearance of which Sevillanos have compared to mushrooms (*Las Setas*), accommodate an archaeological museum, shops and restaurants, as well as providing shade and panoramic views of the city. The structure is said to be the largest in the world held together soley by glue.

Doñana Visitor Centre of the Marine World, 2002 **Cruz y Ortiz**
Carretera A-494, km51, Doñana National Park, 21760 Almonte ◑
Appearing to hunkered down among sand dunes is the jagged form of this marine museum, its low-slung volume designed to have a minimal visual impact on its landscape. A long hallway with a faceted concrete ceiling runs the length of the building, with each 'tooth' accomodating a separate gallery.

Baelo Claudia Visitor Centre, 2007 **Guillermo Vázquez Consuegra**
Ensenada de Bolonia, 11380 Tarifa ◑
Built over two levels and cut into the landscape, this centre situated in an archaeological site frames views of the adjacent Roman ruins, houses exhibitions and provides space for the archaeologists and conservationists still working on site. The remains discovered so far include an impressive temple and basilica.

517

Woerman Tower and Plaza, 2005 **Ábalos & Herreros**
Calle Eduardo Benot con Albareda, 35008 Las Palmas ●
This development sits on the narrow isthmus joining the peninsula of La Isleta to Las Palmas. A new, tree-lined public square separates a residential tower and seven-storey commercial block. Coloured glass enlivens the tower's facade, while cantilevered top floors create a cranked profile.

518

Magma Art and Congress Centre, 2005 **AMP**
Avenida de Los Pueblos, 38660 Costa Adeje ◐
Conceived as an expression of the surrounding hills and ocean, this massive structure provides large, flexible areas for events and exhibitions. Thirteen concrete blocks support a curvilinear steel canopy faced with fibre-cement panels, with punched-out openings and narrow fissures admitting natural light.

Spain   281

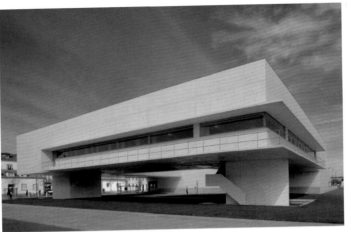

Municipal Library, 2008   Álvaro Siza Vieira
Avenida Marginal 50, 4901-877 Viana do Castelo ◑
Supported at one end by two L-shaped piers and on the other side by a ground-floor structure, the library's main volume is raised above ground and organized around a central, square void, enabling interior spaces to be naturally lit. The exterior comprises exposed concrete and areas clad in faceted stone.

Centro de Artes Nadir Afonso, 2013   Louise Braverman
Rua Gomes Monteiro 3, 5460-304 Boticas ◑
Built as a single-artist gallery to showcase the work of painter Nadir Afonso, this project is carved into a hillside, the excavation of which provided the stone for its surrounding retaining walls. The gallery is topped by a green-roof park, further integrating the building with its landscape.

Braga Stadium, 2003   Eduardo Souto de Moura
Montecastro Parque Norte, 4710 Braga ◑
This stadium lies adjacent to a disused granite quarry and is framed by parallel grandstands, each divided into two overlapping tiers. Granite was blasted from the hillside to accommodate the stadium and re-used as aggregate on site. Circular apertures perforate concrete piers to facilitate horizontal circulation.

MIEC, 2012   Eduardo Souto de Moura and Álvaro Siza Vieira
Avenida Unisco Godiniz 100, 4780-366 Santo Tirso ◑
Situated next to the meticulously restored eighteenth-century monastery of São Bento, this stone and concrete museum extension is a sublimely minimal, low-slung wing that sits easily within its historic context. Consisting of a café and exhibition space, it shares an entrance with the Municipal Museum Abade Pedrosa.

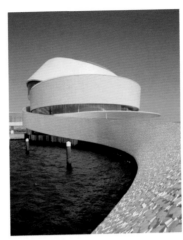

Terminal de Cruizeiros, 2015   Luís Pedro Silva
Avenida General Norton de Matos, 4450-208 Matosinhos ◑
Accommodating liners up to 300m long, this cruise ship terminal is bounded by sinuous curves that direct passengers around a bend in the jetty. Spiralling ramps envelop the structure like a spooled ribbon, while its facade's ceramic blocks are angled and rotated, evoking barnacles and reflecting the sunlight in myriad directions.

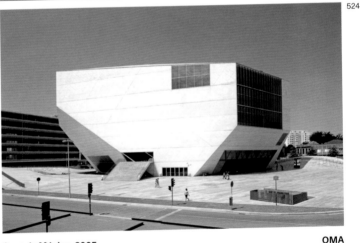

Casa da Música, 2005   OMA
Avenida da Boavista 604-610, 4149-071 Porto ◑
This white concrete polyhedron is integrated into the city through a continuous public route within and around the building. Public functions are elevated and exposed as glazed rectangular voids that puncture the shell. The intersecting auditoriums define the exterior's oblique planes.

Igreja de Santa Maria, 1996 **Álvaro Siza Vieira**
Avenida Gago Courtinho, 4630-206 Marco de Canaveses ◑
Situated 60km west of Porto, this 1997 church is among Siza Vieira's later works, which are characterized by white marble and surfaces that funnel natural light at varying times of the day. The soaring interior is a sculptural space with a simple off-centre cross, exaggeratedly tall steel doors and a top-lit, tiled baptism area.

Pavilion of Portugal, 2000 **Eduardo Souto de Moura and Álvaro Siza Vieira**
Avenida Lousã, 3000 Coimbra ●
This pavilion, designed for the World Exposition in Hannover, is a pre-fabricated and dismantleable building that was later rebuilt in Coimbra. The facade features 55 tons of cork, of which Portugal is the main source of production, while lias stone and glazed tiles are also integrated.

Adega Mayor Winery, 2006   Álvaro Siza Vieira
Herdade das Argamassas, 7370-171 Campo Maior ◑
This winery's long axis is perpendicular to the contours of its sloping terrain, sitting the grape delivery at a level above the production floor without terracing the ground. A large overhang shades the wine loading bay. The top floor aligns with the building's long roof, transforming it into a panoramic terrace.

Mythos Building, 2012   ARX Portugal
Parque das Nações, Lisbon ●
This residential building was designed as an opaque orthogonal shell with an emphasis on privacy. Deeply recessed balconies are cut into the black facade, housing a series of small gardens and ponds, and protecting the inside of the building from harsh sunlight.

MAAT, 2016 AL_A
Avenida Brasília, 1300-598 Lisbon ◑
Facing the banks of the Tagus River, the low-slung arched facade of this museum
is clad in crackle-glazed trapezoidal tiles. Galleries are arranged around a central
elliptical circulation path and the roof forms a riverside promenade that spans the
museum's length and connects to outdoor terraced seating at the rear.

Maritime Control Tower, 2002 Gonçalo Byrn
Terrapleno de Algés, Doca de Pedrouços, 1495-165 Lisbon ●
Positioned at the end of a breakwater in Algés, just west of Lisbon, this leaning tower signals the entrance to the city's new harbour. Above a stone plinth housing the
entrance and boathouses are five copper-clad floors containing offices. By night,
the tower effectively becomes a lighthouse.

Portuguese National Pavilion, 1998　　　　　　　　**Álvaro Siza Vieira**
Avenida do Indico 10503a, 1990-221 Lisbon ◑
The Portuguese Pavilion was built for Expo '98, the theme of which was 'The Oceans, A Heritage for the Future'. Fittingly, the roof at its centre resembles both a shell and the billowing sail of a ship. Impressively fashioned from concrete, it has a light, supple quality, which contrasts dramatically with the heavy porticos at either end.

GS1 Portugal, 2016　　　　　　　　　　　　　　　　**Promontorio**
Estrada do Paço do Lumiar, Campus do Lumiar, Edifício K3, 1649-038 Lisbon ●
Housing the Portuguese headquarters of a global non-profit organization, this project began with the conversion of an 1980s concrete office block, introducing floor-to-ceiling windows to the original facade. The interior emphasizes the raw materials of the existing building, using concrete and exposed wiring as an aesthetic feature.

Europe

Casa das Histórias Paula Rego, 2009   **Eduardo Souto de Moura**
Avenida República 300, 2750-475 Cascais ◑
This museum, with its two pyramid-shaped towers and red-coloured concrete facade, is easily identifiable among the surrounding trees. The building is made up of
four wings of different heights and sizes, and circulation revolves around a central
room housing temporary exhibitions.

Museum of Mechanical Music, 2016   **Miguel Marcelino**
Rua dos Alegrias, Quinta do Rei, Arraiados, 2955-281 Pinhal Novo ◑
An opaque volume rendered in a sand coating, the hermetic exterior of this museum
disguises the collection of musical instruments displayed within. Only the principal
facade, with its sharply delineated concave entrance, defers from the uniform envelope. Inside, the plan is organized around a central courtyard.

Alcácer do Sal Residences, 2010　　　　　　　　**Aires Mateus**
Rua Torres 1, 7580 Alcácer do Sal ●
This complex consists of a series of private 'houses', or rooms, each with its own terrace, and public spaces for the elderly. The long concrete building features a checkerboard-like facade, and snakes along the southeast limit of the site, responding to the topography of the landscape.

Museum of Luz, 2003　　　　　　　**Pedro Pacheco and Marie Clément**
Largo da Igreja de Nossa Senhora da Luz, 7240-100 Mourão ◑
Located by the reservoir now covering the drowned village of Luz, the Luz ('light') room provides the focal point to this museum's dark limestone boxes. A café and entrance porch define the open sides of a patio. Light enters an atrium through the porch's glazing, and is channelled into exhibition spaces by 'light chimneys'.

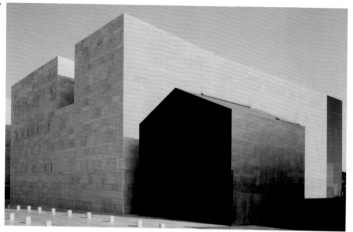

Sines Cultural Centre, 2005 **Aires Mateus**
Rua Cândido dos Reis 33, 7520-177 Sines ◑
These monolithic stone boxes flanking the route to a castle contain an exhibition centre, theatre, library and regional archive. Oversized castellations split the volumes, while arrow-slit apertures and parallel strips of street-level glazing allow light into the archive.

Vulcanism Pavilion, 2004 **Paulo David**
Sitio do Pé do Passo, 9240-039 São Vicente ◑
This geological exhibition centre is adjacent to a network of volcanic caves on the north coast of Madeira. Partially embedded in the valley's rocky hillside, rough blocks of local volcanic basalt form the building's envelope. Outside, a gently sloping path zigzags up to the caves.

Europe

589–594
546
563
576
560 561 562
564 565
574
570 571
540 541 542
543 544 545
575 547
539
579
548–559
572
587
581–585
573

Hamburg

Germany

Berlin

645
646–653
580
656
654 655

568 569
566 567 588
595–607
616

Switzerland
Bern

Vienna

Austria

Liechtenstein

628 627
624
625
626
619 629
608 609
620
617
610–615
618
623
633–637
631 632
621 622
586
578
630 577
638
643 644
639 640
641 642
660
657
658 659

Germany, Switzerland, Liechtenstein and Austria

Europe

Rostock IGA Pavilion, 2003   **Atelier Kempe Thill**
IGA Park Rostock, Mecklenburg-Vorpommern, Rostock ○
With this pavilion, an entry in Rotterdam's International Garden Exhibition (IGA)
2003, the architects sought to display the poetry inherent in the rigorously logical
model of Dutch farming. Walls of ivy are grown on smart screens, which are usually
used in commercial glasshouses.

540

Edel Music Headquarters, 2002   **Antonio Citterio and Patricia Viel**
Neumühlen 17, 22763 Hamburg ◑
Overlooking the River Elba, this record company headquarters is reminiscent of the
modernist tradition, with glass being the primary material on three of the building's
facades. A sunken garage is topped by a ground floor containing reception, bar,
restaurant and auditorium, with three levels of offices above.

Dockland Office Building, 2005   **BRT**
Van-der-Smissen-Strasse 10, 22767 Hamburg ●
This building was designed to appear like a ship, situated as it is by the Elba River. The glass parallelepiped has seven levels extending 40m. The vicinity of the river also affected certain aspects of the project, such as the need for a system for preventing flooding of the lower floors, should the river overflow its banks.

Dock 47, 2004   **Spengler Wiescholek**
Pinnasberg 47, 22767 Hamburg ●
Asymmetrical Dock 47 springs out of the urban St Pauli landscape like a flame. This dynamic office building, with its deep-red panels and outward-leaning walls on two sides, is a beacon that stands on a sloping site at a hectic traffic intersection opposite the 300-year-old Fischmarkt.

Europe

Erweiterung des Polizeireviers Davidwache, 2004
Davidwache, Spielbudenplatz 31, 20359 Hamburg ●

Winking Froh

Updating a well-loved Hamburg landmark, this project adds an extension to the rear of the original 1914 police station. The structure alludes to the clinker-brick character of pre-war Hamburg, while large windows on the top storey give the police a better vantage point over the town.

Tanzende Türme, 2011
Reeperbahn 1, 20359 Hamburg ●

BRT

Standing 80 and 90m tall respectively, these two high-rises lean towards and then shy away from each other, slanting by up to 3m from the vertical, conveying the impression of a flirting couple. This device is a reference to the nineteenth-century Trichter dancehall that once stood here.

Hamburg Elbphilharmonie, 2016　　　　　　　　　**Herzog & de Meuron**
Platz der Deutschen Einheit 1, 20457 Hamburg ◑
Consisting of an original 1960s brick warehouse and a new, glazed upper section, this complex accommodates a philharmonic hall, a chamber music hall, restaurants, bars, a panoramic terrace, apartments and a hotel. The extension's glass facade is formed from 1,100 panes, and the undulating roof rises to a height of 108m.

Archaeological Museum and Park, 2002　　　　　**Annette Gigon/Mike Guyer**
Venner Strasse 69, 49565 Bramsche ◑
These buildings act as signs, references and aids with which to try and imagine the 'Battle of Varus' between the Teutons and the Romans — thought to have taken place here in 9 AD. Pavilions called 'Seeing', 'Hearing' and 'Questioning' are used interactively to help re-create the sights and sands of the time.

Phaeno Science Centre, 2005   **Zaha Hadid**
Willy-Brandt-Platz 1, 38440 Wolfsburg ◑
The centre's funnel-shaped cones support its main volume, which sits above
a covered public plaza. The building's jagged angles, looming curves and daring
projections could not have been realized without the use of individually fabricated
formwork sections for the concrete.

Biosphere and Flower Pavilion, 2001   **Barkow Leibinger**
Georg-Hermann-Allee 99, 14469 Potsdam ◑
Situated near Postdam's Sanssouci Palace on an ex-military site, the design of
this giant greenhouse is based on the defensive earthen berms made here by
the occupying Soviet Army at the end of WWII. The structure is sunk into a series
of berms clad in oak logs, turf, slate and poured concrete.

Europe

Swiss Embassy Extension, 2004
Otto-von-Bismarck-Allee 4a, 10557 Berlin ●

Diener & Diener

Providing diplomatic and consular services, the Swiss Embassy's eastern wing pays homage to the scale of its neoclassical neighbour, but without the embellishment. Panels of coquina stone aggregate encase the four-storey cubic extension, their flat finish broken by the entrance courtyard and two tall openings in the north facade.

Forum Museumsinsel, 2016
Tucholskystrasse 2, 10117 Berlin ●

David Chipperfield

Occupying a site with eight listed buildings, the Forum Museumsinsel is located on the banks of the Spree River. The complex includes a new building that nods to the composition of the main hospital building behind it, characterized by a repeating motif of tall arched windows across its three-storey brick facade.

Campus Joachimstrasse, 2013   David Chipperfield
Joachimstrasse 11, 10119 Berlin ●
This conversion project, comprising an exhibition gallery and event spaces, as well as a three-level apartment, studio and office, adds four new building volumes to a former piano factory. Concrete walls have been left unfinished, and are punctured on the facade by six large windows.

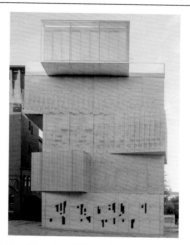

Museum for Architectural Drawing, 2013   Sergei Tchoban and Sergei Kuznetsov
Christinenstrasse 18a, 10119 Berlin ◑
The concrete facade here emulates parchment and is covered with architectural sketches in relief, while the irregularly stacked floors resemble open drawers; the top floor is a glass box with a terrace. The museum's collection ranges from eighteenth-century architectural blueprints, right through to sketches by Frank Gehry.

Apartment House Prenzlauer Berg, 2016   **Barkow Leibinger**
Prenzlauer Berg, Berlin ●
Shaped by historic and council restrictions, this apartment building abuts an urban residential block. Almost square in plan, like its predecessor, the multi-coloured brick-clad cube rises to a hefty pyramidal roof punctuated by irregularly sized and placed windows that respond to neighbouring buildings.

554

Netherlands Embassy, 2003   **OMA**
Klosterstrasse 50, 10179 Berlin ◑
This building's corner site faces a park and the Spree River. A continuous pedestrian route travels through all eight floors, leading visitors from the entrance, via the library, meeting rooms, fitness area and restaurant, to the roof terrace. From the outside, it is possible to see diagonally through the building.

Parkside Apartments, 2004   **David Chipperfield**
Beisheim Centre, Potsdamer Platz, 10785 Berlin ●

A vertical slice emphasizes this apartment building's entrance, while dividing the two volumes that rise from its four-storey plinth. A facade composed of irregular and roughly sanded stone slabs is given a contemporary character by the free composition of recessed balconies and french windows.

Daimler Chrysler Skyscraper, 2000   **Hans Kollhoff**
Potsdamer Platz 1, 10785 Berlin ●

The 27-storey, 101m tall Daimler Chrysler building in Potsdamer Platz draws inspiration from Chicago's early skyscrapers. Fitting a tight corner site, the brick-clad building is triangular in plan with its end elevation only four bays wide. There is a panoramic viewing platform on the top floor.

Europe

Potsdamer Platz, 2000   **Renzo Piano Building Workshop**
Marlene-Dietrich-Platz, 10875 Berlin ●
Renzo Piano's masterplan for a 7.5 hectare site within Potsdamer Platz, a focus for urban renewal, includes offices, housing, cultural amenities, shops and restaurants. The complex is based on the traditional Berlin block dimensions and integrates extensive public spaces and water features.

Jewish Museum, 1999   **Studio Libeskind**
Lindenstrasse 9–14, 10969 Berlin ◑
Replacing the formal facades of Berlin's Lindenstrasse, this urban void represents notions of absence, memory and loss. With its deep-cut riveted zinc walls, the building's material and compositional strength suit its urban scale. Inside, public spaces are arranged around a cavernous route.

559

Labels 2, 2010
Stralauer Allee 12, 10245 Berlin ◑   **HHF**

Behind a wave-patterned concrete facade lies this complex of fashion showrooms and event spaces. The building was constructed with a network of tubes containing water from the Spree River, which is heated during winter and cooled during summer, reducing energy consumption by 40 per cent.

560

Landesarchiv NRW, 2013   **Ortner & Ortner Baukunst**
Schifferstrasse 30, 47059 Duisburg ●

Converted from a former grain store, this building houses a 70m tower of state records, located in a brick structure without openings, which protects the archive from daylight. Stepped masonry bricks, scaled identically to its historic neighbour, create its finely articulated cladding.

Museum Folkwang, 2009 **David Chipperfield**
Museumsplatz 1, 45128 Essen ◑
Complementing the existing listed 1950s building, this extension is composed of six rectilinear buildings of varied heights and four inner courtyards. The translucent alabaster-like facade of recycled-glass panels is set on a cement stone base, which is a continuation of the existing plinth.

Urban Waterfalls Subway Canopies, 2014 **Despang**
Schauspielhaus, 44789 Bochum ○
This series of louvred canopies, set in low concrete walls around street escalators, are formed of rows of thin steel supports enclosed by glass sheets. The rib structures are tough enough to resist the impact of being hit by a truck, yet delicate enough to register cascading rainwater over their 'urban waterfall' exteriors.

Jüberg Observation Tower, 2010   **Birk Heilmeyer und Frenzel**
Sauerlandpark Hemer, 58675 Hemer ◑
Surrounding a spiral staircase and formed of 240 larch laths, this lookout marks the
boundary between urban and rural landscapes. Organized as a hyperboloid and anchored by steel needles, the tower's mesh structure expands towards the top with
more widely spaced timber rods, allowing increasingly panoramic views out.

Colorium Office Building, 2001   **Alsop Sparch**
Speditionstrasse 9, 40221 Düsseldorf ●
Part of Düsseldorf's waterfront, this 17-storey office block occupies a long, narrow
site. With plans for a taller tower constrained by planning restrictions, Alsop radical-
ized the facade, using coloured-glass panels to transform the standard orthogonal
structure. A crimson plant installation projects from its summit.

Langen Foundation Art Centre, 2004   **Tadao Ando Architect & Associates**
Raketenstation Hombroich 1, 41472 Neuss ◑
This complex houses a collection of 800 Japanese screens and scrolls, as well as modern Western art. Visitors pass through an arch cut into a semicircular concrete wall, framing a long concrete gallery, which is enclosed by a fully glazed steel cage. A ramp leads down to two semi-buried galleries.

Kolumba Museum, 2007   Peter Zumthor
Kolumbastrasse 4, 50667 Cologne ◑
Providing exhibition space for the Cologne diocese's extensive collection of religious art, a band of perforated openings allow air and light into this double-height space, which incorporates an existing chapel and archaeological remains. Second-floor galleries and a reading room are laid out like buildings around a town square.

Wallraf-Richartz Museum, 2001   **Oswald Ungers**
Martinstrasse 39, 50667 Cologne ◐
This museum, sited between the historic Gürzenich and the Rathausplatz, is composed of two volumes linked by a common circulation zone. The smaller volume is integrated into the existing buildings and the larger, a cubic block, houses all the exhibition areas. On the northeast, panoramic windows provide city views.

Bruder Klaus Field Chapel, 2007   **Peter Zumthor**
Iversheimer Strasse, 53894 Mechernich-Wachendorf ◐
Dedicated to a fifteenth-century mystic, this chapel stands in a field southwest of Cologne. Recalling Brother Klaus's cell, a soot-blackened interior was created using a wigwam of tree trunks, which were set alight when the concrete had hardened. The exterior's smooth rectangle was cast by the clients' family and friends.

Europe

Arp Museum, 2007　　　　　　　　　　　**Richard Meier & Partners**
Hans-Arp-Allee 1, 53424 Remagen ❶
Housing works of Dada artists Hans Arp and his wife, Sophie Taeuber-Arp, this building looks over the Rhine Valley from its lofty site. An underpass incorporates the main museum lobby and shop, leading visitors towards the exhibition spaces via glass lifts that rise up through a tower.

Autobahnkirche Siegerland, 2013　　　　**Schneider+Schumacher**
Elkersberg, 57234 Wilnsdorf ❶
Identified by its stylized white silhouette resembling a traditional village chapel, the Autobahn Church provides a quiet place for a break, unlike the usual motorway services. The exterior, cloaked in white polyurethane damp-proofing, contrasts with the interior, which opens to a vault formed from a cross-ribbed grid of timber framing.

Europe

571

Braun Headquarters, 2001   **Wilford Schupp**
Werksanlagen Pfieffewiesen, 34212 Melsungen ●
This latest addition to the Braun headquarters, designed by Wilford, houses offices.
Accessed by a bridge from the existing administration block, the volumes relate to
office functions. The various cladding materials emphasize the disparity between
the different volumes.

572

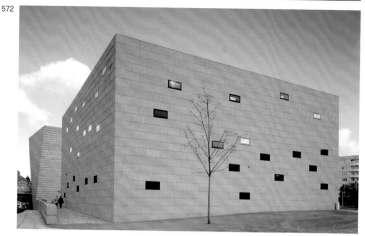

Synagogue Dresden, 2001   **Wandel Hoefer Lorch**
Hasenberg 1, 01067 Dresden ◑
Built next to the site of the previous synagogue, which was designed by Gottfried
Semper and destroyed on Kristallnacht in 1938, this building is a curvilinear stone
structure, its bevelled shape resulting from the gradual layering of the 41 levels of
coursing. Opposite stands the lower volume of the community hall.

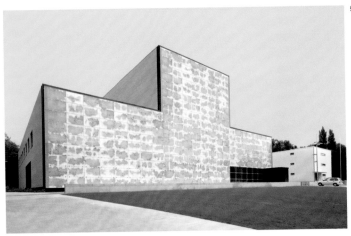

Deutsche Bundesbank Office Building, 2004 **Mateo**
Zschopauer Strasse 49, 09111 Chemnitz ●
Occupying the site of the former Park of the Victims of Fascism, this building was in-spired by fossilized tree trunks. The first floor is suspended from the two upper-floor walls by cables, leaving the ground floor without load-bearing columns and giving the white structure an airy, floating quality.

Städel Museum Extension, 2012 **Schneider+Schumacher**
Schaumainkai 63, 60596 Frankfurt am Main ◑
Submerged beneath a grassy knoll, this museum extension adjoins the twentieth-century garden wing and houses contemporary art. The roof is supported by 12 rein-forced concrete columns and spans the entire exhibition space. Circular skylights in the lawn admit light to the galleries below while also being strong enough to walk on.

Europe

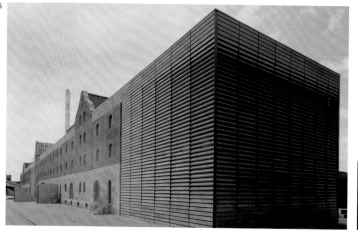

Art Depot Gallery, 2002
Veitschöchheimer Strasse 5, 97080 Würzburg ◑

Brückner & Brückner

Set along the harbourside, this art gallery is a conversion of a former grain silo. The wings have been extended with boxes composed of slender horizontal stone slabs set at angles that subtly shift over the height of the building. Freestanding galleries are inserted inside the elongated void of the interior.

Mensa Moltke, 2007
Moltkestrasse 12, 76133 Karlsruhe ◑

J Mayer H

A college canteen and café near the Hartwald Forest, this strikingly organic building takes it cue from nearby trees — its perimeter is marked by forest-like full-height columns. Coated with polyurethane, the laminated wooden columns support an internal core of solid concrete.

Europe

Museum of Modern Literature, 2006   David Chipperfield
Schillerhöhe 8, 71672 Marbach am Neckar ◑
This building sits by the Schiller Museum in a scenic park. An external structure re-interprets the classical loggia form with thin rectangular columns. Beyond, a series of tiered spaces descend a hill in a gesture of architectural reticence. Inside, timber-panelled exhibition spaces are artificially lit to protect fragile documents.

Mercedes-Benz Museum, 2006   UNStudio
Mercedesstrasse 100, 70372 Stuttgart ◑
Overlooking a motorway, this curved-shaped museum has a floorplan divided into three 'leaves' emanating from a central 'stem'. The interior is organized in a spiral-ling, double-helix formation whose intersections allow visitors to navigate between the various exhibitions.

St Peter's Church, 2003   Brückner & Brückner
Hauptstrasse 4, 93173 Wenzenbach ◑
This addition to an existing church, located in the centre of a small Bavarian town, creates a nave curving towards the altar to form a point, giving the plan a boat-like shape. Steel posts higher than the roof itself surround its perimeter and the interior is flooded with blue light from the blue glass on the upper half of the nave walls.

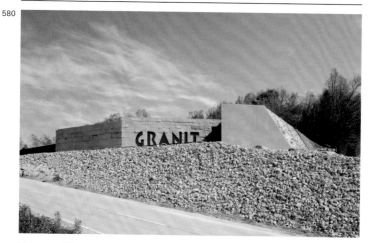

Museum of Granite, 2005   Brückner & Brückner
Passauer Strasse 11, 94051 Hauzenberg ◑
This building's plan corresponds to the natural rock formations of the site, formerly a granite quarry. Granite from various stages of the manufacturing process was used in the building's structure, demonstrating a diversity of finishes and displacing a variety of by-products and raw materials.

BMW Welt Exhibition Centre, 2007   **Coop Himmelb(l)au**
Am Olympiapark 1, 80809 Munich ◑
This marketing building serves as a stage for events and a platform for the delivery of new cars. One roof warps upwards, cantilevered out at one end; another twists down, to meet the ground at the other, following the profile of a glass-walled, double-cone pavilion. The glass is partially screened by perforated metal.

Church of the Sacred Heart, 2000   **Allmann Sattler Wappner**
Lachnerstrasse 8, 80634 Munich ◑
This elegant church comprises two boxes, one placed inside the other. The nave is clad with vertical maple louvres set close to each other at the entrance and becoming more widely spaced down the nave. The outer glass skin is gradually less transparent.

       Germany

NS Dokuzentrum, 2015   **Georg Scheel Wetzel**
Brienner Strasse 34, 80333 Munich ◑
This five-storey building formed of white concrete marks the former headquarters of the National Socialist German Workers' Party. Containing permanent and temporary exhibitions, seminar and conference rooms, a library and offices, its perfect cubic form is incised with vertical concrete louvres that extend around the corners.

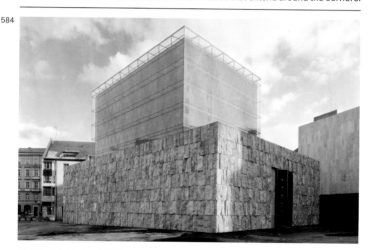

The Jewish Center, 2007   **Wandel Hoefer Lorch**
Sankt-Jakobs-Platz 16, 80331 Munich ◑
This project combines three buildings within a public space in the centre of Munich: a synagogue, a museum and a community centre. A glass and steel cube rises from the synagogue's monumental stone base, while the museum has a glazed ground floor with an opaque cube above.

Europe

Mortuary and Cemetery, 2000 **Meck**
Strasse am Mitterfeld 68, 81829 Munich ●
Located in a park opposite the old graveyard, this contemporary mortuary and cemetery stands as an austere composition of stone, concrete, rusting steel and oak. A canopy floats above the linear structure that comprises a chapel, mourning rooms and tranquil, stone-paved courtyards.

Porsche Museum, 2009 **Delugan Meissl**
Porscheplatz 1, 70435 Stuttgart ◑
Hovering above ground level and supported by three concrete bases, this floating form houses Porsche's exhibition hall, with a large window in its angular perimeter. The museum's ramped entrance reveals a restaurant, museum shop and coffee bar, as well as an extensive underground car park.

Europe

Marktoberdorf Gallery, 2001   **Bearth & Deplazes**
Kemptener Strasse 5, 87616 Marktoberdorf ◐
Three gallery spaces, each square in plan, connect to an existing villa by a glazed linking building. The largest space is an open-air forecourt for the display of sculpture. Two cube-shaped volumes are joined directly along one side of the complex, with a wide portal in the wall connecting the space within.

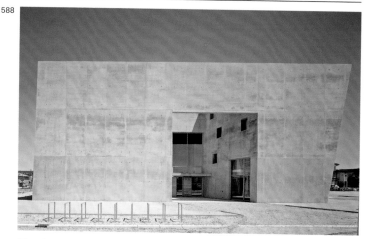

Church for Two Denominations, 2012   **Kister ScheithAuer Gross**
Maria-von-Rudloff-Platz 1, 79111 Freiburg im Breisgau ◐
Both a Protestant and Catholic church, this concrete building — freestanding in an open square — is the focal point of a new residential district. Inclining from the vertical, two approximately parallel, zigzagging concrete walls define the building. Movable internal walls delineate the two churches sacristy and prayer space within.

Conference Pavilion, Vitra Campus, 1993   **Tadao Ando Architect & Associates**
Charles-Eames-Strasse 2, 79576 Weil am Rhein ○
This structure, a large portion of which is concealed below ground, features a sunken courtyard at its centre, from which a series of corridors and ramps lead to a sequence of conference rooms. Its exposed concrete and wood finishing establishes an atmosphere of calm.

VitraHaus, Vitra Campus, 2010   **Herzog & de Meuron**
Charles-Eames-Strasse 2, 79576 Weil am Rhein ○
Grouped around a central wooden deck, this five-storey building, comprising 12 'houses', showcases Vitra's Home Collection. The cantilevered volumes stack up on one another. Inside, showrooms replicating the shape and scale of domestic homes have glazed gable ends.

Germany

Factory Building, Vitra Campus, 2012 **SANAA**
Charles-Eames-Strasse 2, 79576 Weil am Rhein ◑

Elliptical in plan, this factory building features an oval form that maximizes the periphery for truck docks, as well as allowing an open floorplan suitable for large events. It is cloaked in a white facade of vacuum-moulded acrylic glass affixed to metal framing, while the interior is illuminated by roof lights.

592

Fire Station, Vitra Campus, 1993 **Zaha Hadid**
Charles-Eames-Strasse 2, 79576 Weil am Rhein ◑

The long, narrow structure of this fire station is formed of concrete panels, enclosing three layered angular volumes that appear devoid of typical functional details. Similarly, the interiors are stripped of skirtings and door frames, and fluorescent tubes starkly light bathrooms, changing rooms and engine bays.

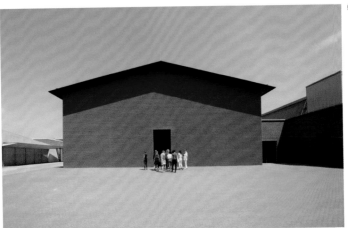

Vitra Schaudepot, Vitra Campus, 2016
Charles-Eames-Strasse 2, 79576 Weil am Rhein ❶

Herzog & de Meuron

Set above a vast basement warehouse, this storehouse, used to display selections of Vitra's collection, mimics the site's former industrial shed. Built from handmade clay-brick masonry, with an oversailing gabled roof, the volume provides a modest vessel for the triple-height modular display racks inside, built of timber and metal.

Factory Building, Vitra Campus, 1994
Charles-Eames-Strasse 2, 79576 Weil am Rhein ❶

Álvaro Siza Vieira

This simple, rectilinear brick structure is reminiscent of nineteenth-century factory architecture — and considerably less flashy than its neighbours in the Vitra campus. It is connected to the adjacent building by an arched, bridge-like roof construction, which automatically lowers during rainfall to provide shelter.

Germany

Europe

Europe

Shopping Center Stückfärberei, 2009 **Diener & Diener**
Hochbergerstrasse 70, 4057 Basel ◐
This two-storey shopping mall and six-level hotel complex are knitted together
within a white envelope, punctuated by four windowless entrance towers. Both mall
and hotel open to the southern courtyard, framed by a green wall and the rhythmic
banks of windows that differentiate the hotel's facade.

Asklepios 8, Novartis Campus, 2015 **Herzog & de Meuron**
Elsässerrheinweg 101, 4056 Basel ●
This riverside office building is composed of two cubes of similar height, placed on
top of each other. Between these two sections, a high atrium provides a spacious
venue for meetings and events. At the side facing the Rhine, the tower is supported
by two horizontal volumes, which house a public restaurant and café.

Novartis Campus, Visitor Centre, 2006
Fabrikstrasse 6, 4056 Basel ●

Peter Märkli

This building is bound by regulations regarding position, appearance and the provision of a colonnade, but unconventional elements imbue sophistication. A trellis of moving letters by artist Jenny Holzer horizontally divides the front colonnade, and is framed on other facades by the diamond-pattern grille of the mezzanine.

Novartis Campus Forum 3, 2005
Forum 3, Fabrikstrasse 3, 4056 Basel ●

Diener & Diener

This modern revision of the office building type provides a spectrum of working environments. A colourful, open facade contrasts with the nature of the work carried out within. An internal landscape of screens and curved, curtained glass capsules for private meetings modulate views inside.

Messe, 2013
Messeplatz, 4058 Basel ●

Herzog & de Meuron

An extension to the Basel Messe exhibition centre, this huge hall features a brushed-aluminium, basket-weave facade. Bridging a neighbouring public square, the hall provides a partly covered urban space and a connection between the site's different exhibition halls, while at its centre sits an enormous, circular rooflight.

Novartis Square 3, 2009
Strasse 5, 4056 Basel ●

Maki & Associates

This four-storey office building for Novartis showcases the company's principles for interactive working environments. Its translucent curtain wall is composed of layers of glazing, ceramic frit and white aluminium, which appears diffuse or opaque according to the angle of the light.

Jazzcampus, 2013
Utengasse 15, 4058 Basel ●

Buol & Zund

The rounded arches, pitched roofs and oriel windows of this music complex are a perfect counterpoint to the traditional architecture of its surroundings. Its uniform pale-brick facade, meanwhile, places it firmly in the twenty-first century. Built on the site of a former factory, it comprises 49 practice rooms and recording studios.

Roche Building 1, 2015
Grenzacherstrasse 124, 4058 Basel ●

Herzog & de Meuron

Housing the headquarters of pharmaceutical giant Roche, this 41-storey, 178m-tall skyscraper is heated entirely with waste heat from on-site manufacturing. As Switzerland's tallest tower, it is visible from all over Basel, yet its tapered, tiered shape provides entirely different silhouettes depending on the angle at which it is viewed.

Museum der Kulturen, 2010   Herzog & de Meuron
Münsterplatz 20, 4051 Basel ◑
This museum extension adds a 600 sq m column-free attic gallery to the original
building. The addition is an irregular volume with a folded roof and totem-like vines
hanging down from the cantilever. The hexagonal tiles which form the facade,
meanwhile, are inspired by the mosaics of nearby Münster cathedral.

Kunstmuseum Basel, 2016   Christ & Gantenbein
St Alban-Graben 8, 4010 Basel ◑
An extension to the 1930s art gallery it faces, this new space for exhibitions and
events is clad in a gradated grey brick skin that rises from dark to light, and mimics
its neighbour's height and window numbers. Inside, cast-concrete floors are linked
by a grand Carrara marble staircase illuminated by a broad circularrooflight.

Basel Train Station, 2003   **Cruz y Ortiz**
Centralbahnstrasse 10, 4051 Basel ◑
A steel and glass pedestrian bridge provides a route across the tracks below. The
roof steps up and down, depending on the function of the area below, providing
shops and cafés, a four-storey commercial space, and public square at street level.
Its folded, organic roof echoes the surrounding mountains.

Signal Box Auf dem Wolf, 1994   **Herzog & de Meuron**
Walkeweg 61, 4053 Basel ○
This tall, copper volume contains a signal box. Six floors contain mainly electronic
equipment for the control of signals to the depot and the related tracks, as well as a
few workstations. The building's concrete shell is wrapped with copper strips that
are twisted at certain places in order to admit daylight.

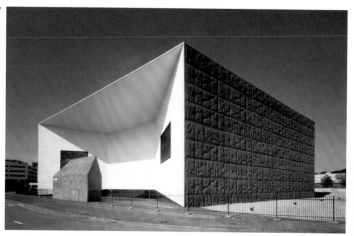

Schaulager, 2003 **Herzog & de Meuron**
Ruchfeldstrasse 19, 4142 Basel ●

Part museum, part warehouse and research centre, the Schaulager (Viewing Warehouse) contains the Emanuel Hoffmann Foundation's art collection. Basement and ground levels house exhibitions and a large auditorium, while three levels above store artwork in touch-screen-activated display cells.

Färberplatz Market Hall, 2002 **Miller & Maranta**
Färbergässli, 5000 Aarau ◑

The lightweight timber structure of this market hall contrasts with the surrounding medieval buildings. It sits atop a concrete podium, negotiating a level change and extending at the back into an open-air terrace. The ambiguous material quality results from the metallic, brown-painted surface of the rigorously machined timber.

Aarau City Museum Extension, 2015 **Diener & Diener**
Schlossplatz 23, 5000 Aarau ◑
An almost lozenge-shaped annex inserted between the Renaissance Saalbau and stone medieval tower, this extension provides staff workspaces, exhibition areas, a connection to the tower's labyrinthine corridors, and a new entrance hall. The principal facade is marked by 134 portraits cast in rectangular cement tablets.

Leutschenbach School, 2009 **Christian Kerez**
Saatlenfussweg 3, 8050 Zürich ●
Not unlike a high-rise, this project stacks classrooms, a library, a multi-purpose hall and a gymnasium into a single volume with a small footprint. All levels are composed as structural steel frameworks, but the location of the bracing differs from one level to another, allowing various layouts of the interior spaces.

Allianz Headquarters, 2014 **Wiel Arets**
Richtiplatz 1, 8304 Wallisellen ●
The twenty-storey tower and five-storey annex which comprise this office complex
are linked by a series of bridges. Inspired by Mies van der Rohe's famous Barcelona
Pavilion, the project's facade is clad with patterned glass, which has been through
a process of fritting to give the appearance of onyx marble.

Freitag Flagship Store, 2006 **Spillmann Echsle**
Geroldstrasse 17, 8008 Zürich ◑
These stacked freight containers accommodate a shop. Cut-out floors have an
internal metal staircase running the height of the tower to a viewing platform at the
top, as well as an external steel staircase. The containers on the sales levels have
their ends replaced by glazing.

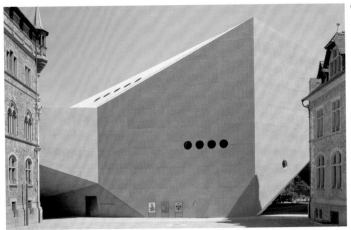

Swiss National Museum Extension, 2016
Museumstrasse 2, 8001 Zürich ◑

Christ & Gantenbein

Extending the original nineteenth-century gallery, this new wing bridges the interior courtyard and adjacent park, its zigzagging plan pierced by a double-height triangular void. Constructed in an abstract geometry from raw concrete, its thick walls are cut by deep-set ribbon windows and circular glazing.

Giesshübel, Track 3, 2013
Wolframplatz, Zürich ●

Burkhalter Sumi

This reclaimed industrial site adjacent to Giesshübel station contains apartments arranged beside the railway lines. Ranging from seven to eight storeys in height, the sober facade is composed of recessed panoramic windows arranged in bands, marked by grey stone transoms.

Zellweger Park, 2015 **Herzog & de Meuron**
Weiherallee 11a, 8610 Uster ○
A cast-concrete apartment block in a former industrial park, this eight-storey build-ing contains 32 homes. Saving the space normally consumed by shared corridors, the homes are accessed via private central circulation cores or spiral staircases that flank each corner giving the appearance of a fortified castle.

CentrePasquArt Extension, 1999 **Diener & Diener**
Seevorstadt 71, 2502 Biel ◑
This building is approximately L-shaped in plan and interlocks with its neoclassical neighbour, adding gallery space. The project creates continuity between old and new, extending pathways from the existing staircase and organizing floor heights according to the nineteenth-century tradition.

Europe

Jaquet Droz Swiss Watch Manufactory, 2004　　　　　**Atelier Oï**
Allée du Tourbillon 2, 2300 La Chaux-de-Fonds ●
Comprised of a single rectilinear volume, this structure accommodates a workshop. A highly reflective glazed facade lets natural light into the interior, while allowing the structure to mirror its hillside setting — it has been finished with a metallic coating designed to maximise reflectivity.

Friedrich Dürrenmatt Museum, 2000　　　　　**Mario Botta**
Chemin du Pertuis-du-Sault 74, 2000 Neuchâtel ◑
Set into a hillside, this museum contains the drawings of Friedrich Dürrenmatt (1921–90). Within the complex, his old house accommodates his library, a cafeteria and a bookshop. The fortress-like exterior is dominated by a tower and a semicircular wall, at the top of which is a viewing platform.

619

Zentrum Paul Klee, 2005 **Renzo Piano Building Workshop**
Monument im Fruchtland 3, 3000 Bern ◑
Only a few metres from Klee's tomb, this building's wave-like form encloses galleries, a basement auditorium and an archive. Parallel rows of curved steel girders define three structural hills, while an internal 'street' containing a café, restaurant and museum shop links the hills at ground level.

620

Cultural and Congress Centre, 2000 **Ateliers Jean Nouvel**
Europaplatz 1, 6005 Luzern ◑
This building's dominant feature is a sharp cantilevered roof, which reaches over a lakefront public plaza and fountain. The roof's reflective underside is raised clear of the building on three sides. A conference hall inside separates galleries and an auditorium from a symphony hall, bar and restaurant overlooking the lake.

Graubünden Museum of Fine Arts, 2016　　　　　　　**Barozzi Veiga**
Bahnhofstrasse 35, 7000 Chur ◑
This extension to Villa Planta, a museum dedicated to fine arts, also accommodates the Bündner Kunstmuseum. The project's logical order has been inverted, with a series of exhibition spaces being placed below ground level so as to reduce the structure's exterior volume. Its cubic form is clad in sculptural concrete slabs.

Bergbahn Arosa Chairlift, 2001　　　　　　　**Bearth & Deplazes**
Carmenna, 7075 Arosa ◑
These three chairlift stations, spaced between a valley and the top of a mountain ridge, are located in the alpine resort of Arosa. The valley station has a long rectangular hall with an entrance of translucent polycarbonate panels. Tent-like roofs are covered with a layer of soil and planted with vegetation.

Chesa Futura Apartment Building, 2004 **Foster + Partners**
Via Tinus 25, 7500 St Moritz ●
This curved house, clad in wood shingles, is elevated off the ground, offering views towards the valley, lakes and mountains beyond. The floorplan take its shape from two circles centred around a circular lift and stair cores. The building's north and south facades are formed by convex and concave arcs adjoining the circles.

Rolex Learning Centre, 2010 **SANAA**
École polytechnique fédérale de Lausanne, Route Cantonale, 1015 Lausanne ◑
In plan, this building resembles a slice of Swiss cheese, while in section its undulating form fluctuates between being a floating plane to being anchored to the ground. Inside, rounded openings reveal fragments of the building's unusual internal topography, with its sloping floors, through full-height glass facades.

École Polytechnique Fédérale de Lausanne, 2006 **Dominique Perrault**
Route Cantonale, 1015 Lausanne ●

An office and research building for mechanical engineering, this project is arranged in two wings, with a central rooflit atrium. Each wing connects through the broad entryway via footbridges, informal meeting areas and staircases. All but the north facade is screened with tilting, storey-height mesh that creates a woven pattern.

ArtLab EPFL, 2016 **Kengo Kuma & Associates**
1015 Ecublens, Vaud ◑

The new campus for the Swiss Federal Institute of Technology consists of three boxes tucked under a grand pitched roof, which stretches 235m. The roof provides shelter to pedestrian's walking from the north esplanade plaza down to the south residences throughout the day.

Europe

JTI Headquarters, 2015   **SOM**
8 rue Kazem-Radjavi, 1202 Geneva ●
Shaped by its triangular site, this headquarters consolidates offices from four disparate premises. Elevated opposing corners of the form gives it a tilted profile, and it's clad in a curtain wall of tessellated glass triangles. The building has a large central courtyard, and its torsional tube structure gives column-free office spaces.

Société Privée de Gérance Headquarters, 2017   **Giovanni Vaccarini**
Route de Chêne 36, 1208 Geneva ●
An innovative triple-layered glass facade provides this office conversion with both solar shading and visual transparency. On the exterior, strips of screen-printed glass, described by the architects as 'fins', provide a sense of pattern and depth. At night, when the building is lit with LED lights, it has a shimmering appearance.

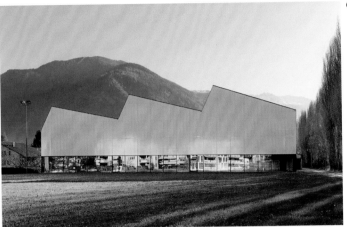

Three-in-One Sports Center, 2012
3930 Visp ◐

Savioz Fabrizzi

Three adjacent but independent sports halls are housed in this single building, its division into distinct areas emphasized by three saw-toothed roofs. Clad in cast-concrete panels, the spacious halls benefit from clerestory lighting and storey-height glass along their north and west faces.

MAX Gallery, 2005
Via Dante Alighieri 6, 6830 Chiasso ◐

Durisch & Nolli

A renovated hangar provides a central gallery space with four large rooflights, with a new two-storey building defining the site's roadside edge. A plaza for open-air exhibitions leads to the main entrance under the cantilevered floor of the fluted-glass gallery. An auditorium occupying one end of the basement seats 60 people.

Forum Gardens and Parliament, 2008 **Hansjörg Göritz Studio**
Peter-Kaiser-Platz 3, 9490 Vaduz ●
The ensemble for the Principality of Liechtenstein's forum, gardens and parliament
is comprised of a square, an enclosed garden, and two buildings — the 'Long House'
and, with its double-pitched roof, the 'High House' — connected by a third. The former two buildings are built in custom-made Swiss brick, with the latter in glass.

Liechtenstein Art Museum, 2000 **Morger & Dettli**
Städtle 32, 9490 Vaduz ◑
Smooth, light stone links museum facade and plaza in a restructuring of this open
space within the dense urban fabric of Vaduz. A low slot marks the entrance to the
museum building, leading into an unexpectedly large atrium. Generous windows
at ground level allow passers-by to glimpse exhibitions.

Europe

Kunsthaus Bregenz, 1997   **Peter Zumthor**
Karl-Tizian-Platz, 6900 Bregenz ◑
Designed without windows, this four-storey home for contemporary art and archives is designed to focus attention within. Clad in etched-glass shingles that refract the daylight, each rectilinear gallery of polished concrete is washed with traces of light that enter through translucent glazed ceilings.

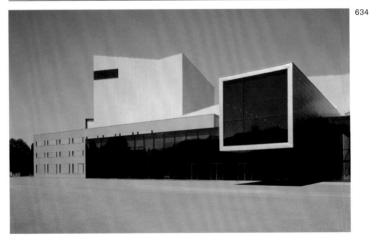

Bregenz Festival House, 2006   **Dietrich Untertrifaller**
Platz der Wiener Symphoniker 1, 6900 Bregenz ◑
Combining a range of functions, this centre comprises a stack of structurally interdependent volumes clad in striking dark glazing. A large square volume juts out from the main facade between the indoor theatre and the outdoor event space, which overlooks a floating stage on Lake Constance.

635

Europe

SIE Headquarters, 2002   **Marte.Marte**
Millennium Park 12, 6890 Lustenau ●
Accommodating the headquarters of a computer-manufacturing firm, this cube-shaped tower is built primarily in white concrete. Its storeys vary in height and transparency: some floors feature glass windows and balconies, offering views of the surrounding landscape, while others are almost entirely opaque.

636

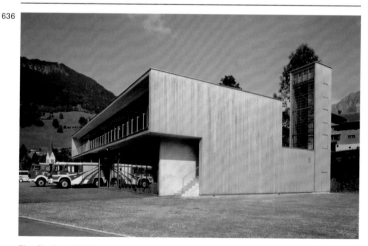

Fire Station, 2005   **Dietrich Untertrifaller**
Platz 292, 6881 Mellau ●
The ground floor of this building is located on the Mellenbach River, and is connected to the road on its first-floor level via a footbridge. This jump between levels is mirrored in the shift of the building's two main volumes. Large windows and a balcony along the facade allow for uninterrupted views of the river and mountains.

Music Kiosk, 2002   **Marte.Marte**
Furxstrasse 1, 6832 Zwischenwasser, Batschuns ●
Weathered plywood panels clad the exterior walls of this rehearsal space for a local orchestra. The entrance leads to a half landing, where stairs occupying one side of the building access the lower and upper floors. Two large projected windows and a rooflight above the conductor's stand illuminate the upper floor.

Galzigbahn Lower Terminal, 2006   **Driendl**
Kandaharweg 9, 6580 St Anton ◑
This ski-lift terminal's curved glass roof, supported by beams and cables on the outside and a steel truss inside, shows off inner mechanics that glow at night. A concrete pedestal anchors the building, acting as counterweight to a new funicular that enables the boarding of gondolas at ground level, via a giant wheel.

Nordpark Cable Railway, 2007   **Zaha Hadid**
Höhenstrasse 147, 6020 Innsbruck ◑
All four stations of this cable railway follow the architect's design concept of 'shell and shadow'. The shell is a curved roof above a concrete plinth — its shadow. Thermoformed glass elements wrap the roof's steel ribs, while lighting integrated into the concrete illuminates it from underneath.

Innsbruck Town Hall Gallery, 2002   **Dominique Perrault**
Maria-Theresien-Strasse 18, 6020 Innsbruck ◑
The grid-like panelled facade of the Town Hall Gallery, which houses mixed public and commercial services, echoes the fenestration of surrounding buildings and provides a new city landmark. A glass circulation tower provides a focal point and a reflective glazed wall opens onto a plaza.

Europe

Bergisel Ski Jump, 2002   **Zaha Hadid**
Bergiselweg 3, 6020 Innsbruck ◐
This intriguing Olympic-standard ski-jump consists of a bridge, tower, terrace, café
and athletes' area, with the jump twisting down from the apex. Fluorescent lighting
transforms the dramatic structure at night. The project celebrates the collaboration
between architecture and structural engineering.

Swarovski Kristallwelten, 2015   **Snøhetta**
Kristallweltenstrasse 1, 6112 Wattens ◐
This project includes a play tower, shop, playground and café-restaurant. The 20m
tower is covered by 160 facets that create zones for children to climb, alongside a
playground of steel and timber. A sculpted concrete volume encloses the dining
space, while the shop is entered via a tunnel lined with glowing fibres.

643

Special School and Dormitory Mariatal, 2007   **Marte.Marte**
Mariatal 15, 6233 Kramsach ●
Upgrading and extending this school housed in a historic former monastery, the
architects inserted two new buildings — one for classrooms and sport, the other
a boarding house — beside a modified structure for administration. New exposed
concrete facades feature golden aluminium joinery.

644

Festival Hall of The Tiroler Festspiele Erl, 2012   **Delugan Meissl**
Mühlgraben 56a, 6343 Erl ◑
A new winter concert venue for the Tyrol Festival, this jagged volume contrasts with
the existing white playhouse and was inspired by the rock formations behind it. The
dark timber-lined concert hall sits at the centre of the plan and connects to a white
faceted double-height lobby via two galleries on each level.

St Franziskus Church, 2001   **Riepl Riepl**
Werner-von-Siemens-Strasse 15, 4400 Steyr ◑
With its simple floorplan and concrete planes, this Catholic church is located in an
outer urban area of Steyr. Inside, varying room heights produce spatial hierarchies
and changing atmospheres. A glass cube substitutes for the conventional church
tower and contains a dramatic light installation.

Spittelau Viaduct Housing Project, 2005   **Zaha Hadid**
Spittelauer Lände 10, 1090 Vienna ●
This structure winds itself like a ribbon through, around and over the bays of a viaduct. Restaurants and offices occupy the lower floors and apartments on the third
and fourth floors spectacularly bridge the tracks, supported by groups of tilted columns. Strips of windows punctuate white plastered facades.

647

Gasometer Urban Entertainment Centre, 2001　　　**Rüdiger Lainer**
Gulglasse 43, 1030 Vienna ◑
Part of a regeneration project, the centre combines cinema, shopping and leisure
in decorative and animated interior spaces. A new edge to this well-worn formula
is created by an interweaving of functions, layers and platforms. Winding ribbons of
material define internal and external spaces.

648

WU Campus, 2013　　　**Zaha Hadid**
Welthandelsplatz 11, 1020 Vienna ●
One of seven buildings that form a new campus for the Vienna University of Economics and Business, this polygonal block, clad in black and white concrete panels,
cantilevers over a public square at the site's main entrance. Housing a library, as well
as function rooms, its curvilinear interior evokes canyon-esque grandeur.

Museum of Modern Art Ludwig Foundation, 2001   **Ortner & Ortner Baukunst**
Vienna Museum Quarter, Museumsplatz 1, 1070 Vienna ◑
One element within a cultural complex, this modern art gallery is an art object in its own right, presenting an almost-impenetrable basalt facade punctuated by narrow incisions. Entrance is via an elevated terrace. Inside, the shallow barrel-vaulted roof is sliced along its length to let in light.

MISS Sargfabrik Apartment Building, 2000   **BKK-3**
Goldschlagstrasse 169, 1140 Vienna ●
Making no attempt to blend in, MISS Sargfabrik represents a radical approach to residential building design, with each of the 39 flats opening onto a street-like communal loggia with a green courtyard. Varying room heights allow maximum density and unorthodox room divisions. Communal facilities include pool, library and disco.

Apartment and Office Building, 2005 **Coop Himmelb(l)au**
Schlachthausgasse 28-30, 1030 Vienna ●
Two slim volumes, placed in line with the Schlachthausgasse, re-establish the original urban block form. Existing trees are preserved to form an acoustically separated
yard. A chunky three-dimensional grid contains a youth centre and a bright red volume cantilevers over the garden, increasing in size as it projects further.

Gasometer B Apartment Building, 2000 **Coop Himmelb(l)au**
Guglgasse 6, 1110 Vienna ●
One element in an urban mega-project of post-industrial regeneration, Gasometer B, a shield-like structure, reclines against a former gas tank to provide popular
apartments. A large, airy courtyard now brings light into the gasometer, and a caged
fire escape follows the oblique angle of the building.

Wienerberg City Apartment Towers, 2004
Herta Firnberg-Strasse 16, 1100 Vienna ●

Coop Himmelb(l)au

This complex consists of two towers and a five-storey block containing loft-style apartments with flexible floorplans and parking below ground. Connected on the ninth floor by a steel truss, the volumes form a triangle around a public square. A silver disc on the lower block's roof contains a round swimming pool and spa.

Podersdorf Parish Centre, 2002
Seestrasse 67, 7141 Podersdorf am See ◑

Lichtblau Wagner

A contemporary religious building rather than a church, this Parish Centre has a glass facade inscribed with biblical quotations and thoughts on the topic of family. Natural light sources and white walls create an atmosphere of simplicity and purity inside, particularly in the mass room, which is almost featureless.

Steinbruch St Margarethen, 2008   **AllesWirdGut**
Festspielgelände, St Margarethen im Burgenland ◑
The carved cliffs of this quarry provide a dramatic backdrop for an open-air theatre. Long angled ramps lead down to the performance pit, and walkways are clad in corrugated steel, used for its corroding properties that will allow it to blend in to the surroundings. Wood and concrete are left rough to attract moss growth.

Semperit F&E Building, 2000   **Najjar & Najjar**
Triester Bundesstrasse 26, 2362 Wimpassing ●
The sleek, curved aluminium envelope of Semperit's research and development centre reflects the company's innovative profile in the plastics and rubber industry. The laboratories on the ground floor are entirely glazed and arranged around a central hall. A slanted cut-off end looks towards the busy road.

Europe

Franz-Liszt Chamber Music Hall, 2006   **Atelier Kempe Thill**
Franz Liszt Strasse 48, 7321 Raiding ◑
This concert hall adapts to the style of the region, with white walls, low windows and
a box-like shape. The auditorium walls are spruce wood. From the foyer, a full-height
window overlooks the garden and the adjacent house, where composer Franz Liszt
was born.

Mur Island Inhabited Bridge, 2003   **Acconci Studio**
Mariahilferplatz 2, 8020 Graz ○
Vito Acconci's idea was to bring the previously neglected Mur River into the public
sphere with this shell-like installation, which accommodates an open-air theatre,
children's playground and café. Created to celebrate Graz as European Culture
Capital 2003, the project proved technically challenging.

Fresach Protestant Diocesan Museum, 2011   Marte.Marte
Museumweg 32, 9712 Fresach ◑
Showcasing the treasures of the diocese church, this concrete museum is organized as two squares set symmetrically atop each other. The lower level houses
the glazed foyer and temporary exhibit area. Above, the permanent exhibits sit in
a taller, smaller volume, pierced by a cross-shaped incision that acts as a skylight.

Residential DNA Apartment Building, 2001   Weichlbauer/Ortis
Koloniegasse 11a and 11b, 8101 Gratkorn ●
Located in the suburbs of Graz, and surrounded by more conventional neighbours,
this housing unit is based on computer-generated patterns. Elements are simple,
restricted and regularly arranged — with one format for windows and doors — yet
the building's bright yellow adds an element of playfulness.

661 662 663

664 665

666 667 668

669 670 671

672

673

674

Milan

Turin

Italy

675

678

676 677

679

680–687

688

689

Rome

Italy

Lakeside Baths, 2006   **the next ENTERprise**
St Josef am See 15, 39052 Caldaro ◑
An artificial landscape, this lido incorporates a lake, spa facilities, restaurant and bar. Pools and sundecks are elevated onto a concrete plane resting on six structural cores, while glass openings in the floor of the pool allow visitors to gaze up from the space below. The restaurant is converted from a 1950s lido building.

Vigilius Mountain Resort, 2003   **Matteo Thun & Partners**
Monte San Vigilio, 39011 Lana ◑
Reached by cable car or foot, this hotel accommodates a restaurant, spa and library, with many facilities buried into the sloping ground. A traditional shingle-roofed timber building has been remade, incorporating beams from a 300-year-old barn. A long block containing 37 rooms and six suites is accessed from a central corridor.

Firebrigade Margreid, 2010   **Bergmeisterwolf**
Via Johann Steck 34, Margreid ●
A new volunteer fire station for Margreid, this two-bay garage is excavated from the base of a steep rock face. Charcoal in hue, the concrete structure encases the building, giving necessary support and protecting against falling stones. Three glazed steel portals that house garaging, offices and administration incise the wall.

Museum of Contemporary Art, 2002   **Claudio Silvestrin**
Via Modene 16, 10141 Turin ◑
Occupying the site of a former factory in a Turin suburb, this minimalist art museum clothes its cavernous volume in an immaculate, soft limestone skin. The long, pure facade is scored by vertical cuts, allowing light to slice through internal spaces, and is punctuated by timber doors cut out in rhythmic sequence.

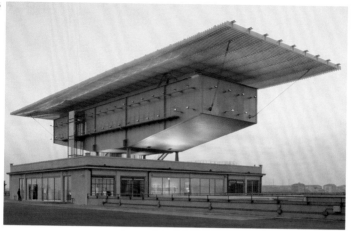

Pinacoteca Giovanni e Marella Agnelli, 2002   **Renzo Piano Building Workshop**
Via Nizza 230, 10126 Turin ◑
Hovering above the landmark 1917 Fiat Factory, this gallery displays the Agnelli family's art collection in a calm and minimalist interior. The body is a partly cantilevered wedge-shaped box, with no apparent openings in its steel skin. The roof is made of 16,000 glass fins.

Fiera Milano, 2005   **Fuksas**
Strada Statale del Sempione 28, 20017 Milan ●
This complex is one of Europe's largest exhibition facilities, occupying the site of a former refinery, northwest of Milan. An undulating roof covers the central axis, flanked by exhibition halls and supported by tree-columns. The lightweight roof consists of a mesh structure of precast steel covered with laminated glass.

Bosco Verticale, 2014   **Boeri Studio**
20124 Milan ●
Conceived as a 'vertical forest', this complex comprises two residential towers
in the Porta Nuova area of Milan, set perpendicular to each other, surrounded by
20,000 sq m of trees and undergrowth. The towers reach 80.5m respectively and
are planted with around 900 trees.

Fondazione Giangiacomo Feltrinelli, 2016   **Herzog & de Meuron**
Viale Pasubio 5, 20154 Milan ◑
This research centre and archive features reinforced concrete ribs, which articulate
the repeated skewed gable. Marching along the narrow site, the building is split in
two, with the foundation occupying one half, and offices the other. The facade is clad
in glass panes that reveal the inner workings, including a café and bookshop.

Galleria Lia Rumma, 2010   **CLS**
Via Stilicone 19, 20154 Milan ◑
Constructed from marble-like concrete, this gallery is set back from the street, allowing for outdoor exhibitions uninhibited by height restrictions. An external iron staircase links its five storeys, while a rooftop deck is topped by a series of cage-like steel beams.

Luigi Bocconi University, 2008   **Grafton**
Via Sarfatti 25, 20136 Milan ●
This university addition comprises a cantilevered auditorium rising from the lower-ground to the second floor, a library and research offices. The complex is arranged around in-between zones, creating a maze of courts, bridges, terraces and corridors. The comb-like structure of the offices filters light down to the lower floors.

671

Fondazione Prada, 2015   **OMA**
Largo Isarco 2, 20139 Milan ◐
Located in a former gin distillery, this project consists of seven existing buildings,
and three new structures: Podium, a space for temporary exhibitions; Cinema, a
multimedia auditorium; and Torre, a nine-storey permanent exhibition space for displaying the foundation's collection. An existing building is covered entirely in gold leaf.

672

Lido on Lake Segrino, 2004   **Studio di Architettura Marco Castelletti**
Via Luigi Panigatti 3, 22030 Eupilio ◐
This L-shaped lido sits on the shore of Lake Segrino, partly dug into the bank behind.
A tower marks the entrance, and gates of staggered horizontal steel offer glimpses
into a colonnade of laminated timber, enclosing the bathing area. Changing rooms
are lit and ventilated by glass-louvred clerestory lights.

Church and Pastoral Centre, 2004   **Mario Botta**
Via Po 1, 24068 Seriate ⊙
Clad in red marble, this facility includes a public plaza and church connected to a one-storey volume housing the centre's classrooms and residence. In plan, the church is a square; in section each of its four facades rises, then tapers, then rises again, forming four towering volumes. Inside, rooflights flood the space with natural light.

Nardini Performance and Research Centre, 2004   **Fuksas**
Via Madonna di Monte Berico 7, 36061 Bassano del Grappa ⊙
A stepped ramp carved into the earth provides entry to this research space and auditorium for an adjacent distillery. Grassy steps lead to a large arena below, where glass stairs and a slanting lift connect to the two bubble-like volumes above that appear to hover over the water.

Enzo Ferrari Museum, 2012   **Future Systems**
Via Paolo Ferrari 85, 41121 Modena ➊
Comprising the renovation of an existing brick building and a new structure that
curves around it, the Ferrari Museum stands out for its curvaceous yellow livery. Its
aluminium roof is sliced by 10 glazed incisions, like automobile intake vents. Inside,
a ramp gently slopes into a vast white-panelled vault showcasing signature vehicles.

MAST Foundation, 2013   **Maria Claudia Clemente and Francesco Isidori**
Via Speranza 42, 40133 Bologna ➊
This mixed-used complex houses the headquarters of an institution that promotes
art, technology and innovation. Clad with glass and concrete panels, it provides staff
facilities and public spaces, including a technology museum. At the entrance, a large
rectilinear canopy, supported by thin columns, extends out over a water feature.

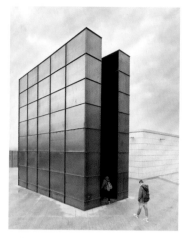

Bologna Shoah Memorial, 2016   **SET**
Via Giacomo Matteotti, 40129 Bologna ○
This Holocaust memorial consists of two symmetrical Corten steel parallelepiped blocks of 10 sq m each; the blocks sit adjacent to one another, perpendicular to the existing walls of the square. Their position converges to create a path, which begins with a width of 1.6m, before drastically narrowing to just 80cm.

San Michele Complex, 2002   **Massimo Carmassi**
Via Degli Orafi, 56127 Pisa ◑
This project comprises two restored sides of a medieval square and a new third side in traditional brick construction with recessed openings that faces an existing thirteenth-century church. The modern element houses shops and dwellings, and uses glass and steel structures faced with masonry.

Sandro Penna Library, 2004 **Studio Italo Rota & Partners**
Viale San Sisto, 06156 Perugia ◑
The lower floor of this project comprises a theatre and multimedia areas. A glazed circular reading area occupies the first floor and forms the pedestal to the pink, disc-like volume above, containing a gallery. The disc's skin is composed of sheets of tinted glass mounted onto a curved metal frame with gaps in between.

Fiumicino Town Hall, 2002 **Alessandro Anselmi**
Via Portuense, 00054 Fiumicino ◑
Located at the entrance to the city centre and facing a canal, this municipal complex forms a reinforced concrete hill, with administrative, political and retail functions and a public plaza arranged underneath. The smooth brick covering layer is supported on invisible pillars and hides the main aluminium and glass structure below.

MAXXI National Museum for XXI Century Arts, 2009　　　　**Zaha Hadid**
Via Leopardi 24, 00185 Rome ◑
This sinuous, concrete building contains two museums within its L-shaped plan. Gallery spaces and walkways intertwine as defined by curving concrete walls, and a black snaking stairwell circulates visitors. Using louvres and skylights, a complex roof system controls natural and artificial light.

Città del Sole, 2016　　　　**Labics**
Via della Lega Lombarda/Via Arduino, Rome ●
Marking the edge of an existing Roman neighbourhood, this series of angular buildings forms a mixed-use complex woven through with a system of urban paths. Linked by ground-level retail, offices and a library, raised volumes accommodate offices and residences, with glazed facades protected by aluminium or glass brises-soleils.

Stazione Tiburtina, 2011   **ABDR**
Tiburtina, 00162 Rome ◑
This angular station features a glass-fronted main hall stretching 300m high and
covered by a jutting roof. Inside, suspended pods house a bar and lounge, and office
space. It was conceived as a multi-use hub for various means of transport, and to
accommodate the new Italian high-speed train system.

Church of San Carlo Borromeo, 2011   **Monestiroli**
Via Edoardo Amaldi 215, 00134 Fonte Laurentina ◑
This church hall and annex was conceived to be visible from afar. Double-height perimeter walls of stone enclose the monolithic liturgical hall, which has a symmetrical
rectangular floorplan. Set on an axis with the altar, the presbytery bell tower rises
directly above; its two tall, perforated walls admit light to the interior.

Europe

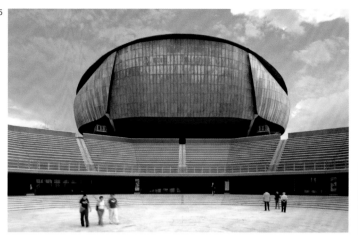

Parco della Musica, 2002 **Renzo Piano Building Workshop**
Viale Pietro de Coubertin 30, 00196 Rome ◑
The bulging volumes of these three concert halls are accessed from a central piazza
with an open-air amphitheatre. Exterior surfaces are clad with lead tiles coated in a
pearly protective lacquer. A museum containing the remains of a Roman villa is also
located on the site.

Parrocchia Santa Maria Josefa del Cuore di Gesù, 2002 **Garofalo Miura**
Via Marcello Candia, 00132 Rome ◑
Located in a suburb to the west of Rome, this church forms part of a social and
sports complex. The caustic red of the community centre pinions the modest and
neutral church building. Subdued and formal green marble and cherry wood deco-
rate the church interior.

New Rome-Eur Convention Center 'La Nuvola', 2016　　　　　　　　**Fuksas**
Quartiere XXXII Europa, 00144 Rome ◑
This complex comprises three distinct architectural concepts: the 'Theca', a metal, glass and reinforced-concrete outershell; the 'Cloud', a cocoon-like structure covered in 15,000 sq m of fibreglass and silicone membrane, supported laterally at points by the 'Theca'; and the 'Blade', an adjacent 17-storey hotel.

Community Center, 2015　　　　　　　　**Burnazzi Feltrin**
Via Benedetto Croce, 67026 Poggio Picenze ◑
Zigzagging across the site and down a gentle slope, this community centre is arranged around two large, square-planned rooms linked by oblique glazed walls. Clad with larch boards, the project encompasses a library, multi-purpose spaces and music room, as well as gardens on the roof, a sheltered terrace and vehicle bays.

Ortona Cemetery, 2006   **Giovanni Vaccarini**
66026 Ortona ○
Referencing a traditional Italian cemetery, recesses arranged in straight lines are
built in neat two-storey blocks. Each long block is cut into cubes, leaving gaps
filled with light. Limestone cladding juxtaposed against white-plastered inner
walls enhances the impact of the cut-out openings.

Salerno Maritime Terminal, 2016   **Zaha Hadid**
Stazione Marittima di Salerno, 84121 Salerno ◑
This maritime terminus, housed in an undulating concrete shell, provides border control offices and docking for vessels. Its asymmetric form envelops ramped paths
that lead visitors in and out of the building, with international departures and arrivals
passing through channels for security, customs and luggage retrieval.

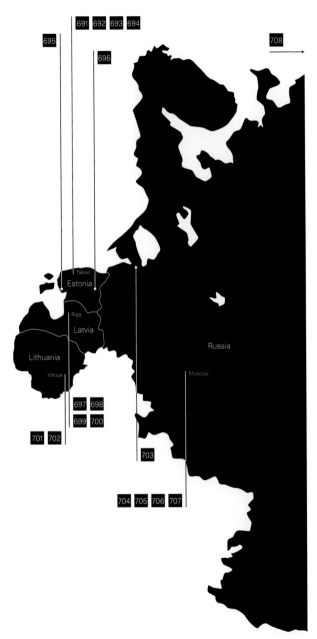

Estonia, Latvia, Lithuania and Russia

Viimsi St James Church, 2007   **Martin Aunin**
Haabneeme, 74001 Harju ◑
Located on a plinth of local stones, this church in Viimsi, a rural maritime parish in
northeastern Estonia, commemorates those lost at sea. A folded roof covers a sacristy, lobby and church hall. A tall reinforced-concrete belfry faces the sea, and the
building's exterior is clad in spruce weatherboarding.

Kumu Art Museum, 2006   **Vapaavuori**
Weizenbergi 34, 10127 Tallinn ◑
Positioned on the limestone slope of Lasnamäe Hill, the circular floorplan of this art
museum takes up 7,620 sq m. An atrium rises through the seven floors, two of which
are below ground. The museum is constructed of dolomite, wood and copper, which
are traditional local materials.

Europe

Koidula 24 Apartments, 2007   3+1
Lydia Koidula 24, 10125 Tallinn ●
Spanning a long, narrow site beside a landscaped courtyard in the heart of Tallinn,
this apartment block is distinguished from its neighbours by the angular steel facade it presents ot the street. The three-storey apartment block unfolds inside its
armoured shell, revealing large windows that overlook walkways and green spaces.

Museum of Occupations, 2003   **Head**
Toompea tänav 8, Kesklinna linnaosa, 10142 Tallinn ◑
This reinforced-concrete steel-frame structure appears as a neutral form which explores the qualities of brightness, lightness and fragility. Its main floor is a continuous surface divided between different functions. Visitors entering the building pass
under the main floor slab into an enclosed tree-lined, memorial courtyard.

Pärnu Stadium, 2017   **Kamp**
Pärnu, 80012 Pärnu County ◑
All 1,500 seats of this grandstand are located under a cantilevered awning, which has an unsupported span of 28m. Its facade is clad in wood and white concrete, while on the ground floor, there are dressing rooms for the athletes, as well as auxiliary rooms, including a 4m-wide tartan-covered corridor extending 62m.

Estonian National Museum, 2016   **DGT**
Muuseumi tee 2, 60532 Tartu ◑
This glass and concrete museum rises from the runway of a former Soviet airbase. Visitors enter at the highest point, after which the museum gradually decreases in height, culminating in an exit of just 3m. The glazed facade features a motif of eight-pointed stars — a reference to Estonia's national flower, the cornflower.

Art Academy of Latvia Extension, 2012　　　　　**Andis Sīlis**
Kalpaka bulvāris 13, Centra rajons, Riga ◑
Extending a neo-Gothic house, this project takes an existing 1940s redbrick storage block, lowers it by 3m and adds glass walls, a concrete access ramp and a cantilevered roof, which, along with the original shell, protects the interior from direct sunlight. The lecture rooms and exhibition halls are often open to the public.

National Library of Latvia, 2014　　　　　**Gunārs Birkerts**
Mūkusalas iela 3, Zemgales priekšpilsēta, Riga ◑
The sloping form of this building is inspired by a Latvian legend, and represents a glass mountain. With the exception of the curtain wall, the building was manufactured using local materials. The 13 floors are arranged around a large interconnecting atrium, and the interior colour scheme is derived from old Latvian banknotes.

Day Centre for the Homeless, 2009   **8AM and Mikus Lejnieks**
Katoļu iela 57, Latgales priekšpilsēta, Riga ●
Located on a small plot near a railway embankment, this compact volume is
wrapped in tin sheeting, arranged vertically and diagonally, which refracts sunlight
off the surface at varying angles throughout the day. By night, a warm orange interior is revealed through irregularly spaced and differently sized windows.

Žanis Lipke Memorial Museum, 2012   **Zaigas Gailes Birojs**
Mazais Balasta dambis 8, Kurzemes rajons, Riga ◑
This black shed-like structure commemorates Žanis Lipke, who saved the lives of
more than 50 Jews in WWII by hiding them in a bunker in his backyard. A passage
leads to a shaft connecting the three levels of the building. From the attic, visitors
peer down into a well symbolizing the bunker, with its original three sq m dimensions.

Life Sciences Center, 2016 Architektūros linija
Vilnius University, Saulėtekio al 7, Vilnius 10223 ●
A modern addition to the oldest university in Lithuania, this centre accommodates labs, lecture theatres and an auditorium. The facade is influenced both by technology and the verticality of the pine trees which surround the campus, while glass-fibre-reinforced concrete cladding helps to protect the interior from the sun.

Litexpo Exhibition Pavilion, 2006 Paleko Arch Studija
Laisves Prospektas 5, 04215 Vilnius ◑
The pavilion, a simple triangle in plan, has a glazed diagonal facade looking towards the surrounding mountains. The other two sides are concrete walls which fold over the roof, projecting over the glazing and forming a canopy in front of the building, ending at the point of the triangle.

Quattro Corti, 2010   Piuarch
Pochtamtskaya ul 3, 190000 St Petersburg ●
This business centre is defined by four internal courtyards behind two restored facades from the eighteenth and nineteenth centuries. Each quadrangle — a gold-hued entrance, a blue plaza with a pool, a green garden square and a red space with a Corten sculpture — is faced with angled panels of tinted, mirrored glass.

704

Skolkovo Golf Club House, 2014   Shigeru Ban
Skolkovo Village, 143025 Moscow ●
Situated at the upper reaches of a golf course, the club house's curving plan frames expansive views across the course. Guests enter through the 72m-long arced entrance screen of timber columns, descending to the main hall. This timber structure accommodates the reception, shop and restaurant, and an exterior terrace.

Moscow School of Management, 2010　　　　　　**Adjaye Associates**
Novaya Ulitsa 100, Skolkovo Village, Odintsovsky, 143025 Moscow ●
This gargantuan complex is predominantly assembled as a single entity in which
a range of facilities are accessible without going outside — a response to the cold
winters. A 150m wide circular disc houses learning spaces; above this, four huge
towers are suspended, alongside more stout towers for offices and sports facilities.

City of Capitals, 2009　　　　　　**NBBJ and Erik van Egeraat**
Presnenskaya Naberezhnaya 8, 123317 Moscow ●
This project accommodates an entertainment complex, offices, luxury apartments,
and a fitness centre and spa. Its twin skyscrapers resemble a series of stacked
offset cubes. Among the tallest buildings in Europe, the pair are connected by a
ground-floor lobby, situated on top of seven subterranean storeys.

Garage Museum of Contemporary Art, 2015   **OMA**
9/32 Krymsky Val Street, 119049 Moscow ◑
Enclosing an existing Soviet-era concrete structure, this art gallery preserves original elements, including a mosaic wall, tiles and brick. It's all enclosed within a new
translucent double-layer polycarbonate facade raised 2.25m from the ground in
order to visually reconnect the pavilion's interior to the adjacent park.

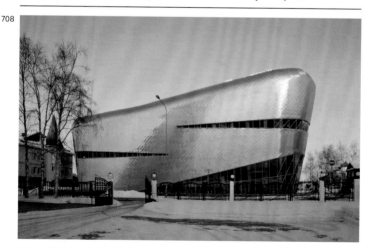

Billiard & Chess Club, 2010   **Erick van Egeraat**
1 Lopareva Street, 628000 Khanty Mansiysk ●
Conceived as a signature building for the 2010 Chess Olympiad, this club house
unfolds around a central double-height playing hall with terraced seating, flanked
by rooms for administration or individual matches. Its skin of zinc-painted shingles
wraps the curving form, spliced by narrow bands of ribbon windows.

709 710

711

712 713

714

715 716 717 718 719

720

Europe

Warsaw

Poland

Prague

Czech Republic

Slovakia

Bratislava

Budapest

Hungary

721

722

723 724

725

726

Europe

National Museum, 2016   **Robert Konieczny KWK Promes**
Plac Solidarności 1, 70 515 Szczecin ◑
This museum for Szczecin history is partially embedded below ground, arranged by
a quarter-circle plan that shapes an undulating public plaza of precast concrete —
which also functions as the building's roof. Its raised edge to the north houses the
entrance lobby and leads to orthogonal concrete galleries painted black.

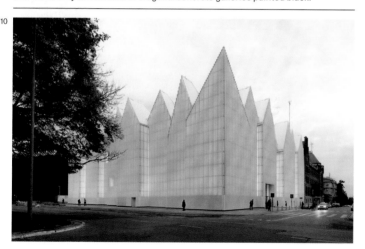

Philharmonic Hall, 2014   **Barozzi Veiga**
Małopolska 48, 70 515 Szczecin ◑
The translucent ribbed glass cladding of this concert hall contrasts dramatically
with the conditions of its surrounding environment. Its most prominent feature is
its zigzagging roofline, made up of a series of sharply pitched gables. It comprises
a 1,000-seat symphony hall and a smaller venue for chamber music.

CKK Jordanki, 2015   **Menis**
Aleja Solidarności 1–3, 87 100 Toruń ◑
Situated in green parkland, this concert hall emerges from its environment like a
huge boulder. Concrete and broken redbricks were mixed — a technique the architect calls 'picado' — to create the cave-like interior of the building, which is intended
to provide optimal acoustics during music performances.

Museum of the History of Polish Jews, 2013   **Lahdelma & Mahlamäki**
6 Mordechaja Anielewicza Street, 00 157 Warsaw ◑
On the site of a former ghetto, this museum for Jewish heritage is housed in a cubic
concrete shell, pierced by a triple-height void that forms the entrance hall. Rising in
a bulging shape from the travertine floor, the panelled double-curve surface defines
the spaces for exhibitions, a library, auditorium and classrooms on the upper levels.

Eko Park Expo Pavilion, 2001
Chodkiewwicza Street, Mokotów, Warsaw ◑

Kuryłowicz & Associates

Originally a temporary structure in downtown Warsaw, this pavilion was saved by its simplicity and now provides permanent exhibition space. The galvanized-steel skeleton is clad with white polycarbonate panels creating a soft light suited to displaying artworks.

Arthur Rubinstein Philharmonic Concert Hall, 2005
Rubinsteina Ulitsa Naruto 20–22, 90 135 Łódź ◑

Atelier Loegler

Standing on the site of a nineteenth-century concert house, the project features an architectural drawing of the original edifice serigraphed onto an arch in front of the glazed south facade, which wraps over the entire building. Daylight enters a full-height foyer through a lattice brise-soleil.

Europe

Kolbenova Metro Station, 2000   **Chalupa**
Kolbenova Metro, 190 00 Prague 9 ◑
This new concourse for an existing station on Prague's metro system provides an inviting exterior. Light floods in through a surface facade that combines metal mesh, distorted glazing and fibreboard panels. Inside, a polished stainless-steel wall intensifies the light and reflects the street outside.

Pathway through the Deer Moat, Prague Castle, 2002   **Josef Pleskot Atelier**
Jelene Prikop, 118 00 Prague 1 ◑
This underground tunnel provides pedestrian access from the Vltava River to the grounds of Prague Castle. Egyptian-style entrances with rectangular portals and inclined retaining walls lead into a tall oval brick tunnel with high vaulted ceilings, with a stream running below the floor.

The Dancing House, 1996   **Frank Gehry**
Jiráskovo náměstí 1981/6, 120 00 Prague 2 ◑
Consisting of two adjoining structures, this project's unusual 'dancing' shape consists of a glass tower supported by curving pillars and a second building that runs parallel to the river. On the top of one building is a large twisted structure of metal that is nicknamed *Medusa*.

Nový Smíchov Shopping Centre, 2001   **D3A and Fiala-Prouza-Zima**
Plzeňská 8, 150 00 Prague 5 ◑
Part of an ambitious renovation scheme spanning several city blocks in the Smíchov district of Prague, this shopping centre addresses two streets from its corner location with a series of glass and titanium volumes. Much of the bulk of the complex is hidden beneath a gently sloping grass hill.

Europe

Former Smíchov Synagogue, 2004   **Znamení Čtyř**
Stroupežnického 290/32, 150 00 Smíchov, Prague ◑
The reconstructed and extended Smíchov Synagogue is now used as the archive of the Jewish Museum. Original floors and wall paintings have restored, while a newly built wing houses contemporary offices, as well as research rooms on the ground floor. The former synagogue lobby functions as a bookshop.

Javornik Distillery, 2015   **ADR s.r.o.**
Javornice, 384 22 Dub ●
Most of the original features of existing buildings have been retained and restored across this project such as red roof tiles. New buildings mimic the old in their facades and roof shape, and feature materials that complement original elements, including similar roofing material but in black.

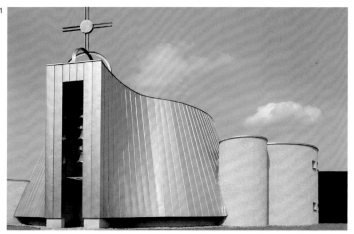

Church of St Francis Minorities Monastery, 2002   **Justus Dahinden**
Kláštor minoritov, Námestie svätého Františka 4, 841 04 Bratislava ◐
The Church of St Francis Minorities Monastery sits on a circular plaza near the University of Bratislava. Three cylindrical chapels open through arched incisions off a central liturgical space. A continuous rooflight around the top of the cone allows daylight to flood the interior.

Heat Exchanger Važecká, 2012   **Architektonické štúdio Atrium**
Važecká 2, 040 12 Kosice ◐
Angular concrete-panelled walls that include a rock-climbing surface provide a striking foil for the public cultural and sports centre contained inside this former heat exchange. The project includes five split-level floors, and an open timber roof deck provides the ultimate reward for triumphant climbers.

Central European University (Phase 1), 2016   O'Donnell + Tuomey
Nador utca 15, 1051 Budapest ●
Situated on a World Heritage site in Budapest, this project unites the university, connecting disparate buildings into an open campus arranged around a series of courtyards. A new building clad in lattices and solid courses of local limestone forms the primary entrance, housing the library, auditorium and conference facilities.

Parish Church of the Celestial Queen, 2015   **4 plusz Építész Stúdió**
Szent István Square 21, 1041 Budapest ◑
Converted from a 1920s school, this church features a new wing, crafted from brick and white fibre-cement and capped with a gabled slate roof. From the front entrance, you can see right through a courtyard and an expanse of glass to the garden, while the building's perforated facade references Hungarian embroidery patterns.

Füleky Winery, 2010   **Félix Zsolt**
Tokaj ◑
On a plot directly adjacent to a fifteenth-century church, this winery produces Tokaj wines. Elements from the original stone building have been retained, including laid stone interior walls. New facades, as well as the roof, have been made from a yellow-grey stone, originating from nearby Mád.

Cultural Centre, 2000   **Imre Makovecz**
4 Posta Utca, Makó, 6900 Csongrád ◑
Traditional local styles and materials were used to transform a dilapidated existing cultural centre into this stunning new auditorium. The slate and timber roof of the central space is flanked by bulbous, partially glazed towers. References to the natural world continue inside, with tree-like supporting columns.

727
728
729 730
731
732

Ljubljana
Slovenia
Zagreb
Croatia

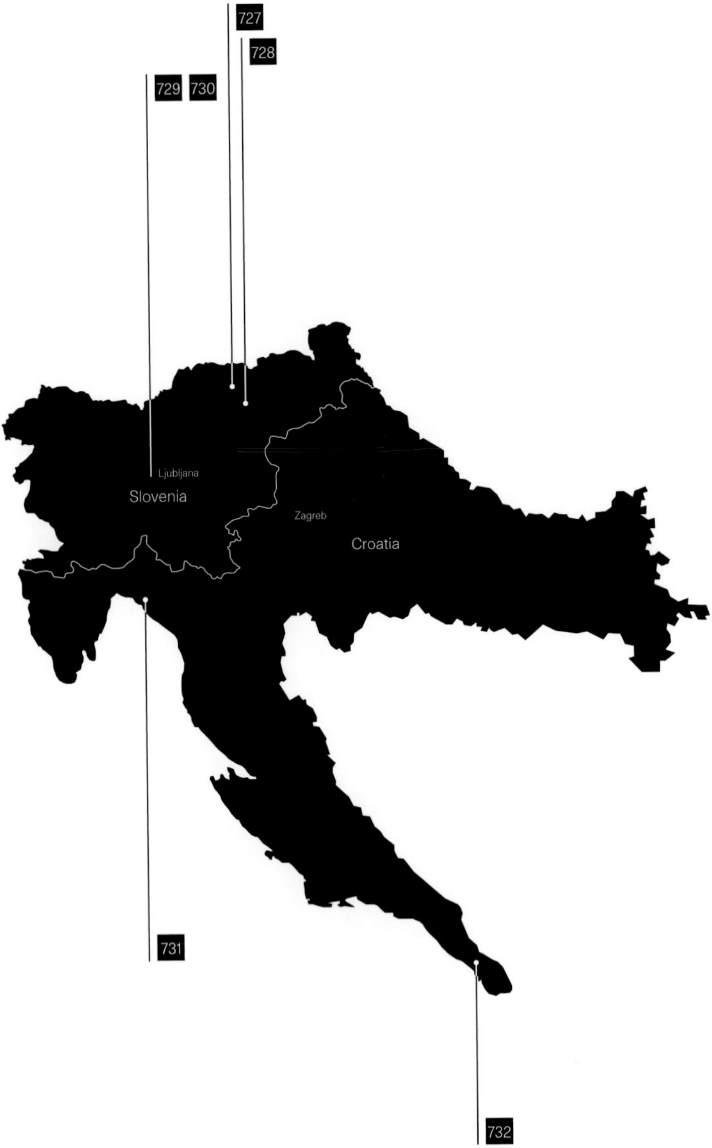

Cultural Centre of European Space Technologies, 2012   **Bevk Perović**
Na vasi 18, 3205 Vitanje ◑
This cultural and scientific building integrates a local community centre with a multipurpose hall, library and space technology museum, and is inspired by rocket sci-
entist Herman Noordung. Conceptually derived from his tilting 'habitation wheel',
the metal-clad exhibition spaces are arranged in a series of interlocking rings.

Celjska Lodge, 2006   **Arhitektura Krušec**
Pečovnik 31, 3000 Celje ◐
Comprising an inner layering of wood panelling and glazing and an outer skin of horizontal timber laths, this building has a dual presence. Seen from the valley side, its
imposing solidity dominates the landscape. Seen from the slope, it sits lightly on the
site with minimal visual impact in this alpine panorama.

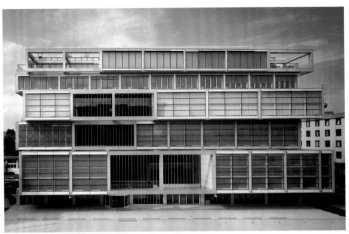

Chamber of Commerce and Industry of Slovenia, 1999   **Sadar + Vuga**
Dimičeva ulica 13, 1504 Ljubljana ●
A 'megastore' to house public service offices, this hybrid project also provides semi-public amenities including restaurants, a library, archival reading room and exhibition areas. Five levels of cantilevered glazed boxes of various sizes and heights contain semi-public services, while the offices sit within a regular glazed skin.

Parking Garage Šentpeter, 2005   **A.biro**
Zaloška cesta 1, 1000 Ljubljana ●
This is a multi-storey car park and commercial building next to the University Medical Centre of Ljubljana. The perforated facade permits natural ventilation of the car park. From particular vantage points, the aluminium cladding appears to be three-dimensional.

731

Memorial Bridge, 2001   **3LHD**
51000 Rijeka ○
This Memorial Bridge in the Croatian port of Rijeka provides pedestrian access over a canal between a city park and the historic centre, and it commentators those Croatians lost in the Balkan conflicts. The relationship between the vertical sentine slabs and horizontal bridge sections creates a powerful presence.

732

Public Lavatory, 2002   **Nenad Fabijanic**
Old Port of Dubrovnik, 20000 Dubrovnik ○
Part of the Dubrovnik reconstruction project, the site for this public lavatory demanded a long, narrow structure. Nestling between ancient city walls and the Austro-Hungarian port authority building, its smooth facade of local sandy limestone contrasts with the surrounding rough-hewn stone.

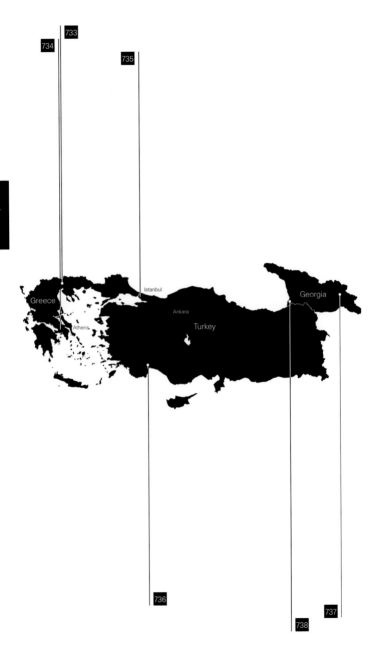

733

734

735

Europe

Istanbul

Greece

Athens

Ankara

Turkey

Georgia

736

738

737

Greece, Turkey and Georgia

733

Cultural and Recreation Centre, 2001   **AM Kotsiopoulos & Partners**
Naousa 59200 ❶
Adjacent to the ancient School of Aristotle, this centre comprises two boxes, with a pergola on a shallow plinth that forms the roof of the basement, which houses an auditorium. The facade is made up of glazed windows and translucent wooden shutters, while the ground floor contains a museum, shop and restaurant.

734

Athens Olympic Velodrome, 2004   **Santiago Calatrava**
Kifisias 37, Athens 15123 ❶
Originally constructed in 1982, this complex was refurbished for the 2004 Olympics, with entrance plazas, boulevards, gathering places and sculptural elements that integrated sports areas with surrounding public spaces. A new roof that overhangs the sides of the main stadium is suspended from double steel arches.

Europe

Vakko Fashion Center, 2010   **REX**
Kuşbakışı Caddesi 35, Nakkaştepe, Istanbul ●
Vakko's offices occupy the core — a 'showcase' of tilted steel boxes clad in mirrored surfaces — and the two-storey glass-walled 'ring' (really a square). Underground are the Power Media offices, a public design library and galleries for Vakko's fashion collection, which dates back to the 1950s.

Minicity Model Park, 2004   **Emre Arolat**
Arapsuyu Mahallesi, 07030 Antalya ◐
This park exhibits quarter-scale models of some of Turkey's historic buildings. The low-slung entrance building, which houses shops, a restaurant and an exhibition hall, forms an artificial blue-grey landscape reminiscent of the nearby Taurus Mountains, while a pavilion and bar sit at the opposite edge of the park.

Rest Stop, 2011   J Mayer H
Gori ◑
A series of roadside service stations along the Georgian highway connecting Azer-baijan and Turkey, these huge concrete structures provide shelter for petrol filling stations and were commissioned to reflect the country's new identity. Partially en-closed by dark glazing, the services also include plazas for farmers' markets.

Border Checkpoint, 2011   J Mayer H
Sarpi ○
The unusual silhouette of this Georgian checkpoint near the Turkish border aims to illustrate a new sense of identity for the country. Housing customs facilities and staff accommodation, as well as a café, the tower's cantilevered, elevated terraces provide viewing platforms across the vehicle bays and to the coastline.

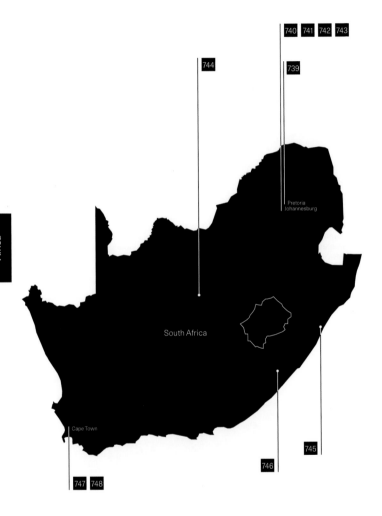

740 741 742 743

739

744

Pretoria
Johannesburg

South Africa

745

Cape Town

746

747 748

Africa

Freedom Park, 2011   **GAPP, Mashabane Rose and MMA**
Koch Street/7th Avenue, Salvokop, Pretoria ◑
This monument to democracy comprises a landscaped park and memorial, interactive museum and archive, commercial precinct and administration facilities. Sikhumbuto, the major memorial element, sits on the crest of Salvokop, a natural quartzite ridge. Isivivane (Garden of Remembrance) contains a burial ground.

Alexander Forbes Headquarters, 2003   **Paragon**
115 West Street, Sandton, Johannesburg ●
The bulk of this eight-storey financial building, car park, crèche and gym sits on concrete columns, with a large concrete canopy running along the top of the building. Big grey 'scallop' wings scoop light into the back of the building, while the horizontal louvres on the glass-fronted Rivonia Road facade curb its penetration.

Africa

Constitutional Court, 2004   **Janina Masojada and Andrew Makin**
1 Hospital Street, Constitution Hill, Johannesburg ●
Imposing carved wooden doors lead to a foyer incorporating more than 500 stained-glass windows, and mosaic elements that reflect the traditional seating pattern of village elders. The structure is built from bricks reclaimed from a prison wing that previously occupied an adjacent site.

Apartheid Museum, 2001   **GAPP**
Northern Parkway/Gold Reef Road, Ormonde, Johannesburg ◑
This museum is crafted almost entirely from sand- and adobe-coloured stone and brick. The exterior is punctuated by seven large pillars, each symbolising a tenet on which the present South African constitution is based. Inside is a series of chambers, consisting of tiny cells, lofty halls and silos.

Africa

Maropeng Visitor Centre, 2005   **GAPP**
R400, Mogale, Gauteng ◑
Most of this museum, situated in the Cradle of Humankind site, is buried beneath a hill-shaped mound. The building is composed of a concrete frame covered with earth and grass. Upon entry one passes an excavation site, before descending into an arrival court and then rising towards the mound, suggesting a ritualistic process.

Africa

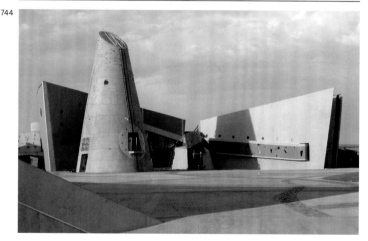

Legislature Building, 2002   **Luis Ferreira da Silva + Johnston**
Galeshewe, Kimberley, Northern Cape ◑
Arranged around an open-air forum for speeches and rallies, these earthy, sculptural buildings contain administrative offices, a library and a debating chamber. A triple-height lobby hosts functions and temporary exhibitions. An ochre-hued conical tower provides a local reference point.

Denis Hurley Centre, 2014   **Ruben Reddy**
2 Cathedral Road, Durban Central, Durban ◑
Triangular in form, this community centre uses its unusual configuration to bind all areas to a centralised atrium, creating an integrated community space. The building is clad in thick, sand-hued brick, and long, narrow windows ventilate and illuminate the centre.

Nelson Mandela Museum, 2000   **Cohen and Judin**
Nelson Mandela Drive/Owen Street, Bhunga Building, Umtata ◑
The Mveso monument, one element of the Nelson Mandela Museum, preserves Mandela's birthplace in a simple open-air structure of concrete, brick and gum poles under a steel sheet roof. Existing fencing and traditional lattice weaving skills were used in the project, and training was given in stone-building techniques.

Thusong Service Centre, 2010 **Makeka Design Laboratory**
Steve Biko Road, Khayelitsha Mall, Cape Town ◑
Located in a township southeast of Cape Town, this service centre, alongside sports facilities and a social centre, is a focal point for an impoverished area of the city. Its distinctive saw-tooth roof is a striking presence, while its translucent exterior and wooden pergolas create a sense of lightness.

Zeitz MOCAA, 2017 **Heatherwick Studio**
V&A Waterfront, Cape Town ◑
Occupying a former grain silo, this project consists of a hotel and cultural institution housing contemporary art from Africa. The conversion retains much of the building's industrial origins, such as its concrete exterior. Pillowed glazing panels, inserted into the existing geometry of the upper floors, bulge outward as if gently inflated.

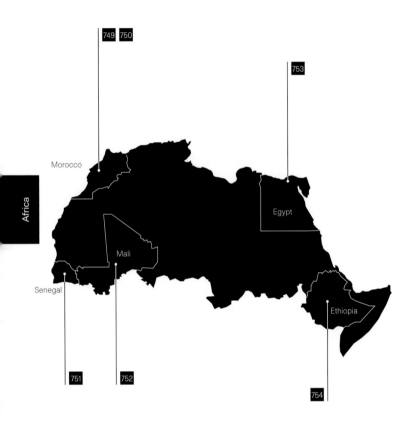

749 750

753

Morocco

Africa

Egypt

Mali

Senegal

Ethiopia

751 752

754

749

Menara Airport, 2008 **E2A**
Ménara, Marrakech ◐
This airport extension's superlative Maghreb modern design, based on a grid of inter-locking rhomboids clad in white aluminium, incorporates an arabesque pattern in the glass that dapples the light, and a cantilevered roof fitted with photovoltaic pyramids arranged in stylised Islamic motifs.

750

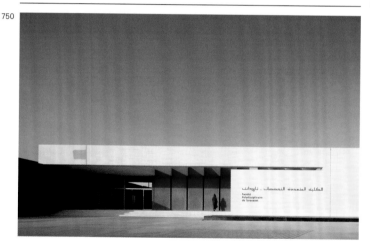

Faculté Polydisciplinaire de Taroudant, 2014 **Saad el Kabbaj**
Hay El Mohammadi, Taroudant ●
Clad predominantly in ochre-hued concrete, this university campus consists of a series of low-slung structures positioned as individual volumes, maximizing natural ventilation. Given the climate, different sun protection devices have been employed throughout the site, such as brise-soleil and protected walkways.

Thread, 2004   **Toshiko Mori**
Sinthian ◑
A community hub, this cultural centre offers artists residencies and creative programmes, as well as hosting markets and meetings. Constructed by local builders
using native materials of brick and bamboo, its rough figure-of-eight plan is crowned
by a sweeping, inverted thatched roof, which channels fresh rainwater for villagers.

Centre de l'Architecture en Terre, 2010   **Kéré**
Quartier Komoguel I, Avenue du Cinquantenaire, Mopti ◑
This project — mainly constructed from compressed earth blocks — features a sleek
cantilevered roof, which unites the three different volumes that comprise this centre,
as well as aiding insulation. Its low-slung form ensures views of the adjacent mosque
aren't compromised.

Bibliotheca Alexandrina, 2001   **Snøhetta**
Al Azaritah WA Ash Shatebi, Qesm Bab Sharqi, Alexandria ◑
Adjacent to Alexandria University's Arts Campus, this building recreates the library founded around 2,300 years ago. Inscribed with texts from around the world, a massive granite wall protects about four million volumes inside. Terraces divide the collection into subject areas, and allow views to the Mediterranean.

Africa

Lideta Market, 2016   **Vilalta**
Liberia Street, Addis Ababa ◑
Based on traditional market principles, this contemporary shopping mall tackled the problems of glass-fronted shops absorbing too much heat by using a lightweight concrete for its facade. A series of openings provide light and ventilation, and riff on a traditional Ethiopian fractal pattern, which is normally found in local fabrics.

765

766 767 768

769

Cyprus

Lebanon

Tel Aviv

Palestine

Israel

771 772

773 774

775 776

Middle East

Saudi Arabia

Riyadh

UAE

770

763

755-762

764

Terminal 3, Ben Gurion Airport, 2002   **SOM**
Ben Gurion Interchange, Tel Aviv ◑
This airport is divided into two connected volumes, one housing ticketing, departure and arrival halls, with a smaller volume for security control that contains a rotunda with a central waiting lounge, food and retail facilities. The rhythmic light cast by the glazed northeast entrance facade creates a calm interior.

Palmach Museum, 1992   **Zvi Hecker and Rafi Segal**
Chaim Levanon Street 10, Tel Aviv ◑
This museum, commemorating the underground Jewish army that fought for the establishment of the state of Israel, is set in a building formed of oblique intersecting blocks of smooth reinforced concrete, part clad in bricks made of kurkar limestone. In the basement, an intricate floor plan serves the innovative exhibition settings.

Amir Building, Tel Aviv Museum of Art, 2010   **Preston Scott Cohen**
Golda Meir Compound, Sderot Sha'ul HaMelech 27, Tel Aviv ◑
This new wing for the Tel Aviv Museum of Art is situated on a tight triangular site. In order to create large rectangular galleries inside, the architects conceived subtly twisting geometric surfaces that connect the disparate angles between the galleries. Each space is organized around an 26.5m-tall spiralling atrium.

Azrieli Center, 1998 and 2007   **Eli Attia**
Derech Menachem Begin 132, Tel Aviv ◑
Three towers in the shape of a triangle, a square (both completed in 1998) and a circle (2007) are connected at the base by a mall, and form a monumental trio over Ayalon Freeway. The 187m cylindrical tower is the highest in Tel Aviv, and has a restaurant and observation deck on the 49th floor.

First International Bank Tower, 2009   **Pei Cobb Freed & Partners**
Baron Edmond de Rothschild Boulevard 42-44, Tel Aviv ●
Five stacked triangular glass prisms form a stepped asymmetric tower standing 132m tall. The double curtain wall, which allows air to circulate within the facade, also has automated blinds. Set in the centre of the financial district, the structure is raised at ground level to form a sheltered plaza adjacent to two low-rise buildings.

Peres Center for Peace, 2010   **Fuksas**
Kedem Street 132, Tel Aviv ◑
This building's facade is constructed from alternating layers of concrete and translucent glass. Rising seven storeys, the centre is dedicated to cross-cultural coexistence within the Middle East, and houses archives, a press hall, an auditorium and a library in the atrium. The Mediterranean-facing gardens are accessible to the public.

Design Museum Holon, 2010   **Ron Arad**
Pinkhas Eilon Street 8, Tel Aviv ❶
This museum showcases works encompassing fashion, jewellery, textiles and fur-
niture, by native and international creatives, across a split-level space. The building's swooping, sculptural facade is made up of reddish Corten ribbons formed in
a rough figure of eight, which provides a series of perspective-shifting routes.

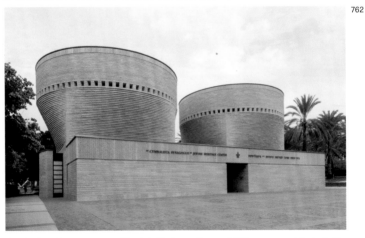

Cymbalista Synagogue and Jewish Heritage Center, 1998   **Mario Botta**
Tel Aviv University, Tel Aviv ❶
From the base plinth of the synagogue, a pair of circular towers rise close to 13m
high, one functioning as a place of worship, and the other as a secular lecture hall.
Lessinia stone from the Dolomites was used for the exterior, while the interior
utilises golden Tuscan stone.

Yad Vashem Holocaust Memorial, 2005   **Moshe Safdie**
Har Hazikaron, Jerusalem ◑
This Holocaust memorial occupies a sweeping site overlooking the village of Ein Kerem. A 2005 makeover of the History Museum features an 180m-long raw concrete arcade, which cuts through the hilltop, and at one tip culminates in a pair of curved 'wings' that thrust dramatically outwards from the hillside.

The High-Tech Park Bridge, 2016   **Bar Orian and Rokach Ashkenazi**
Beer Sheve, Negev ○
Providing a pedestrian path between Be'er Sheva train station and the city's Advanced Technologies Park, this 210m-long bridge incorporates over 200 steel-beam cross sections. The structure of the bridge is exposed, and its four arches intersect to create two oval shapes resembling eyes.

Bethlehem Cultural Centre, Hall and Restaurant Building, 2003   **Juha Leiviskä**
Paul VI Street, Bethlehem ◑
Surrounded by historical buildings, a series of levels across the site connect this new academy complex to existing church spaces. The progressive retraction of lounge and restaurant volumes creates a dynamic glass and sandstone facade with rhythmic balconies and pergolas.

Nestlé Waters Beirut Headquarters, 2014   **Bernard Mallat and Walid Zeidan**
Jir El Basha, Beirut ●
Informed by the turning circle of delivery trucks, this headquarters and storage building is organized into a long brick delivery warehouse set perpendicular to three office buildings stacked on top. The offices have progressively larger cantilevers that culminate in a forest of steel columns, which support the largest upper level.

Middle East

Aïshti Foundation, 2015 **Adjaye Associates**
Sea Side Road, Antelias, Beirut ◑
This foundation, situated on a brownfield coastal site, replaces a number of existing warehouses, and also fronts a seaside promenade. Taking the form of a simple
block, it is rotated on one edge so that it appears tilted. The eye-catching facade —
made of ceramic louvres — uses a geometric 'thunderbolt' pattern.

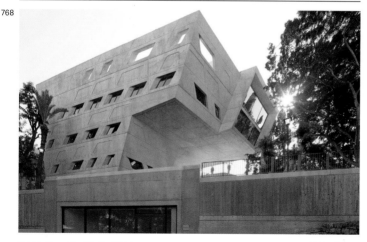

Issam Fares Institute, 2014 **Zaha Hadid**
Riad El-Solh, Beirut ●
An institution for public policy and international relations, this five-level concrete
edifice is largely concentrated in a cantilevered form incised by angular windows
and reliefs. The building hovers above the entry courtyard and an elevated pathway
that connects to the first-floor entrance, preserving the existing topography.

Oroklini Coastal Promenade, 2002 **Margarita Danou and Sevina Zesimou**
Dhekelia Avenue, Voroklini ◑
A threshold between a resort development and the coastal edge, this promenade
bounded by the sea and an artificial lake provides leisure activities for the public.
A series of platforms, canopies and lighting unified by a path accommodates chang-
ing facilities, a kiosk and places to sit along the way.

Middle East

The Palestinian Museum, 2016 **Heneghan Peng**
Museum Street, Birzeit ◑
This museum — a long, narrow building of concrete, clad in local limestone — has
been compared to a Bedouin tent, notable for its complex geometries. Set within
four hectares of landscaped gardens, the project houses space for exhibitions
and performance, as well as research and education.

King Fahad National Library, 2013   **Gerber**
King Fahd Branch Road, Al Olaya, Riyadh ◑
This extension to Saudi Arabia's national library, which surrounds the original building entirely, accommodates one of the country's most important institutions. Its facade is influenced by traditional Arabian patterns, formed by rhomboid textile awnings. At night, the exterior glows with changing colours.

Middle East

Kingdom Centre Building, 2003   **Omrania and Associates**
2239 Al Urubah Road, Al Olaya, Riyadh ◑
This tower is the tallest building in Saudi Arabia. Its fluid, curved form and distinctive parabolic opening at its apex houses the global headquarters of the Prince's Kingdom Holding Company, a 10-storey hotel, offices, luxury apartments and a bridge with a public observation deck, which crosses the void at the top.

Concrete, 2017   **OMA**
Street 8, Alserkal Avenue, Al Quoz 1, Dubai ◑
Situated in Dubai's most important art hub among twenty-five galleries and art spaces, this building functions as a public space that hosts a diverse programme of events. Facing a public square, it's enclosed behind a facade of tall polycarbonate doors. Inside, four pivoting, sliding walls allow for varied internal configurations.

Middle East

Cayan Tower, 2013   **SOM**
Dubai Marina, Dubai ●
Each of this skyscraper's 75 floor plates is rotated slightly from the one below, resulting in a 90-degree twist from bottom to top. This helps combat wind load and solar gain, but the benefit for the observer is the way it captures and reflects sunlight at different times of day, adding tremendous aesthetic appeal.

Sheikh Zayed Bridge, 2010   **Zaha Hadid**
Al Shahama Road, Abu Dhabi ○
This third gateway crossing links Abu Dhabi Island to the Gulf south shore. A four-lane highway bridge, it features cantilevered road decks suspended from symmetrical steel arches, which form a sinusoidal waveform — giving the large structure a fluid silhouette.

Hazza Bin Zayed Stadium, 2014   **Pattern Design**
Al Tawia, Al Ain, Abu Dhabi ◑
This stadium's facade features a pattern inspired by the geometry of the date palm, a tree native to the region, and also acts as a cooling device. The white, undulating parasol roof was designed specifically for the desert climate and provides shade for both players and spectators.

777
778
779 780 781 782
783 784

Québec City
Montréal
Toronto

North
America

Canada

785 786 787

788–794

Canada

777

National Music Centre of Canada at Studio Bell, 2016   **Allied Works**
850 4 Street South East, Calgary ◑
Arranged as interlocking towers across two city blocks — and linked by a curvaceous sky bridge — the National Music Centre includes a concert hall, exhibition
spaces, and recording and broadcast studios. The new-builds are clad in glazed
bronze-hued terracotta tiles, alongside a refurbished historic brick building.

778

OMS Stage, 2011   **5468796 Architecture Inc**
124 King Street, Winnipeg ◑
Nicknamed 'The Cube', the OMS Stage is an open-air performance venue located in
Winnipeg's Exchange District. Built from concrete and enclosed in a flexible metal
mesh that, when pulled back, reveals the stage, this structure functions as both
performance space and outdoor sculpture.

Squish Studio, 2011　　　　　　　　　　　　　**Todd Saunders**
Turpin's Trail, Tilting, Fogo Island ◑
This white trapezoid studio, built from painted wooden planks, rises to 6m in height at the south entrance, descending to 3m on the other side. Designed to fend off winds from the North Atlantic, the downward angled roof frames a window that faces the shoreline, with narrow windows dotted on the side.

North America

Bridge Studio, 2011　　　　　　　　　　　　　**Todd Saunders**
Deep Bay, Fogo Island ◑
Accessed by a 5m-long footbridge, this studio stands on four pins, and overlooks an inland pond. The building is composed of concrete and painted spruce planks, and features a glass entrance. Although contemporary in style, inspiration was drawn from Newfoundland's fishing traditions.

Fogo Island Inn, 2013 **Todd Saunders**
Joe Batt's Arm, Fogo Island ◑
Perched like a marooned ship atop slender, angled columns, this timber-clad hotel is comprised of two volumes: the first is two storeys and accommodates public areas, while the other four-storey block houses the guest rooms — all of which offer sweeping views of the often wild North Atlantic.

Long Studio, 2011 **Todd Saunders**
Joe Batt's Arm, Fogo Island ◑
Standing on stilts facing the sea, this studio features a rectangular form, which draws in light from large windows at either end. Inspired by the seasons, an open but sheltered entrance represents Spring, the exposed centre connotes Summer, and the enclosed space, with views of the surroundings, marks the Autumn and Winter.

High House, 2017 **Delordinaire**
Québec City ●
Raised on thin black metal stilts, the High House lives up to its name, elevated one storey off the ground. It is cloaked in white concrete and corrugated metal, and is accessed by a narrow steel staircase entering the centre of the plan. The two-bedroom cabin receives ample daylight through broad windows in its east and north faces.

784

Pierre Lassonde Pavilion, 2016 **OMA**
179 Grande Allée Ouest, Québec City ◑
Formed of a stack of steel-trussed, translucent glass volumes that step down towards a park, becoming progressively wider in plan, this extension knits together green space, street and existing buildings. A 14m-high transparent Grand Hall acts as a gateway to the galleries, courtyard and auditorium.

115 Studios for Cirque du Soleil, 2003   **FABG**
8333 2e Avenue, Montréal ●
Located in the Cirque du Soleil headquarters, this residential building, comprising a five-storey tower and three-storey wing, is clad in corrugated metal-panels. The ground floor contains social spaces. Cantilevered rooms above have full-height corner windows offset on each floor to resemble irregularly stacked containers.

Bibliothèque du Boisé, 2014   **Lemay**
2727 Boulevard Thimens, Montréal ◐
Sunken into the site's slope and wrapped in a shell of cast concrete and glazing, this low-slung building sits unobtrusively in its surroundings. The southern wing holds the library's collections and reading areas, with a café and foyer at the centre, and exhibition spaces are located to the north.

Mies van der Rohe Gas Station, 2011 FABG
201 Rue Berlioz, Montréal ◑
This project transformed a 1960s petrol station by Mies Van der Rohe into a community centre for both teenagers and senior citizens. Two large rooms, one for each age group, are connected by a steel roof. The monochrome effect of the fluorescent lighting and black steel beams accentuates the sleek lines of the original design.

Vaughan Civic Centre Resource Library, 2016 ZAS
2191 Major MacKenzie Drive West, Vaughan ◑
Clad in slanting panels of aluminium and glass, this public library is configured as an irregular pentagon with bowed elevations. Visitors enter beneath the highest point of the roof into a one-storey structure arranged around a central reading garden. Places to socialize and study, as well as a café, are organized along the perimeter.

Aga Khan Museum, 2014　　　　　　　　　　　**Fumihiko Maki**
77 Wynford Drive, Toronto ◑
Built to house the Islamic art collection of philanthropist Aga Khan IV, this lunar-like two-storey museum features canted walls of white Brazilian granite centred on a deep courtyard shrouded in mashrabiya-patterned glass. The building is orientated at 45 degrees to the compass so that all four facades receive direct sun.

North
America

Renaissance ROM Galleries, 2007　　　　　　　**Studio Libeskind**
100 Queens Park, Toronto ◑
Called the Michael Lee-Chin Crystal, this dramatic extension comprises five inter-locking prismatic sections clad in shiny brushed aluminium and glass that project out of the original building. It's supported on a complicated skeleton of steel beams and considered one of the most challenging construction projects in North America.

Student Learning Centre, 2015 **Snøhetta and Zeidler**
Ryerson University, 341 Yonge Street, Toronto ●
Resembling an uncut diamond, this centre was inspired by the agoras of Ancient Greece, where education was inherently social. Signposted by a triangular swathe of hand-folded aluminium panels, the structure is finished in iridescent blue paint that stretches from the exterior to the soffit and over the lobby ceiling.

Sharp Center for Design, 2004 **Will Alsop**
100 McCaul Street, Toronto ◑
In addition to the multicoloured columns, a concrete core containing lifts and exit stairs supports this two-storey box of studios and teaching spaces. The elevation of the building allows visual and physical access to the adjacent park, while a stairwell, set within a red, sloped tube, connects it to the concrete core.

Absolute Towers, 2012   **MAD**
50-60 Absolute Avenue, Mississauga ●
In order to achieve the twisted silhouettes of these towers, each floor rotates between one and eight degrees. They are also ringed by continuous balconies, allowing the glass facades to be recessed and protected from the sun, and lending the design a ribbed effect. The two buildings top out at 170m and 150m respectively.

Centre for International Governance and Innovation, 2014   **KPMB**
67 Erb Street West, Waterloo ●
Situated on the site of a former distillery, this academic complex uses brick as its primary material — a tribute to the neighbourhood's industrial past. The central courtyard features a contemporary stone bell tower, while a glazed curtain wall and cantilevered roof make for a dramatic entrance.

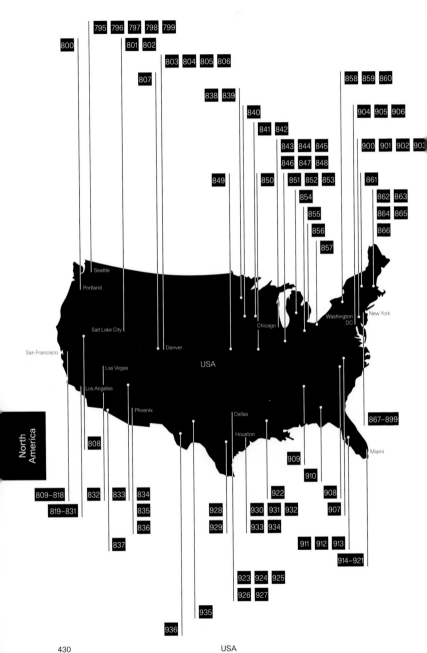

USA

Experience Music Project, 2000   **Frank Gehry**
325 5th Avenue North, Seattle, WA 98109 ◑
The Experience Music Project at the Seattle Center celebrates the history of American popular music. The project inhabits a cluster of fragmented and undulating forms suggesting a trashed Fender Stratocaster guitar. Looping steel cables are reminiscent of guitar strings.

Olympic Sculpture Park, 2007   **Weiss/Manfredi**
2901 Western Avenue, Seattle, WA 98121 ◑
A Z-shaped pedestrian path leads past art installations, and bridges the roadways and railroad tracks that slice through this new sculpture park. Concrete retaining walls mask mechanically stabilized earth, while a transparent pavilion frames views of Puget Sound and the Olympic Mountains.

Seattle Central Library, 2004   **OMA**
1000 4th Avenue, Seattle, WA 98104 ◑
With mountain views from a tenth-floor rhomboid reading room, this library incorporates ramps and floating platforms wrapped in steel and glass as principal features. The exterior is composed of a triple-glazed structural curtain wall overlaid
with an expanding aluminium mesh.

Bellevue Arts Center, 2000   **Steven Holl**
510 Bellevue Way North East, Bellevue, WA 98004 ◑
The organizing concept of this museum, which has an educational rather than a col-
lecting focus, is 'tripleness': three slightly warped main lofts contain dramatically
curved volumes with distinctive lighting conditions. The outer walls, in a 'shotcrete'
construction, support the lightweight steel framework.

Tacoma Art Museum, 2003   **Antoine Predock**
1701 Pacific Avenue, Tacoma, WA 98402 ◑
The two wings of the Tacoma Museum hover on slender piloti, mediating between the vehicular scale of the adjacent freeway and the pedestrian scale of the immediate context. Stainless steel and smoked glass evoke grey skies. Fissured openings connect the interior galleries to the urban environment outside.

Portland Aerial Tram, 2007   **AGPS**
3303 South West Bond Avenue, Portland, OR 97239 ◑
This aerial tram system links Oregon Health and Science University campus with the ground at a lower level, reducing congestion. Clad in aluminium panels, the higher station's covered platform is supported on steel legs. Shiny, bulbous tramcars, hung from cables by a stem, are fabricated in aluminium and glass.

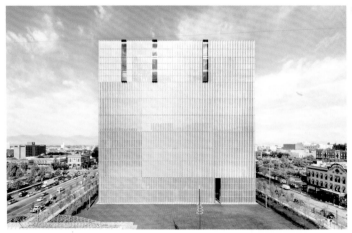

United States Courthouse, 2014   **Thomas Phifer & Partners**
351 South West Temple, Salt Lake City, UT 84101 ◑
Connected by a raised garden terrace, the United States Courthouse and the existing Federal Courthouse form a federal precinct in downtown Salt Lake City. Accommodating ten courtrooms and federal offices, it is bound by glass and aluminium in a quilt-work pattern — the glass transmits light, while the aluminium deflects heat.

Marcia and John Price Museum Building, 2000   **Machado Silvetti**
Utah Museum of Fine Arts, Salt Lake City, UT 84112 ◑
The centrepiece of this museum, on the University of Utah's hillside campus, is crowned with distinctive green glass. A series of five rectangular volumes, resting on a concrete plinth, step up and around the tall central space of the Grand Gallery, which is built out of various shades of redbrick.

Frederic C Hamilton Building, Denver Art Museum, 2006   **Studio Libeskind**
100 West 14th Avenue Parkway, Denver, CO 80204 ◑
Visitors enter this museum extension, which is clad with titanium and glass panels
on a cantilevered concrete frame, via a rooflit atrium with dramtically sloping walls.
They climb to the galleries up a perimeter staircase, which becomes more intimate
in scale as it ascends.

Denver Union Station,2014   **SOM**
Union Station, Denver, CO 80202 ◑
Built to expand the existing station, the open-air terminal hall is the main focus of
this project. Manufactured from 11 steel arch trusses spanning 55m, the canopy
rises to 21m in height and sweeps down to 7m at the centre, providing cover for passengers and expansive views of the historic site.

Center for Character & Leadership Development, 2016　　　　**SOM**
Polaris Hall, US Air Force Academy, CO 80840 ●
An angular glazed structure aligned with the North Star distinguishes this education and research centre, located at the US Air Force Academy — a campus originally designed by SOM in 1954. The heart of this building, flooded with daylight, contains the Forum, a space for academic and social interaction.

North
America

Robert Hoag Rawlings Public Library, 2003　　　　**Antoine Predock**
100 East Abriendo Avenue, Pueblo, CO 81004 ◑
This library facility rises five storeys, taking advantage of views over the Arkansas Valley. A lobby, which features glass lifts that extend past the building's height, overlooks the entrance courtyard. Concrete walls anchor a sky wing, while a glazed bronze-clad volume contains reading areas.

Aspen Art Museum, 2014　　　　　　　　　　**Shigeru Ban**
637 East Hyman Avenue, Aspen, CO 81611 ◑
Partially wrapped by a woven wooden screen, made of a composite material called Prodema (an amalgam of paper and resin encased within a wood veneer), this museum consists of six galleries, a shop, and an education centre. A rooftop sculpture garden provides views of Ajax Mountain.

North America

Nevada Museum of Art, 2003　　　　　　　**Will Bruder+Partners**
160 West Liberty Street, Reno, NV 89501 ◑
Inspired by the nearby Black Rock Desert and clad in sun-absorbing, charcoal-grey zinc panels, this four-storey building contrasts with the glitzy neon facades of its downtown neighbours. As well as gallery space, the museum houses a multimedia theatre, a roof-lit atrium, library, shop and café.

Jan Shrem and Maria Manetti Shrem Museum of Art, 2016   **SO-IL**
254 Old Davis Road, Davis, CA 95616 ◑
United by a canopy of perforated-aluminium triangular beams, this structure extends over the site and buildings, creating a permeable roof that modulates light and shade. Beneath, galleries, offices and classrooms are arranged around an interior courtyard clad in corrugated concrete panels and glazing.

Berkeley Art Museum and Pacific Film Archive, 2015   **Diller Scofidio + Renfro**
University of California, 2155 Center Street, Berkeley, CA 94720 ◑
This gallery is an interface between the university and the town, with a mashing together of a 1939 printing plant and a stainless-steel extension that slithers over the top. The saw-tooth roof of the modern building allows light to penetrate the ground-floor galleries. At one end, there's an LED screen and lawn for public viewings of films.

SFMOMA, 2016   **Snøhetta**
151 3rd Street, San Francisco, CA 94103 ◑
Set at the rear of the existing Mario Botta-designed build, this 10-storey extension forms a new east entrance for the museum and provides facilities for education, conservation and archives, as well as 9,290 sq m of gallery space. It's clad in a rippling skin of fibreglass-reinforced panels, punctuated by horizontal windows.

North
America

Contemporary Jewish Museum, 2008   **Studio Libeskind**
736 Mission Street, San Francisco, CA 94103 ◑
This museum is distinguished by its abstract form, clad in luminous blue steel panels. Contrasting with an existing nineteenth-century redbrick power plant, the angular building accommodates a lobby, auditorium and principal gallery at ground floor, with a double-height exhibition space above.

Federal Building, 2007   **Morphosis**
90 7th Street, San Francisco, CA 94103
Standing 72m tall, this slender edifice accommodates government office space, a plaza, and a daycare and fitness centre accessible to the public. Its perforated metal facade has a natural cooling effect, while inside, skip-stop elevators lead to a series of lobbies, promoting both physical exercise and social encounters.

1028 Natoma Street, 2006   **Stanley Saitowitz / Natoma**
San Francisco, CA 94103 ●
Inspired by terraced housing and an industrial aesthetic, this structure, accommodating four apartments, comprises ground-floor parking and an entrance lobby, with living spaces stacked above. The exterior's aluminium grating shields the interior yet allows it to glow from within at night.

California Academy of Sciences, 2008   **Renzo Piano Building Workshop**
55 Music Concourse Drive, San Francisco, CA 94118 ◐
This project's green roof billows over an aquarium, planetarium, exhibition spaces and a rainforest habitat. Sustainably designed, the roof's curved form and rooflights aid in regulating the temperature inside the structure, and incorporate 60,000 photovoltaic panels that supply electricity to the building.

UCSF Regeneration Medicine Building, 2011   **Rafael Viñoly**
707 Parnassus Avenue, San Francisco, CA 94143 ●
This cantilevered research lab snakes for 180m along a bend in the road. The slope it resides on reaches 45 degrees, making a build nigh on impossible, yet a steel-truss system connected to the concrete base supports the structure, allowing a wobble of 66cm in case of an earthquake.

Apple Store, Stanford, 2013   **Bohlin Cywinski Jackson**
379 Stanford Shopping Center, Palo Alto, CA 94304 ●
This two-room, pavilion-like store features some 55m of storefront glass, which extends from floor to ceiling, and three entrances marked by a stainless-steel canopy. The transparent display room is made column-free by the integration of slender structural glass fins.

Windhover Contemplative Centre, 2014   **Aidlin Darling Design**
370 Santa Teresa Street, Stanford, CA 94305 ●
This student sanctuary at Stanford University houses paintings by Nathan Oliveira, with a meditation path worked around it. Located in an oak glade, the expansive glass wall on the east side allows for natural light, while the use of straight lines, wood and earthen walls blends the building into its surroundings.

New United States Courthouse, 2016   **SOM**
312 North Spring Street, Los Angeles, CA 90012 ●
Housing 24 courtrooms, this structure combines features of traditional civic architecture — grand public places, the use of limestone and processional steps — with
modern elements. A highly reflective glass volume cantilevers over a stone base,
creating the impression of a floating cube.

North
America

Caltrans District 7 Headquarters Office Building, 2004   **Morphosis**
100 South Main Street, Los Angeles, CA 90012 ●
This government building comprises 13 storeys, stretching an entire city block and
facing a plaza bordered by another four-storey volume. Floor plates cantilever over
the street, and perforated-aluminium panels open and close in response to the
weather and the sun's position.

Star Apartments, 2014   **Michael Maltzan**
240 East 6th Street, Los Angeles, CA 90014 ●
These prefabricated housing modules are set above an existing low-rise concrete
building, separated by a recreation terrace with gardens, a running track and a communal kitchen. Concrete columns and two interior concrete stairways brace the
new buildings, which were craned on site and linked by steel-framed walkways.

Inner-City Arts, 2008   **Michael Maltzan**
720 Kohler Street, Los Angeles, CA 90021 ◑
Providing art education for disadvantaged youth, this arts complex houses a wide
range of facilities, from ceramics and animation studios to a black-box theatre. A
series of connected plazas and courtyards allow it to function as an open-air urban
village, while white walls encircle the campus.

North
America

Emerson College, 2014   **Morphosis**
5960 Sunset Boulevard, Los Angeles, CA 90028 ◑
The West Coast campus for the Boston arts and communication school is comprised of a 10-storey metal, glass and aluminium square that frames a cluster of classrooms and interlocking walkways. The building features a series of automated fins on the glass-curtain wall, which respond to shifting weather conditions.

Matthew Marks Gallery, 2012   **Zellnerplus**
1062 North Orange Grove Avenue, Los Angeles, CA 90046 ◑
This structure references California Minimalism and the low-rise commercial buildings next door. The gallery is comprised of a single monolithic block, finished in white stucco and featuring a slim glass door. A grid of rectangular skylights allow natural light to permeate the interior.

Petersen Automotive Museum, 2014　　　　**Kohn Pedersen Fox Associates**
6060 Wilshire Boulevard, Los Angeles, CA 90036 ◑
Ribbons of stainless steel and aluminium wrap an inner shell of red corrugated metal sheet that houses the renovated Petersen Automotive Museum. A new 'body' for the existing 'chassis', the three-storey interior includes galleries showcasing the history, industry and artistry of cars.

Our Lady of the Angels Cathedral, 2002　　　　**Rafael Moneo**
555 West Temple Street, Los Angeles, CA 90012 ◑
This sandblasted concrete building replaces a predecessor damaged in the 1994 earthquake. It is the third-largest cathedral in the world, and is built to last for 500 years. A carved concrete Franciscan cross is its focus, and it occupies one end of a plaza defined by fortress-like walls.

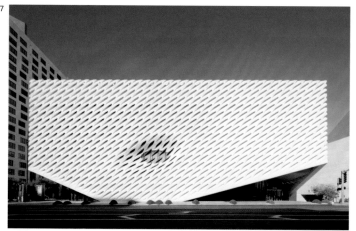

The Broad, 2015 **Diller Scofidio + Renfro**
221 South Grand Avenue, Los Angeles, CA 90012 ◑
With a honeycombed, concrete exo-skeleton, this contemporary art museum's self-titled 'veil-and-vault' structure reflects the two ambitions of the project: an acre of column-free exhibition space on the third floor and the storage of The Broad's 2000-strong collection, visible through portholes as you take the exit stairwell.

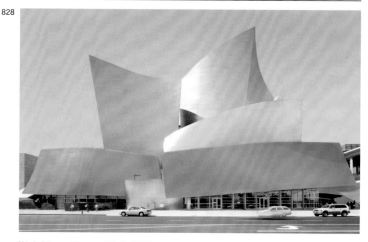

North
America

Walt Disney Concert Hall, 2003 **Frank Gehry**
111 South Grand Avenue, Los Angeles, CA 90012 ◑
This building's brushed stainless-steel sails billow around the auditorium, in which there are no acoustically inferior seats. Steeply raked banks of seating embrace the performance area, and a Douglas-fir canopy, which echoes the steel sails, is peeled away at the corners to admit natural light for performances.

Samitaur Tower, 2010 **Eric Owen Moss**
8521 National Boulevard, Culver City, CA 90232 ◑
The five acrylic projection screens wrapped around this information tower act as a canvas for an ever-changing display of public art and locally significant content. The tower is comprised of five vertically stacked steel rings and stands at 17m tall, with each of its levels providing a public viewing platform.

Beehive Office Building, 2001 **Eric Owen Moss**
8520 National Boulevard, Culver City, CA 90232 ●
Partly glazed and partly clad in curved zinc-copper-titanium panels, this office building sits on an uneven bed of grassy landscaping. Eccentric columns, wrapped by a skeleton of hooped steel piping, provide the framework for its distinctive beehive form, while an Escher-like staircase crowns the roof.

Pterodactyl, 2014   **Eric Owen Moss**
3528 Hayden Avenue, Culver City, CA 90232 ●
Consisting of a lower car parking structure and nine rectangular 'boxes' set above, this advertising agency headquarters takes its name from its spiky silhouette. A series of metal-clad boxes jut out obliquely, creating angled spaces at the upper levels, which contain quiet corners or meeting annexes.

North
America

Veer Towers, 2010   **JAHN**
3722 South Las Vegas Boulevard, Las Vegas, NV 89103 ●
Standing 150m tall, these two glass and steel towers lean at opposite angles from each other. As well as creating an interesting aesthetic feature, the coloured glass is designed to maximize the project's energy efficiency. Residents of the tower have access to a rooftop pool and panoramic views of Las Vegas.

Mii Amo Spa, Enchantment Resort, 2001   **Gluckman Mayner**
525 Boynton Canyon Road, Sedona, AZ 86336 ⏺
Surrounded by the red-rock walls of Boynton Canyon, the main building of this resort is organized along a horizontal circulation corridor. A grand hall lit by a continuous rooflight runs along one side. On the other side, five adobe-brick towers contain the tranquil treatment rooms, which are softly lit from above.

Phoenix Art Museum, 2006   **Tod Williams Billie Tsien**
1625 North Central Avenue, Phoenix, AZ 85004 ⏺
A redesigned main entrance, new interior courtyard, sculpture garden and galleries refresh the existing Phoenix Art Museum. A cantilevered parasol signals and shades the entrance, while freestanding concrete walls and falling water mitigate traffic noise.

Health Sciences Education Building, 2012 CO
Phoenix Biomedical Campus, 435 North 5th Street, Phoenix, AZ 85004 ◑
Merging two universities interdisciplinary health sciences education and research, this six-storey building is shaped by its academic intent to share resources, as well as by the desert climate. The two-part structure of burnished concrete enables passive cooling and frames a central circulation 'canyon'.

Sandra Day O'Connor US Courthouse, 2000 Richard Meier & Partners
401 West Washington Street, Phoenix, AZ 85003 ◑
Comprised of steel and a mixture of transparent and frit glass, this six-storey Courthouse in downtown Phoenix features a large atrium as its focal point, backed by an L-shaped masonry block. Framing the glazed atrium are various facilities, including district and magistrates courts, a café and library.

Stone Ridge Church, 2005   **DeBartolo**
6300 East 24th Street, Yuma, AZ 85365 ◑
This rectilinear complex in the desert of Yuma consists of a church raised on a podium, dominating a compact group of single-storey buildings. These contain education spaces and frame an external courtyard. A baptismal pool provides a focus at
the centre of a rectangular spiral pathway.

Walker Art Center Expansion, 2005   **Herzog + de Meuron**
725 Vineland Place, Minneapolis, MN 55403 ◑
Built to provide more room for electronic media and performance art, this conversion project extends an existing art gallery. The project's focus is signposted by the
addition of a new tower, which houses a venue the architect compares to a Shake-
spearean open-air theatre.

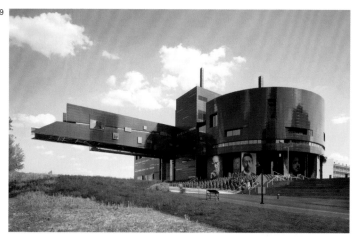

Guthrie Theater, 2006　　　　　　　　　　　　**Ateliers Jean Nouvel**
818 South 2nd Street, Minneapolis, MN 55415 ◑
This replacement theatre is a replica of the original, with its thrust stage, asymmetrical auditorium and slightly staggered balconies, a proscenium stage, and a studio with flexible seating. A walkway is cantilevered over the river, sheltering the entrance and linking the theatre and set-building area.

Des Moines Public Library, 2006　　　　　　　**David Chipperfield**
1000 Grand Avenue, Des Moines, IA 50309 ◑
This new library's aeroplane-shaped plan was decided by public ballot. The exterior is composed of triple-glazed units with expanded copper mesh embedded between sheets of glass. Opaque from the outside in daytime, this reduces glare inside the building. Reading areas are situated along the glazed facades.

Visual Arts Building, 2016   **Steven Holl**
University of Iowa, 107 River Street, Iowa City, IA 52246 ●
The four-storey Visual Arts Building, featuring a facade of weathered zinc and perforated stainless steel, replaces an original arts building that dated from 1936. Natural light and ventilation reach into the building's core via seven vertical cut-outs,
while a central, full-height atrium exposes studio activity throughout.

Figge Art Museum, 2005   **David Chipperfield**
225 West 2nd Street, Davenport, IA 52801 ◑
On the banks of the Mississippi River, this museum is built over a car park to protect
it from floodwaters. External glass panels reflect the grid pattern in which the building sits. The facades are fritted with horizontal banding of varying density, while
a plaza provides a sculpture garden and public space.

Writers Theatre, 2016   **Studio Gang**
325 Tudor Court, Glencoe, IL 60022 ◐
Organized as a cluster of volumes surrounding a central hub, the Writers Theatre
includes two performance venues, rehearsal spaces and amenities. The glazed lobby is framed by broad timber trusses, and accommodates informal performances,
talks and community events. At night, the theatre glows like a lantern.

The Godfrey Hotel, 2014   **Valerio Dewalt Train Associates**
127 West Huron Street, Chicago, IL 60654 ◐
When the 2008 recession hit, this metal-skinned building spent three years covered
with tarpaulin, earning it the nickname 'The Mummy'. Its completed form features
an expressive, exposed structural frame and assembly of shifted, taut, rectilinear
building masses.

Aqua Tower, 2010   **Studio Gang**
225 North Columbus Drive, Chicago, IL 60601 ●
Borrowing from the characteristics of terrestrial topography, this mixed-use sky-scraper was imagined as a vertical landscape made up of hills, valleys and pools. The varying sizes of the floor slabs creating an arresting pattern when viewed as a whole. The rooftop garden above its podium is one of the largest in Chicago.

Chicago Horizon, 2015   **Ultramoderne**
Lakefront Trail, Chicago, IL 60605 ◑
Designed to provide shelter from the elements, this wall-free kiosk also offers views of Lake Michigan and Chicago's skyline. Its expansive flat roof, constructed from cross-laminated timber, is supported by a series of timber columns. The vending kiosk and a viewing platform are demarcated by chain-link fencing.

McCormick Tribune Campus Center, 2003 **Rem Koolhaas**
Illinois Institute of Technology, 3201 South State Street, Chicago, IL 60616 ◑
Squeezed in below an elevated train station — an elliptical tube of corrugated steel and concrete — this structure is a riposte to the previous layout planned by Mies van der Rohe. Desire lines cut across the original grid, while vibrant colours and bold graphics animate the space throughout.

North America

WMS Boathouse at Clark Park, 2013 **Studio Gang**
2754 South Eleanor Street, Chicago, IL 60608 ●
This boathouse creates a key public access point along the river's edge. It features a zigzagging roof, which translates the motion and rhythm of rowing into a sculptural form, and is clad in black zinc and slate, offset by a transparent green screen that faces the water.

Nelson-Atkins Museum of Art, 2007   **Steven Holl**
4525 Oak Street, Kansas City, MO 64111 ◑
This museum addition consists of a series of translucent volumes, which act as lenses, bringing light into underground galleries. They are arranged as a continuous sequence that connect the original buildings to landscaped gardens displaying works of sculpture by Isamu Noguchi.

North
America

Contemporary Art Museum St Louis, 2003   **Allied Works**
3750 Washington Boulevard, St Louis, MO 63108 ◑
A partially glazed facade connects this gallery to the neighbourhood. Its curved corner follows the street line, forming a distinctive profile. With galleries and performance spaces below, sandblasted concrete walls clad in a woven-steel mesh shade offices and lecture theatres.

Cummins Indy Distribution Headquarters, 2017　　　**Deborah Berke Partners**
301 East Market Street, Indianapolis, IN 46204 ●
Housing the headquarters for Cummins Indy Distribution, this office complex includes a tower, conference centre, retail stores and extensive public green space. The tower, with its inflections and projections, provides downtown Indianapolis with a striking landmark, while its system of fins and shades limit interior heat.

Irwin Union Bank

Irwin Union Bank, 2006　　　**Deborah Berke Partners**
707 Creekview Drive, Columbus, IN 47201 ●
A light-box design contrasts with this bank branch's unadorned exterior, signalling its position. Floating above the masonry building, the glowing box spans a drive-through lane and the banking hall inside. Made of structural glass planks, it permits natural light to filter down into the hall.

Speed Art Museum, 2016 wHY
2035 South 3rd Street, Louisville, KY 40208 ◑
This new north wing, organized around a triple-height lobby, exhibits modern and contemporary art, extending the existing Beaux Arts galleries. The upper elevation is wrapped in corrugated aluminium panels, with fritted glass below. Staggered building volumes are linked by a grand staircase, expressed on the entry facade.

Eli and Edythe Broad Art Museum, 2013 Zaha Hadid
547 East Circle Drive, East Lansing, MI 48824 ◑
This art museum features a facade of pleated stainless steel and glass, as well as louvre-type windows that accentuate the unique angle of the building. Based to the north of the Michigan State University Campus, the building offers numerous options for exhibitions.

Driving Park Branch, Columbus Metropolitan Library, 2014 **NBBJ**
1422 East Livingston Avenue, Columbus, OH 43205 ◑
In order to provide various functions, this building is separated into two sections:
interactive social spaces inhabit its perimeter, while the centre allows for focused
reading. Exterior environmental features, such as roof-draining systems and bio-
retention ponds, are made visible to educate visitors about sustainability.

North
America

Toledo Museum of Art Glass Pavilion, 2006 **SANAA**
2445 Monroe Street, Toledo, OH 43620 ◑
This pavilion, comprising a transparent complex of rooms and courtyards, houses
world-renowned glassware collections. The works are displayed in glass-walled
galleries alongside public spaces and two glass-blowing studios. The building itself
is designed to conserve energy.

Akron Art Museum, 2007 **Coop Himmelb(l)au**
1 South High Street, Akron, OH 44308 ◑
This museum is organized around three separate elements. The main entrance lobby, the 'Crystal', provides a venue for art and entertainment. An overhanging second element, the 'Floating Cloud', gives shelter. And the third element, the 'Roof Cloud', is a city landmark that seems to hover above the building.

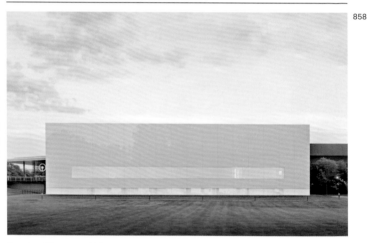

Corning Museum of Glass, 2015 **Thomas Phifer & Partners**
1 Museum Way, Corning, NY 14830 ◑
This glossy white box, clad in opaque glass, houses contemporary glass art. The volume is conceived as a 'vitrine' for five new galleries, ringed by a 'porch' for additional displays, and features a 40m-long window. An adjacent renovated service building is rendered black, and hosts glass-blowing demonstrations.

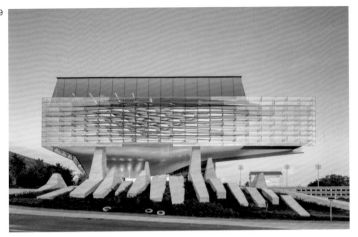

Bill and Melinda Gates Hall, 2014   **Morphosis**
107 Hoy Road, Ithaca, NY 14853 ●
A cantilevered roof extends over the plaza at the entrance to this university building, while sleek stainless-steel panels comprise its exterior. Inside, there is a large,
glass-windowed atrium, from which it is possible to see the activity taking place on
each floor. Throughout, a sense of transparency and light is emphasized.

North
America

Milstein Hall, 2011   **OMA**
Cornell University, 863-883 University Avenue, Ithaca, NY ●
A new home for Cornell's College of Architecture, Art and Planning, Milstein Hall
features a hybrid truss system of 1,200 tons of steel to support two dramatic cantilevers, the underside of which are clad in custom-stamped perforated-aluminium
panels. A sedum-covered green roof is punctured by a cluster of 41 rooflights.

Tang Teaching Museum and Art Gallery, 2000 **Antoine Predock**
Skidmore College, 815 North Broadway, Saratoga Springs, NY 12866 ◑
This modest-sized building placed against a tight semicircle of pine trees at Skidmore College serves as both art gallery and classroom. Three low-profile wings interact in a central atrium, while stone ramps emanate from the earth and culminate in a single ivory tower.

Tozzer Anthropology Building, 2014 **Kennedy & Violich**
21 Divinity Avenue, Cambridge, MA 02138 ◑
Built to combine Harvard University's Archaeology and Anthropology programmes, this building is enveloped by redbrick. A large copper roof volume rotates to capture daylight for a large internal light well, clad in a birchwood panel system, illuminating offices and classrooms.

Harvard Art Museums Expansion, 2014 **Renzo Piano Building Workshop**
32 Quincy Street, Cambridge, MA 02138 ◑
This extension project gives Harvard Art Museums a new gallery wing and improves access at street level, as well as converting an existing courtyard into a glass-roofed indoor atrium. Built using a mixture of steel, concrete and wood, the extension offers a modern contrast to the original building's brick facade.

Honan-Allston Branch, Boston Public Library, 2001 **Machado Silvetti**
300 North Harvard Street, Allston, MA 02134 ◑
This one-storey library is divided into three parallel bands: the front zone contains the book stacks; gardens and glass reading pavilions alternate in the central void; and community functions are housed at the back. The use of natrual materials, including slate, shingles and ironwood, creates a calm environment.

North
America

Simmons Hall, 2002   **Steven Holl and Perry Dean Rogers**
MIT, 229 Vassar Street, Cambridge, MA 02139 ●
Built on a thick concrete slab foundation, this student residence appears to float
above the ground, and its narrow footprint leaves room for outdoor public space.
The exterior walls are prefabricated concrete panels clad in anodized aluminium,
with perforations accomodating the windows.

Institute of Contemporary Art, 2006   **Diller Scofidio + Renfro**
25 Harbor Shore Drive, Boston, MA 02210 ◑
Envisioned as a continuous walkway along the water's edge, this project's timber
boardwalk continues overhead, cladding the galleries' underside. The building's upper level extends prominently towards the water, with a large window on one side
and translucent channel glass that glows at night on the other.

North
America

Grace Farms, 2015   **SANAA**
365 Lukes Wood Road, New Canaan, CT 06840 ◑
Set in a nature reserve, these five pavilions are interlinked by a curving roof that follows the existing topography down a gentle slope. Conceived to be part of the landscape, the glazed pavilions include a sanctuary, library, gymnasium, orientation centre and café. The roof is clad with aluminium panels, and features timber soffits.

North
America

Roy and Diana Vagelos Education Center, 2016   **Diller Scofidio + Renfro**
104 Haven Avenue, New York, NY 10032 ◑
A medical centre for Columbia University, this 14-storey glass, concrete and steel educational building is structured vertically, with classrooms along its north side, and an orange-hued cascading 'study' — largely clad in Douglas fir — extending from the lobby to the top of the building.

Sugar Hill Development, 2015   **Adjaye Associates**
898 St Nicholas Avenue, Harlem, NY 10032 ●
This 13-storey mixed-use development features affordable housing, an early education programme and a new cultural institution. The structure steps back at the ninth
floor to create a terrace and cantilever on opposite sides. The cladding is achieved
with rose-embossed graphite-tinted panels, which create an ornamental effect.

Rose Center for Earth and Space, 2000   **James Polshek**
79th Street Central Park West, New York, NY 10024 ◑
This spherical planetarium floating within a glazed cube has turned the American
Museum of Natural History into a new night-time landmark. The Hayden Planetarium is also the most powerful virtual-reality simulator in the world. Tubular steel
wall trusses support spider fittings that anchor the glazing.

Alice Tully Hall Lincoln Center, 2009   **Diller Scofidio + Renfro**
1941 Broadway, New York, NY 10023 ◑
This renovation creates a dynamic new entrance lobby, adding a three-storey glass foyer to reveal deep-red, wood-clad walls. The entrance is framed by a cantilevered, triangle-shaped structure that houses the Julliard School. Inside the performance space, the auditorium's wood-clad walls incorporate LED lighting.

VIA 57 West, 2016   **BIG**
625 West 57th Street, New York, NY 10019 ●
Dubbed 'The Tetrahedron', the form of this 35-storey residential palace shifts from a pyramid to a glass spire, depending on the vantage point. Cutaways, notably a large courtyard, allow sunlight and views to reach more than 700 apartments. The entrance is marked by Stephen Glassman's eight-storey, serpentine steel sculpture.

North
America

Hearst Tower Office Building, 2006   **Foster + Partners**
300 West 57th Street, New York, NY 10019 ●
A triangulated structural system creates generously lit meeting spaces with views over Manhattan. Expansive rooflights soar above an elevated interior plaza, connecting this steel and glass tower to the shell of the existing building below, which was built by and William Randolph Hearst completed in 1928.

One57, 2014   **Christian de Portzamparc**
157 West 57th Street, New York, NY 10019 ●
Working within the tight constraints of an L-shaped site, this elongated 75-storey tower features a hotel at lower levels and lofty apartments behind a distinctive glazed facade. Like subtle chequerboards, its east and west faces are composed of glass panels in two contrasting colours.

North
America

432 Park Avenue, 2016   **Rafael Viñoly**
432 Park Avenue, New York, NY 10022 ●
The gridded concrete facade of this rectilinear 96-storey skyscraper was, report-edly, partly inspired by a metal trash bin designed by the Austrian architect Josef Hoffmann. The tower has an exposed concrete structural frame, which enables col-umn-free interiors, while openings in the facade at 12-storey intervals reduce sway.

North America

The Westin Hotel New York at Times Square, 2002   **Arquitectonica**
270 West 43rd Street, New York, NY 10036 ◑
On 8th Avenue at Times Square, the striking 863-room Westin Hotel sits on top of E-Walk, a retail podium. A recessed curve in the south facade incorporates a slit of moving light that appears to split the building in two and transforms a rectangular tower into something much more dynamic and alive.

New York Times Office Building, 2007   **Renzo Piano Building Workshop**
620 8th Avenue, New York, NY 10018 ●
Set back from the street to create a public garden and ampitheatre, this building's main newsroom has a tall roof-lit well connecting third and fourth floors. A 14th-floor café has a balcony suspended from its double-height ceiling, and external glass walls are screened with horizontal ceramic tubes.

Morgan Library Extension, 2005   **Renzo Piano Building Workshop**
225 Madison Avenue/36th Street, New York, NY 10016 ◑
Comprised of three pavilions added to an ensemble of historic buildings, the library now features an entrance that sits under suspended exhibition and reading rooms. A cube-shaped, second pavilion is a gallery, while the third, a four-storey pavilion, accommodates offices and a café.

North America

10 Hudson Yards, 2016   **Kohn Pedersen Fox Associates**
10 Hudson Yards, New York, NY 10001 ●
An angled triangle sits atop this 273m tall skyscraper, while a cantilevered bridge extends over West Manhattan's High Line. Part of a massive regeneration project for the Hudson Yards area, the building accommodates the headquarters of fashion brand Coach and features a 15-storey glass atrium.

David Zwirner 20th Street, 2013   **Selldorf**
537 West 20th Street, New York, NY 10011 ◑
One of David Zwirner's two Chelsea-based galleries, this energy-efficient new-build has an industrial edge, notably due to its raw exposed concrete facade, which is tempered by teak window frames and panelling at the entrance. There are two exhibition areas, including a 465 sq m column-free room.

North America

InterActiveCorp Office Building, 2007   **Frank Gehry**
555 West 18th Street, New York, NY 10011 ●
Exploring glass as an expressive skin, this building evokes a yacht in full sail. The concrete frame, with a curtain wall wrapped tightly around it, articulates the first five floors as a quintet of angular bays. Upper and lower portions of the glass wall are screened for privacy, leaving a band of clear glass between.

The High Line, 2009   **Diller Scofidio + Renfro**
West Side Line, New York, NY 10001 ◑
A strip of elevated parkway by the Husdson River in Chelsea has been the regeneration project on everyone's lips for the past decade. This disused 1930s freight rail track was threatened with demolition in the 1990s, but is an inspired public space. The first section, from Gansevoort Street to West 20th Street, opened in 2009.

The Whitney Museum of American Art, 2015   **Renzo Piano Building Workshop**
99 Gansevoort Street, New York, NY 10014 ◑
Anchoring the south end of the High Line, this building provides a new location for the 22,000-piece art collection of Gertrude Vanderbilt Whitney. Its asymmetric form, resembling a stack of differently sized blocks, draws on the Meatpacking District's historically industrial character, and utilizes concrete, steel and low-iron glass.

The New School, 2014   **SOM**
66 West 12th Street, New York, NY 10011 ●
This multipurpose building, clad in brass shingles, was conceived as an entire campus within one structure. The upper nine floors provide student accommodation, while lower floors house a range of facilities, including an 800-seat auditorium and a library. Social spaces are visible from the street through large, diagonal windows.

Cooper Union for the Advancement of Science and Art, 2006 **Morphosis**
30 Cooper Square, New York, NY 10003 ●
This new edifice for Cooper Union unites its faculties of Art, Architecture and Engineering in one volume, skinned in perforated stainless-steel panels offset from glass and aluminium window walls. At its heart is a 'vertical plaza' — a full-height atrium encouraging interdisciplinary dialogue.

North America

10 Bond Street, 2015 **Selldorf**
10 Bond Street, New York, NY 10018 ●
This residential building echoes the low-rise scale and large windows of the surrounding historic buildings. It is clad in copper-coloured terracotta panels, which form a pleasing geometric pattern, while the lobby is lined in mahogany and features tinted terrazzo flooring.

New Museum of Contemporary Art, 2007   **SANAA**
235 Bowery, New York, NY 10002 ◑
This museum is organized as a series of stacked, box-like volumes. These volumes vary in height and size depending on programmatic needs. A ground-floor lobby with a glass facade invites visitors inside, while upper volumes are wrapped in a steel mesh that changes colour with the light.

North America

Spring Street Salt Shed, 2016   **Dattner and WXY**
336 Spring Street, New York, NY 10013 ●
Hidden inside this crystalline volume is 5,000 tons of road salt, used to treat the city's icy bitumen. Constructed from thick walls of reinforced cast concrete with faceted planes that taper towards its base, it was conceived as an abstracted salt crystal. Trucks access the store through a triple-height door in the eastern face.

56 Leonard Street, 2017   **Herzog & de Meuron**
56 Leonard Street, New York, NY 10013 ●
Resembling a 250m-high stack of Jenga blocks mid-game, this slender, 60-sto-
rey tower consists of a series of cantilevered glass boxes, which appear to teeter
towards the building's apex. An enormous mirror-polished stainless-steel blob by
Anish Kapoor balloons out at the structure's base.

North
America

One World Trade Center, 2014   **SOM**
285 Fulton Street, New York, NY 10007 ●
Adjacent to the World Trade Center memorial, this soaring office tower rises from
a cubic base to a parapet rotated through 45 degrees. Creating a glazed volume
enveloped by eight elongated isosceles triangles with embossed stainless-steel
edges, the building reaches 400m into the sky.

World Trade Center Transportation Hub, 2016   **Santiago Calatrava**
70 Vesey Street, New York, NY 10007 ◑
This $4bn transit hub, nicknamed 'The Oculus', resembles a dove taking flight. The arched, elliptical structure features steel ribs that extend upward. Its 100m-long skylight retracts once a year on 11 September, for 102 minutes — the length of time the attacks lasted.

North
America

Four World Trade Center, 2013   **Maki & Associates**
150 Greenwich Street, New York, NY 10007 ●
Rising 72 storeys, the fourth tower on the World Trade Center site is wrapped in a curtain wall of structural floor-to-ceiling, ultra-clear glass that appears mercurial from afar. Set on a three-storey podium, its form pares back from a parallelogram to a trapezoid, creating a chiselled appearance from below.

New York by Gehry, 2011   **Frank Gehry**
8 Spruce Street, New York, NY 10038 ●
The facade of this 76-storey residential high-rise appears as if draped in billowing fabric, and is made from around 10,500 3D-modelled stainless-steel panels, only 2,000 of which are the same. The skyscraper's stepped profile acknowledges Cass Gilbert's 1913 neo-gothic Woolworth Building.

North
America

Greenpoint EMS Station, 2013   **Michielli + Wyetzner**
303–351 Metropolitan Avenue, Brooklyn, NY 11211 ●
Red roller doors punctuate the zigzagging glazed facade of this emergency medical station, which accommodates ambulances and support facilities for the crews. Its two halves are split in section, with vehicle bays at ground level, and lockers and bathrooms in the taller building.

895

Sunset Park Material Recovery Facility, 2013   **Selldorf**
472 2nd Avenue, Brooklyn, NY 11232 ●
Processing recyclable waste, this facility sits on a waterfront pier. Visitor services
are housed in a small separate building, linked by an elevated pedestrian bridge.
The three-part plan provides operational efficiency, organized sequentially from
the waterside tipping building to processing and bale storage.

896

Stapleton Branch, New York Public Library, 2013   **Andrew Berman**
132 Canal Street, Staten Island, NY 10304 ◐
The Stapleton Branch of the New York Public Library is comprised of the original
1907 building and a modern extension. The latter's roof inclines gently, correspond-
ing with the sloping gradient of the street on which it sits. Floor-to-ceiling windows
and exposed wood provide a sense of rhythm and warmth.

Queen Library at Glen Oaks, 2013   **Marble Fairbanks**
256-04 Union Turnpike, Glen Oaks, NY 11004 ◑
Replacing an existing facility, half of this library's interior space is below ground, yet a two-storey atrium, replete with rooflights, allows natural light to permeate the lower level. At night, its expansive glass facade, through which the word 'Search' is projected, exudes light.

Parrish Art Museum, 2012   **Herzog & de Meuron**
279 Montauk Highway Water Mill, NY 11976 ◑
Situated in a bucolic corner of Long Island, the Parrish Art Museum is formed of two pitched-roof, single-storey wings running parallel to each other. Built in a mixture of concrete and wood, the muted colours of the museum's exterior blend harmoniously with its surrounding landscape.

North
America

Novartis Oncology Building, 2012 **Weiss/Manfredi**
1 Health Plaza, East Hanover, NJ 07936 ●
Providing research and oncology facilities for cancer patients, this five-storey office building features a curtain wall of acid-etched, reflective and low-iron glass,
creating a vertically striated envelope, punctuated by a western double-height entry staircase and terraces at third and fifth floors.

Krishna P Singh Center for Nanotechnology, 2013 **Weiss/Manfredi**
University of Pennsylvania, 320 Walnut Street, Philadelphia, PA 1904 ◑
Unusually for a labororatory, this research facility is airy and inviting, and scientists
can be seen busy at work through panels of orange-tinted, UV-blocking glass. A key
feature is a dramatic 21m cantilever, with views over the campus, while the central
quad houses Tony Smith's *We Lost* sculpture.

Skirkanich Hall, 2006   **Tod Williams Billie Tsien**
210 South 33rd Street, Philadelphia, PA 19104 ●
Rather than deferring to the traditional redbrick architecture of the rest of the campus, Tod Williams Billie Tsien shrouded this bioengineering faculty in shingled glass, aluminium, zinc and glazed brick in a whole spectrum of shades from black to chartreuse. The combination is at once high-tech and organic.

The Barnes Foundation, 2012   **Tod Williams Billie Tsien**
2025 Benjamin Franklin Parkway, Philadelphia, PA 19130 ◑
This foundation houses the art collection of Albert C Barnes, which were previously held on his suburban Merion estate. Here, the architects simply replicated the layout of the Merion galleries. The building is clad in offset Negev limestone panels, and is situated amid public gardens.

1200 Intrepid, 2015   **BIG**
1200 Intrepid Avenue, Philadelphia, PA 19112 ●
The form of this office building responds to the adjacent circular-shaped park, flex-
ing inwards along its curvature. Rising three storeys, the project's core is pierced by
a functioning periscope, which projects natural light and views of the nearby Navy
Yard basin into the lobby.

Mattin Arts Center, 2001   **Tod Williams Billie Tsien**
Johns Hopkins University, 3300 North Charles Street, Baltimore, MD 21218 ●
This arts centre is composed of two short and two long buildings situated around
a grassy courtyard. Ramps and decked areas inside and out encourage student interaction. The sturdy redbrick bases contrast with the luminous quality of the sandblasted glass panels, and art studios open directly onto outdoor terraces

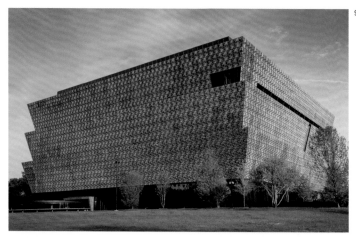

NMAAHC, 2016   **Adjaye Associates**
1400 Constitution Avenue North West, Washington, DC 20560 ◑
This museum is comprised of a three-tiered inverted ziggurat structure and features a lace-like bronze facade — inspired by the history of African American craftsmanship. Interior spaces are free of supporting columns and lined in concrete and timber, while, in the memorial hall, water cascades down through a ceiling aperture.

Francis A Gregory Library, 2012   **Adjaye Associates**
3660 Alabama Avenue South East, Washington, DC 20020 ◑
A neighbourhood library for the District of Columbia, this two-storey building nestles into its parkland context, featuring a mirrored curtain wall skin that amplifies its verdant setting. The broad steel canopy overarching the whole structure admits filtered daylight into the open-plan spaces.

Hunt Library, 2013   **Snøhetta**
North Carolina State University, 1070 Partners Way, Raleigh, NC 27606 ◑
Encased in a skin of fritted glass and aluminium louvres, this four-storey university library is organized around double- and triple-height open-plan spaces, as well as work-studio spaces and a state-of-the-art robotic book-retrieval system on lower floors. Vivid yellow staircases punctuate the white interiors.

Bechtler Museum of Modern Art, 2009   **Mario Botta**
420 South Tryon Street, Charlotte, NC 28202 ◑
This museum houses Andreas Bechtler's collection of artworks. The cube-shaped building is hollow inside to offer an outdoor public courtyard that is outlined by the plastic volumes at the back. A fourth floor gallery juts out from the core of the building and is supported by a huge single column rising from the plaza below.

The Wieland Pavilion, 2005   **Renzo Piano Building Workshop**
Woodruff Arts Center, 1280 Peachtree Street North East, Atlanta, GA 30309 ❿
With a new piazza at its heart, this project includes expanded parking, a residential hall, a restaurant and three museum buildings. The new buildings have floor-to-ceiling windows that provide views in all directions, and over 1,000 rooflights illuminate the top-level galleries with natural light.

Flint RiverQuarium, 2004   **Antoine Predock**
117 Pine Avenue, Albany, GA 31701 ❿
Set next to the Flint River, the RiverQuarium houses an educational tourist attraction, telling the story of the river's history and geology. The building's angular form comprises a labyrinth of monolithic limestone blocks, mimicking the area's particular geography.

North
America

Florida Polytechnic University, 2014   Santiago Calatrava
4700 Research Way, Lakeland, FL 33805 ●
This domed complex surrounded by farmland accommodates labs, classrooms, an amphitheatre and offices, all under its wing-like, louvred roof. Steel pergolas wrap the exterior, forming a filigreed brise-soleil that can be adjusted depending on the position of the sun, while arched beams rib the curved corridors inside.

North
America

The Dalí Museum, 2011   HOK
1 Dali Boulevard, St Petersburg, FL 33701 ◑
Situated alongside St Petersburg's downtown waterfront, this three-storey museum houses the largest collection of Salvador Dalí's work outside Europe. Free-form glass geodesic structures, formed of over 1,000 undulating faceted-glass panels, protrude from the concrete facade, allowing light in and providing views of the bay.

The Center for Asian Art, 2016　　　　　　　　　**Machado Silvetti**
The Ringling, 5401 Bay Shore Road, Sarasota, FL 34243 ◑
This gallery houses the museum's Asian art collection, as well as a lecture hall, offices and seminar rooms. Over 3,000 glazed terracotta tiles envelop the building — the detailing and colour of which pay homage to the Cà d'Zan mansion's ceramic panels — while also complementing the surrounding environment.

Art Deco Project, 2015　　　　　　　　　　**Aranda\Lasch**
103 North East 39th Street, Miami, FL 33137 ◑
A site for four luxury retailers, this development features 'pleated' cladding — zig-zagging reinforced-concrete panels arranged as diagonal ribs — reminiscent of Miami's Art Deco buildings. A series of angular recessed coffers frame individual shop windows.

Pérez Art Museum Miami, 2013   **Herzog & de Meuron**
1103 Biscayne Boulevard, Miami, FL 33132 ◑
Housing over 3,000 sq m of gallery space, this three-story complex is raised on stilts, which is both a necessity, preventing flood damage, and a pleasing aesthetic feature. A shady veranda sits at the entrance, with plants suspended from a wooden canopy — a nod to Miami's tropical climate.

Miami Dade College Academic Support Center, 2012   **Perkins+Will**
300 North East 2nd Avenue, Miami, FL 33132 ◑
Housing both administrative and educational facilities, this concrete structure features a large glazed atrium that, through the provision of space for socializing and studying, enhances the student experience. A series of cisterns harvest and recycle rainwater collected on the roof.

Faena Forum, 2016   **OMA**
3300-3398 Collins Avenue, Miami Beach, FL 33140 ◑
Consisting of two volumes, a cylinder and a cube, this arts complex, clad in a concrete skin incised by irregular apertures, provides performance spaces and meeting rooms. The drum's apex houses a vaulted dome for events, and is pierced by an oculus. A wedge cut from the base reveals the eastern entrance.

North
America

1111, 2010   **Herzog & de Meuron**
1111 Lincoln Road, Miami Beach, FL 33139 ◑
It doesn't make sense to build underground in Miami, where water gushes out of the drains at high tide. So parking garages go up instead. This concrete sculpture, with its irregular supporting wedges, makes quite a statement. Housing retail space and a central plaza at ground level, the structure has no external walls.

New World Center, 2011   **Frank Gehry**
500 17th Street, Miami Beach, FL 33139 ◑
Opening onto a public park, this building's towering glass facade seems to dissolve
when lit from within by a sophisticated lighting system. Inside, the six-storey atrium
reveals geometric volumes, while the auditorium's arching banners, surfaces for
visual displays, and its flexible layout, enrich the theatrical experience.

North America

The Grove at Grand Bay, 2014   **BIG**
2675 South Bayshore Drive, Miami, FL 33133 ●
Two twisted towers rising 20 storeys mark this new seaside residential complex.
Offset concrete floorplates extend on all sides to create generous balconies, and
act as brise-soleils for apartments below. Sheathed with bands of floor-to-ceiling
glazing, the rotated floors are designed to maximize views of the bay.

AH McCoy Federal Office, 2013   **Schwartz/Silver**
100 West Capitol Street, Jackson, MS 39269 ●
Mimicking the meanders of the Mississippi River, the AH McCoy Federal Office
building's canopies bend around the entrance pavilion like ribbons. Supported
by curved metal plates and spines, the ribbons are formed of translucent glass
shingles, poised just in front of the structure's white aluminium skin.

Louisiana State Museum and Sports Hall of Fame, 2013   **Trahan**
800 Front Street, Natchitoches, LA 71457 ◑
Displaying collections pertaining to sport and history, this museum is conceived as
a 'carving', recalling a nearby ancient riverbed. Its undulating foyer is sculpted from
1,100 cast-stone panels that writhe through the centre of the plan. The contrasting
rectilinear steel envelope is clad in pleated copper louvres.

Webb Chapel Park Pavilion, 2012   **Studio Joseph**
11428 Cromwell Drive, Dallas, TX 75229 ⏺
Being held up by only three structural supports, this pavilion gives unobstructed views of the surrounding area, taking in a soccer field and a playground. The concrete canopy has an exaggerated depth that gives it its bold form, and a natural ventilation system is created by the use of four yellow pyramidal voids in the roof.

Nasher Sculpture Center, 2003   **Renzo Piano Building Workshop**
2001 Flora Street, Dallas, TX 75201 ⏺
Five connected two-storey pavilions, defined by parallel stone walls and linked to the gardens through glazed facades, take up little of this extensive green oasis in Dallas. Glass roofs screened against direct sunlight provide perfect viewing conditions for the sculpture collection.

Perot Museum of Nature and Science, 2012　　　　　　　　**Morphosis**
2201 North Field Street, Dallas, TX 75201 ◑
Enclosed in a cube of textured concrete panels, this nature and science museum turns regular circulation upside down. Exhibits are accessed from top to bottom along paths weaving clockwise around the main circulation core. Visitors access the sequence via glazed escalators that break through the concrete facade.

Modern Art Museum of Fort Worth, 2002　　　**Tadao Ando Architect & Associates**
3200 Darnell Street, Fort Worth, TX 76107C ◑
This project arranges five long rectangular volumes in a row surrounded by a large reflective pool of water and landscaped gardens. Each volume is composed of a concrete envelope surrounded by transparent glass walls, forming peaceful spaces in which to view artworks.

North
America

Kimbell Art Museum Pavilion, 2013   **Renzo Piano Building Workshop**
3333 Camp Bowie Boulevard, Fort Worth, TX 76107 ◐
The museum's original building was designed by Louis Kahn in 1972, and this expansion roughly doubles its gallery space. The new-build consists of a 'flying pavilion', which faces Kahn's modern gem across landscaped grounds, and has a three-part facade. At its centre a glazed section serves as the new museum entrance.

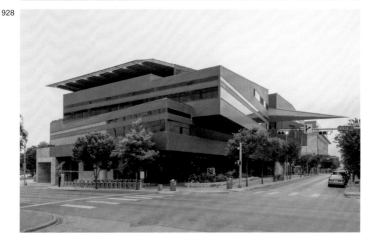

City Hall and Public Plaza, 2004   **Antoine Predock**
301 West 2nd Street, Austin, TX 78701 ●
Built from Texas limestone and clad in copper, this building houses offices for Austin's local government. The adjacent plaza, meanwhile, serves as a public meeting place and performance venue. The building angles away from the nearby streets, contrasting with the surrounding grid system and reflecting its formal character.

St Edward's Residential Building, 2008   **Elemental**
3001 South Congress Avenue, Austin, TX 78704 ●
To gain maximum natural daylight, the living quarters of this residential complex are outward facing, while its common areas look to an inner courtyard, lined with red glass to echo the nearby tiled roofs. The faceted brick walls, which vary in texture, reference the outcrops of Central Texas.

Sicardi Gallery, 2012   **Brave**
1506 West Alabama Street, Houston, TX 77006 ◑
This gallery houses works by Latin American artists. It's clad almost entirely in corrugated Galvalume panels, with a white stucco entrance and one facade of exposed brick. The metal-clad block contains a large square window at its corner, which allows natural light into the top-floor gallery.

Hobby Educational Center for the Performing Arts, 2002   **Miguel Angel Roca**
800 Bagby Street, Houston, TX 77002 ◑
This performing arts complex in downtown Houston is home to the 2,650-seat
Sarofim Hall, the 500-seat Zilkha Theatre and the Humphreys School of Musical
Theatre. The complex is divided into distinctively shaped sections providing an
interesting combination of forms.

North
America

Museum of Fine Arts, 2000   **Rafael Moneo**
1001 Bissonnet Street, Houston, TX 77005 ◑
This four-storey limestone addition fills its available site, more than doubling the
exhibition space of the existing museum. The facade is fragmented by the rooflights, which reflect the arrangement of galleries inside, including the first-floor
sculpture garden originally designed by Isamu Noguchi.

Brochstein Pavilion, 2008   **Thomas Phifer & Partners**
Rice University, 6100 Main Street, Houston, TX 77005 ●
This café pavilion brings new life to a once-desolate area of the Rice campus. Floor-to-ceiling glass and a light-filtering roof create a continuous visual vista between the interior and exterior spaces, drawing attention away from the building and down the row of oak trees that frame the western lawn.

North America

Moody Center for the Arts, 2017   **Michael Maltzan**
6100 Main Street, Houston, TX 77005 ◑
Arcades created by the second floor's cantilevered massing create shaded walkways that make the building's brick-clad upper story appear to levitate. Large picture windows punctuate the articulated brick facade in a playful rhythm and bring light deep into interior spaces.

Wagner Noël Performing Arts Center, 2011   **Bora and Rhotenberry Wellen**
1310 North Farm to Market Road 1788, Midland, TX 79707 ❶
This performance venue is inspired by the desert landscape of West Texas. Its main section is built in locally sourced limestone and patterned with blocks that decrease in size as they near the ground, evoking the process of geological compression. The taller sections are clad in stainless-steel panels that reflect the sky.

North
America

Inde/Jacobs Gallery, 2015   **Claesson Koivisto Rune**
208 East San Antonio Street, Marfa, TX 79843 ❶
A gallery for minimalist artworks, the design of this project is informed by Donald Judd's sparse sculptures. Though the building appears as a continuous wall, it actually comprises two separate white-walled volumes: a gallery and a small home for its owners, linked by an internal courtyard.

937

938 939

940

941

942

Guadalajara

Mexico

Mexico City

Mérida

955

943–953

Guatemala

954

956 957

958

Bioinnova, 2012   **Tatiana Bilbao**
Boulevard Pedro Infante 3773, Congreso del Estado, Culiacán ●
This stack of four cantilevered, glazed volumes forms the biotechnology facility for Monterrey Institute of Technology. The rectangular open-plan floor plates are staggered to create different identities for differing functions, as well as providing passive solar shading to levels below.

Central
America

Parish Church Señor de la Misericordia, 2016   **Moneo Brock**
Carretera Nacional 500, Monterrey ◑
Situated in a large public plaza in the southeast of Monterrey, this church is formed of dazzlingly white concrete shards protruding at different angles. The traditional church tower is given a rectilinear, modern reinterpretation, while enormous cross-shaped windows flood the interior with light.

Centro Roberto Garza Sada, 2013   **Tadao Ando Architect & Associates**
Universidad De Monterrey, Jesús M Garza, San Pedro Garza García ●
This six-storey concrete block has a huge triangular void at its centre, exposing
the underside of the building and creating the appearance of a twisted structure.
This unusual form creates a large sheltered entrance for staff, students and visitors
below, while a trio of cavities in the roof provide natural lighting and ventilation.

Américas 1500, 2016   **Sordo Madaleno**
Avenida de las Américas 1500, Guadalajara ◑
This mixed-use project — housing offices and a hotel — consists of four stacked
geometric volumes. Two of these are slightly offset, although exactly aligned on the
rear face. The building fronts a significant highway, and as such, the facade features
recessed aluminium framing, in the style of a curtain wall.

Vinícola Cuna de Tierra, 2013   **Centro de Colaboración**
San Luis de la Paz, km11, El Rosillo, Dolores Hidalgo ●
Taking inspiration from the vineyard's name — which means 'Soil Cradle' — this project explores the close relationship between wine and its terroir. Locally sourced soil, wood and concrete are used throughout, and the earthen walls have ventilation cavities around the building, which also allow for natural lighting.

Museo Internacional del Barroco, 2016   **Toyo Ito & Associates**
Territorial Atlixcáyotl 2501, Reserva Territorial Atlixcáyotl, Puebla ◑
This museum is dedicated to Baroque art. It features a series of sinuous white concrete walls, with a bush-hammered texture, the highest of which reaches 19.52m. A large fronting plaza welcomes visitors, and an entrance canopy shelters guests waiting to enter the museum.

Museo Soumaya, 2004   **FR-EE**
Miguel de Cervantes Saavedra 303, Mexico City ◑
This distorted hour-glass structure glitters with 16,000 hexagonal aluminium tiles, its singular shape anchored by 28 curved steel columns. The museum's 66,000-strong collection features European and Mexican artists; on the top floor, Rodin's sculptures bathe in sunlight filtered through the glass roof.

Central America

Museo Jumex, 2013   **David Chipperfield**
Miguel de Cervantes Saavedra 303, Mexico City ◑
This museum rotates pieces from one of the largest private collections of global contemporary art in Latin America. The three-storey sand-coloured travertine block is most notable for its saw-tooth roof and, inside, an Escher-like stairwell. Fourteen columns raise the base of the structure, forming a public plaza below.

Fire Station, 2006   **at103 and BGP**
Insurgentes Centro 95, San Rafael, Mexico City ●
This fire station combines public and private spaces behind a reflective facade, which is raised above ground level to provide vehicle access below. Vertical circulation is expressed through glass tubes on one side, allowing firemen to descend quickly, and a stairwell for visitors on the other.

Central
America

Reforma 27 Residential Tower, 2010   **Alberto Kalach**
Paseo de la Reforma 27, Tabacalera, Mexico City ●
Located on one of Mexico City's major thoroughfares, the wood, steel and concrete that form this apartment building have a terracotta-like appearance. The top floor features a tropical greenhouse, as well as a swimming pool with an underwater mural, all of which relate the building to the city's natural history.

Parque España Apartment Building, 2001   **Ten**
Parque España 47, Condesa, Mexico City ●
Clad in translucent plastic panels, this striking building contains five apartments and a ground-floor art gallery. Interior space is flexible: apartments can be open or divided. A laminate stairway zigzags and winds its way up the sealed plane of a plastic panel on the east facade.

Vladimir Kaspé Cultural Centre, 2006   **Broissin**
Benjamin Hill 43, Condesa, Mexico City ◑
This multipurpose university building houses various functions for the student community, including extensive study areas, seminar facilities and multimedia spaces. The exterior ramp runs up the long side of the rectangular building, providing access to the principal floor, which balances on slender piloti.

Arcos Bosques Corporation Office Building, 2008   Teodoro González de León
Paseo de Los Tamarindos 400, Bosques de las Lomas, Mexico City ●
Situated on the western side of Mexico City, this office and retail complex is an elite
urban precinct, built on what used to be sand mines and a rubbish dump. The arched
Torres Arcos Bosques, completed in 1996, is nicknamed El Pantalón (The Trousers).
The twin towers behind it were opened in 2008 and are linked by a glass bridge.

BBVA Headquarters, 2015   LegoRogers
Torre BBVA Bancomer, Juárez, Mexico City ●
This 50-storey office tower — constructed from a steel-and-glass lattice frame that
protects the facade from direct sunlight and heat — occupies the area between
Chapultepec Park and the Paseo de la Reforma. Sky gardens punctuate the facade
every nine floors, and provide views of the adjacent green space and city beyond.

Central
America

Cineteca Nacional Siglo XXI, 2012   **Michel Rojkind and Alberto Villarreal**
Avenida México Coyoacán 389, Xoco, Mexico City ◑
Three decades after a fire ravaged the national film archive, this futuristic facility now consists of four surviving theatres and a pair of new auditoriums, which are united into a coherent ensemble by a geometric white perforated aluminium canopy, nearly 40m high, stretching across a landscaped plaza.

MUAC   **Teodoro González de León**
Escolar, Ciudad Universitaria, Coyoacán, Mexico City ◑
The Museo Universitario Arte Contemporáneo is signalled by a vast 45-degree glass facade that is even more impressive when lit up at night. The interior features a double-height entrance space, and the collection itself shows the evolution of Mexican art since 1952.

Central
America

Tepoztlán Lounge, 2012　　　　　**Eduardo Cadaval and Clara Sola-Morales**
Tepoztlán, Morelos ◑
This three-armed concrete guesthouse features concave elevations that shape the boundaries of two patios at the back and an egg-shaped swimming pool at the front. Walls slide back across each elevation, opening the building's central room out to the garden.

Central
America

Sunset Chapel, 2011　　　　　**Esteban Suárez and BNKR**
34 Jacques Cousteau, Brisas del Marqués, Acapulco ◑
Mimicking a boulder amid scrubland, this chapel is designed as a refuge for mourners. Only a narrow crack in the hexagonal cast-concrete form indicates the entry. Visitors pass through the crypt and ascend to the lofty chapel, which has sweeping views across the Pacific coast.

Fundación Casa Wabi, 2014   **Tadao Ando Architect & Associates**
Puerto Escondido, Oaxaca ◑
In a dramatic setting on the Oaxacan coast, Casa Wabi is a community project
founded by artist Bosco Sodi and directed by Patricia Martín. The silky modernist
concrete complex incorporates the vernacular in the palapa pavilions with thatched
palm-leaf roofs, across six minimalist villas for artists in residence.

Bacsa Corporation, 1999   **Augusto Quijano**
Calle 60 Diagonal, Mérida ●
On an industrial estate to the north of Mérida, this two-storey complex for a construction and engineering company houses offices in an L-shaped block and services
and storeroom in a larger, parallel structure. A curved wall and a freestanding wall
bisecting a pool transform it into a sculptural statement.

Quinta Montes Molina Pavilion, 2015   **Materia**
Avenida Paseo Montejo 469, Centro, Mérida ○
Located within the grounds of a twentieth-century mansion, this pavilion complements its historic context; 36 slim columns, forming a C-shaped promenade, echo
the balconies of the house. The roof reinforces the presence of the 'emptied' space
below contrasting with the solid nature of the existing building.

Central
America

Mexican Embassy, 2003   **Teodoro González de León and Francisco Serrano**
2a Avenida 7–57, Zona 10, Guatemala City ●
Each element of the Embassy —chancery, consulate and cultural centre — is given a
unique geometrical identity within a landscape of pergolas and planting. The stand-
ardized height of enclosing walls and consistent use of materials assures the homo-
geneity of the project.

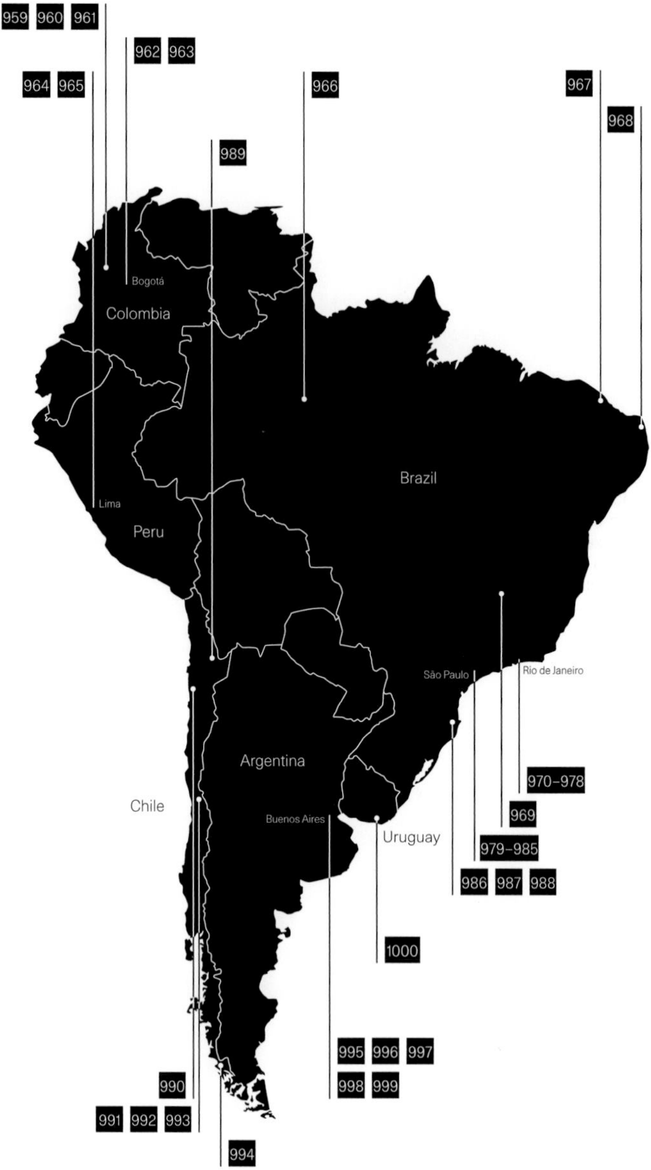

959 960 961

962 963

964 965

966

967

968

989

Bogotá

Colombia

Lima

Peru

Brazil

São Paulo

Rio de Janeiro

970-978

969

Argentina

Chile

979-985

986 987 988

Buenos Aires

Uruguay

1000

995 996 997

998 999

990

991 992 993

994

Library of Spain, 2007 El Equipo Mazzanti
Calle 107a, Carrera 33b, Medellín, Antioquia ◑
Located at the top of a steep hill, this landmark library is formed of three rock-like black boxes with small viewing perforations at the front. Also known as Santo Domingo Park Library, it contains a small auditorium and more conventional reading areas within, while terraces allow for cultural activities outside.

The Wishes Urban Complex, 2004 Juan Felipe Uribe de Bedout
Calle 71, Carrera 53–53, Medellín, Antioquia ◑
This complex contains two facing public buildings — a planetarium and an exhibition and retail building. The main square offers interactive activities such as an 'urban beach' and fountains, as well as installations representing fire, water, wind, sound and time. When fully grown, trees will enclose the space, providing shade.

960

Plaza de La Libertad Civic Center, 2010   **OPUS and Toroposada**
Carrera 53a, Medellín, Antioquia ◑
This project incorporates natural elements, such as indigenous vegetation, as well as patios, bridges, terraces and balconies — traditional elements of local architecture. Two towers accommodate government offices, while an additional two buildings house a television production company and cultural centre.

Four Sport Scenarios, 2010   **El Equipo Mazzanti and Felipe Mesa**
Calle 69, Bogotá ◑
This complex is comprised of four separate volumes that are united under one canopy — a series of movable parallel bars. The north and south facades are open, allowing a breeze to pass through the structure, and the east and west facades have tribunes and eaves to control the morning and afternoon sun.

South America

Gabriel García Márquez Cultural Center, 2008   **Rogelio Salmona**
Carrera 6, Calle 11, Bogotá ◑
This cultural complex accommodates a publishing house, a 324-seat auditorium, an exhibition hall and several libraries. A central outdoor plaza, supported by a series of concrete columns, provides a contrast to the narrow streets of the surrounding neighbourhood.

Place of Remembrance, 2013   **Barclay & Crousse**
Bajada San Martín 151, Miraflores, Lima ◑
Dedicated to the commemoration of modern Peruvian history, this cultural centre houses an auditorium, research facilities and an exhibition space. Recalling the cliffs and gorges of Lima's coastline, it is composed mainly of sand-hued concrete panels — the south-facing facade is glazed, affording views of the ocean.

Ministerio de Educación, 2012   **DLPS**
Calle Del Comercio 193, San Borja, Lima ●
Set within a cultural complex behind the Museo de la Nación, this new home for the Education Ministry clearly signifies what lies within. The structure resembles an uneven stack of books, augmented by slightly protruding floorplates that resemble hardback bindings, and facades of metallic louvres that emulate pages.

Arena da Amazônia, 2014   **gmp**
Avenida Constantino Nery, Flores, Manaus ◑
In response to the humid climate, this arena is shaded by a curving facade and roof of translucent fibreglass. The panels, shaped to appear like flower petals, enfold a cantilevered structure of hollow steel box girders that brace the form and act as gutters to channel torrential tropical rain.

Fortaleza Maritime Passenger Terminal, 2015 **Architectus S/S**
Vicente de Castro Avenue, Praia Mansa, Fortaleza ◑
This structure — featuring a largely glazed facade — was designed as a multipurpose space, functioning as a port for cruise ships, as well as a venue for events and
exhibitions. A sweeping cantilevered roof extends out over the northern side, while,
to the south, brise-soleils accentuate the building's curves.

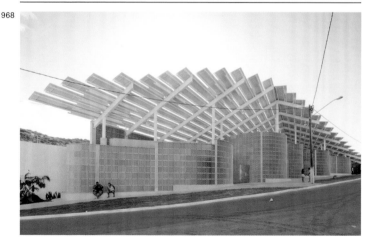

Arena do Morro, 2014 **Herzog & de Meuron**
Rua Camaragibe, Mãe Luíza, Natal ◑
The flagship project of a wider regeneration programme for the area, this complex
features a gymnasium, sports field and terrace with ocean views. The roof, assembled from a series of corrugated-aluminium panels, has slender gaps that let in sunlight, while still preventing rainwater from permeating the interiors.

Galeria Adriana Varejao, 2008   Tacoa
Brumadinho, Minas Gerais ◑
This museum is not housed under one building, but spread out over an area of
350,000 sq m in numerous pavilions. Cut into gently sloping hillsides and encom-
passed by trees, blocks of reinforced concrete are inserted, which house the artwork. Stairways connect the floors, creating a pathway to the water's edge.

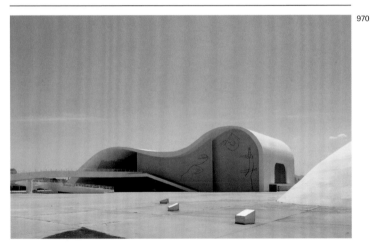

Teatro Popular Oscar Niemeyer, 2007   Oscar Niemeyer
Rua Jornalista Rogério Coelho Neto, Centro, Niterói ◑
A boomeranging ramp brings a sense of drama to entering Oscar Niemeyer's theatre. White concrete swoops over the building like a lazy M, and massive red doors at
the back open to reveal the stage to an outside audience. A spiral staircase drops
like an escape hatch, and sketch-like murals of performers line the walls.

South
America

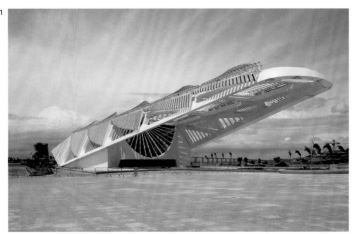

Museu do Amanhã, 2015   **Santiago Calatrava**
Praça Mauá 1, Centro, Rio de Janeiro ◑
Extending out into Guanabara Bay on a long pier, this museum's bright-white facade
shimmers in the surrounding moat, which forms part of a complex recycling system
that cools the building. A tilted roof cantilevers over an expansive plaza, its rows of
steel flaps rising and falling depending on the light.

Olympic Youth Arena, 2016   **Vigliecca & Associados**
Estrada São Pedro de Alcântara, Vila Militar, Rio de Janeiro ◑
The structure and size of seating arrangements within this Olympic stadium — built to
host basketball and fencing — are adaptable according to requirements. The building
is constructed from steel and clad in corrugated iron panels. Thin external columns
support its roof — as a result, the interior is entirely free of structural support.

Nave do Conhecimento, 2012   **RioUrbe**
Parque de Madureira, R Manuel Martins, Madureira, Rio de Janeiro ◑
Otherwise known as the 'Knowledge Ship', this angular concrete structure was inspired by the idea of being adrift in space. The facade dramatically breaks to reveal a floating, UFO-like glass structure, which is supported by metal rods. Inside, there are classrooms, a library and a cinema.

Leblon Offices, 2016   **Richard Meier & Partners**
Avenue Bartolomeu 336, Leblon, Rio de Janeiro ●
This seven-storey sustainable structure is comprised of private interior courtyards, open office spaces and a series of terraces. Its primary facade is shielded by a carefully composed set of louvres along the western elevation designed for both maximum sun shading and privacy.

Capela Joá, 2014   **Bernardes**
Estrada do Joá, São Conrado, Rio de Janeiro ◑
Situated amid the treetops and overlooking the ocean, this chapel provides a tranquil haven for worship. Inside, a series of wooden beams gradually increase in size
as they near the cross, which, rather than simply being ornamental, is formed by the
chapel's supporting steel structure.

Cidade das Arte, 2013   **Christian de Portzamparc**
Avenida das Américas 5300, Barra da Tijuca, Rio de Janeiro ◑
The largest concert hall in Latin America languished unfinished for a decade. Its
great mass of concrete volumes and voids balance between two horizontal planes,
the lower of which acts as a vast terrace, suspended 10m above gardens landscaped by Fernando Chacel. The wave-like shapes are a nod to the sea.

South
America

Museu de Arte do Rio, 2013　　　　　　　　**Bernardes + Jacobsen**
Praça Mauá 5, Centro, Rio de Janeiro ◑
Three disused buildings have been grouped under an undulating roof to create a
new art museum and art school. The canopy shelters a new outdoor bar and events
space on the rooftops. The more modern building had two extra floors, which were
eliminated to balance the set.

South
America

Olympic Handball Arena　　　　**Lopes Santos e Ferreira Gomes and OA**
Rio de Janeiro ●
The core of this project consists of an octagonal area, where games are played, as
well as spectator stands. A temporary metallic structure can be adapted to several
spatial organizations, with the possibility to reuse parts in order to build four schools
in the city of Rio de Janeiro.

Terminal da Lapa, 2003 **Núcleo de Arquitetura**
Rua Guaicurus, Água Branca, São Paulo ⦿
This bus station has two levels — the horizontal terminal is on the lower level, and
a public plaza and service areas are on the higher levels. A unique roof system
dominates the site, comprising three rows of steel and polycarbonate arches with
rooflights that diffuse the sunlight and openings for ventilation.

Praca das Artes, 2012 **Brasil Arquitectura**
Avenida São João 281, Centro, São Paulo ⦿
Situated on a long, narrow urban plot, this complex — predominantly constructed
from pigmented exposed concrete — restores a former concert hall, connecting it to
a set of new buildings, which house venues for music and dance companies, circulation spaces and common areas.

South
America

Studio R, 2012   **Studio Mk27**
Rua 7 de Abril 261, República, São Paulo ●
Housing a photography studio, this structure is formed of three stacked concrete
boxes. The studio occupies the ground floor, where long metal doors at either end
reveal a choice of backdrop — gravel patio or plant-filled garden. The top storey,
offset from the two below, features a rooftop deck.

Casa Triângulo Gallery, 2016   **Metro**
Rua Estados Unidos 1324, Jardins, São Paulo ◑
Providing a new home for one of Brazil's most important art galleries, this structure's single rectilinear volume accommodates two exhibition halls. Its facade is
clad with concrete and, below, translucent panels — at night, lights illuminate this
skin from within.

Nova Leme, 2012　　　　　　　　　　**Paulo Mendes da Rocha and Metro**
Avenida Valdemar Ferreira 130, Butantã, São Paulo ◑
This is a reconstruction of an original gallery, now demolished, which was situated two blocks away. Beyond the reproduction of the original project, a new building was added, connected to the main structure by a footbridge on the upper floor. Both are built from reinforced concrete.

Vitra, 2015　　　　　　　　　　　　　　　　　**Studio Libeskind**
Avenida Horácio Lafer 500, Itaim Bibi, São Paulo ◑
This sculptural, crystalline high-rise residential project features a multi-faceted glass facade that reflects the sky, and is articulated by inlaid balconies, which form a rhythmic pattern across the exterior. Its apex is crowned by a two-storey penthouse.

São Paulo Corporate Towers, 2016   **Pelli Clarke Pelli and aflalo/gasperini**
Avenida Juscelino Kubitschek 1909, Vila Olimpia, São Paulo ●
Set amid lush grounds, this pair of office towers feature soft silhouettes, shaped
by opposing curved corners and slightly offset edges, which creates a twist in the
glazed envelope. Inside, open-plan floors connect via a timber-lined canopy to a
conference centre, café and restaurant.

Museum Oscar Niemeyer, 2002   **Oscar Niemeyer**
Rua Marechal Hermes 999, Centro Cívico, Curitiba ◑
This dramatic annex to the original museum building is constructed from reinforced
concrete and mounted on a cubic plinth. Designed for exhibitions and multimedia
presentations, the ceiling height varies by 9m across its span. Diagonal glazing reveals the interior space at night.

South
America

Aeromovel Porto Alegre, 2015 **OSPA Arquitetura e Urbanismo**
Avenida Farroupilha 8001, São José, Canoas ⦿
This elevated station platform, predominantly built from precast concrete, is one of two termini along the kilometre-long raised Aeromovel track that links Porto Alegre's airport to other transportation. Its canopy of undulating V-shaped steel beams bulge away from the track-side entrance.

Fundação Iberê Camargo, 1995 **Álvaro Siza Vieira**
Avenida Padre Cacique 2000, Cristal, Porto Alegre ⦿
Built on land cut into a hillside, this building holds the work of Brazilian artist Iberê Camargo, as well as providing space for temporary exhibitions and facilities for study and lectures. Visitors enter an interior atrium by passing under a dramatic series of concrete cantilevered ramps.

South America

Hotel Explora, San Pedro de Atacama, 2000　　　　　　**German del Sol**
Domingo Atienza, San Pedro de Atacama, Región de Antofagasta ❶
Within the Atacama Desert, one of the hottest and driest places on the planet, this low-level hotel complex with riding stables is arranged like an oasis settlement. Gently arching overhanging roofs protect the terrace areas from solar glare. Materials are left rough to allow the buildings to mature naturally over time.

ESO Hotel and Information Centre, 2001　　　　　　**Auer+Weber+Assoziierte**
Taltal, Antofagasta Región ❶
In the immense scale and harsh environmental conditions of the Atacana Desert, a unique habitat has been created: a landscape wall embedded below the horizon line contains the entire complex, using small building modules with flexible joins to withstand seismic activity.

Innovation Center UC, 2014   **Elemental**
Vicuña Mackenna 4860, Macul, Santiago, Región Metropolitana ●
This centre functions as a space for investors to meet with researchers. Designed in consideration of the hot climate, it features an opaque facade and deep-set windows — reducing energy costs, assisting ventilation and moderating internal temperatures. The exterior is comprised of starkly geometric concrete blocks.

Viña Las Niñas Winery, 2000   **Mathias Klotz**
Parcela 11, Apalta Casilla 94, Millahue, Santa Cruz ◑
A series of boxes of varied shapes and materials make up this winery in the dramatic Valle de Colchagua. The north elevation of the main building which contains the fermentation tanks, is clad in timber strips and features a continuous ground-floor window; the south elevation is made from full-height polycarbonate sheeting.

Viña Pérez Cruz Winery, 2002   José Cruz Ovalle
Fundo Liguai, Región Metropolitana ◑
This winery in the foothills of the Andes features two parallel barrel-vaulted volumes unified by a sweeping roof. The timber building is broken into three zones by
two wedge-shaped entrance spaces and a central route along each vault provides
access. A bridge in the spandrel leads to the fermentation tanks.

Hotel Remota, 2006   German del Sol
Camino de Puerto a Torres del Paine, Puerto Natales ◑
This remote hotel near the southern tip of South America is a complex of three build-
ings connected by timber-framed corridors and weatherproof shortcuts. Accom-
modation is arranged over several levels, responding to the building's sloping roof.
The rough-hewn timber supports were inspired by Patagonia shearing sheds.

South
America

Museum of Latin American Art, 2001   **AFT**
Avenida Figueroa Alcorta 3415, Buenos Aires ◐
A pale stone-clad wedge with a cantilevered box houses this new museum, now a lively cultural centre. Circulation routes inside begin in a glass-covered double-height atrium. Ground-floor gallery spaces are lit by a glazed walkway opening on to a landscaped area.

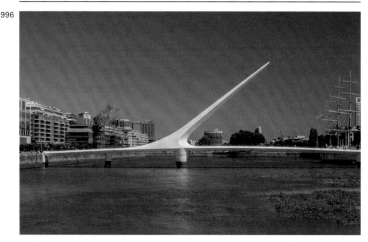

Puente de la Mujer, 2007   **Santiago Calatrava**
Avenida Alicia Moreau de Justo, Buenos Aires ○
'The Bridge of the Woman' is a 170m long pedestrian suspension bridge that connects the west and east sides of the Puerto Madero dock. An inclined 39m-high pylon, intended to evoke the embrace of a duo mid-tango, supports a central section that rotates 90 degrees to allow water traffic to pass underneath.

South
America

Fondación Proa, 2008   **Caruso-Torricella**
Avenida Don Pedro de Mendoza 1929, Buenos Aires ◑
Converted from three nineteenth-century buildings, the centrepiece of this art gallery retains its original Italianate facade — largely left untouched, and flanked on either side by a modern glass exterior. This subtle merging of old and new keeps the gallery in harmony with the historic waterfront around it.

Ciudad Casa de Gobierno, 2015   **Foster + Partners**
Balcarce 50, Buenos Aires ●
This civic centre is notable for its undulating concrete roof, supported by columns, which cantilevers over the entrance and enables full-height glazing, maximizing natural light. Inside, there's a four-storey atrium with staggered tiers of office space; the open-plan layout provides views of the park outside from most desks.

South
America

Museo MAR, 2013   **Monoblock**
Avenida Félix U Camet/López de Gomara, Mar del Plata, Buenos Aires ◑
This cultural institution is situated on a beachfront site, and consists of a series of
large concrete volumes that are connected by a system of metal walkways. The
buildings frame an expansive access and exhibition plaza. Galleries on the top floor
are illuminated by skylights.

Carrasco International Airport, 2009   **Rafael Viñoly**
Ruta 101, Ciudad de la Costa, Departamento de Canelones ◑
This terminal is an addition to Uruguay's largest airport, and features a curved steel
roof spanning over 300m. The interior is spacious and airy, with the glazed mezzanine level at the terminal's entrance permitting abundant natural light. On the
second floor, a landscaped terrace offers a panoramic view of the runway.

South
America

Visitor Information

Australia

1 Wanangkura Stadium
porthedlandleisure.com.au
T +61 8 9140 0400

2 Karijini National Park Visitor Centre
parks.dpaw.wa.gov.au
T +61 8 9189 8121

3 Gallery of Modern Art
qagoma.qld.gov.au
T +61 7 3840 7303

5 Museum of Contemporary Art
mca.com.au
T +61 2 9245 2400

6 Andrew 'Boy' Charlton Swimming Pool
abcpool.org
T +61 2 9358 6686

9 Anzac Hall
awm.gov.au
T +61 2 6243 4211

10 National Museum of Australia
nma.gov.au
T +61 1800 026 132

11 Ilmarinen, Finnish Embassy in Canberra
finland.org.au
T +61 2 6273 3800

12 Huski Hotel
huski.com.au
T +61 1300 652 260

13 High Country Visitor Information Centre
visitvictoria.com
T +61 3 5775 7000

15 Heide Museum of Modern Art
heide.com.au
T +61 3 9850 1500

16 Melbourne Museum
T +61 3 8341 7777

18 RMIT Design Hub
designhub.rmit.edu.au

21 Federation Square
fedsquare.com
T +61 3 9655 1900

22 Southern Cross Station
southerncrossstation.net.au
T +61 3 9619 1624

24 Niagara Galleries
niagaragalleries.com.au
T +61 3 9429 3666

25 Hamer Hall
artscentremelbourne.com.au
T +61 3 9281 8000

26 Australian Centre for Contemporary Art (ACCA)
acca.melbourne
T +61 3 9697 9999

28 Moonah Links Hotel Lodges
peppers.com.au
T +61 7 5665 4426

29 Marion Cultural Centre
marion.sa.gov.au
T +61 8 375 6855

30 Peppermint Bay Visitor Centre
peppermintbay.com.au
T +61 6 267 4088

New Zealand

31 Auckland Art Gallery
aucklandartgallery.com
T +64 9 379 1349

33 Len Lye Centre
lenlyefoundation.com
T +64 3 385 6796

34 Pataka Museum of Arts and Cultures
pataka.org.nz
T +64 4237 1511

35 Christchurch Bus Interchange
metroinfo.co.nz/info/Pages/CentralStation.aspx
T +64 3366 8855

36 Peregrine Winery
peregrinewines.co.nz
T +64 3442 4000

Azerbaijan

37 Heydar Aliyev Centre
heydaraliyevcenter.az

38 Baku Crystal Hall
crystalhall.az
T +994 124 043 152

India

41 Bombay Arts Society
bombayartsociety.org
T +91 222 651 3466

China

43 Harbin Cultural Center
hrbgtheatre.org
T +86 451 8775 1222

44 China Wood Sculpture Museum
zgmdbwg.com
T +86 579 8652 0186

45 Distorted Courtyard House, Commune by the Great Wall
commune.sohochina.com
T +86 108 111 888

46 Airport House, Commune by the Great Wall
commune.sohochina.com
T +86 108 111 888

47 Suitcase House, Commune by the Great Wall
commune.sohochina.com
T +86 108 111 888

48 Bamboo Wall House, Commune by the Great Wall
commune.sohochina.com
T +86 108 111 888

49 Beijing Capital International Airport
en.bcia.com.cn
T +86 109 6158

50 104 Caochangdi Gallery
galerieursmeile.com

51 National Stadium
n-s.cn
T +86 108 437 3060

56 Conrad Hotel
conrad.hilton.com.cn
T +86 106 584 6000

57 Jian Wai SOHO Complex
T +86 105 869 0666

58 Water Cube National Aquatics Center
water-cube.com
T +86 108 437 0112

59 National Grand Theater of China
en.chncpa.org
T +86 106 655 0000

62 Tianjin Grand Theater
tjgtheatre.org
T +86 228 388 2000

63 Dalian International Conference Center
dl-icc.com
T +86 411 3997 3333

64 MOCA Yinchuan
moca-yinchuan.com
T +86 951 842 6106

65 Taiyuan Museum of Art
tymsg.org.cn
T +86 351 608 9616

67 Sifang Art Museum
sifangartmuseum.org

71 Suzhou Museum
szmuseum.com
T +86 512 6757 5666

73 Poly Grand Theatre
shpgt.com
T +86 216 708 8666

75 Long Museum West Bund
thelongmuseum.org
T +86 216 422 7636

77 Natural History Museum
snhm.org.cn
T +86 216 321 3548

79 Shanghai Tower
shanghaitower.com

80 Oriental Sports Center
orientalsportscenter.cn

84 Tiantai Museum
zj.gov.cn
T +86 576 395 8798

102 Dafen Art Museum
dafenart.org
T +86 755 2872 1308

104 Shenzhen Bao'an International Airport, Terminal 3
szairport.com
T +86 755 2345 6789

107 Guangzhou Opera House
gzdjy.org
T +86 400 880 8922

109 Luyeyuan Stone Sculpture Museum
T +86 288 797 6166

111 Clock Museum of Cultural Revolution
jc-museum.cn
T +86 288 831 8000

Hong Kong

115 Kennedy Town Swimming Pool
lcsd.gov.hk
T +852 2817 7973

118 Pacific Place
pacificplace.com.hk
T +852 2844 8900

Taiwan

123 Water-Moon Monastery
ncm.ddm.org.tw
T +886 224 987 171

128 Dadong Art Centre
dadongcenter.khcc.gov.tw
T +886 7743 0011

South Korea

129 White Block Gallery
whiteblock.org/
T +82 319 924 400

131 Dalki Theme Park
ts.dalkicafe.com
T +82 226 382 615

133 Open Books Publishing Company
mimesisart.co.kr
T +82 319 554 404

134 Mimesis Museum
mimesisart.co.kr
T +82 319 554 404

138 Kukje Art Center
kukjegallery.com
T +82 2735 8449

139 Papertainer Museum
sugarcube.tv/papertainer

140 Ann Demeulemeester Retail Store
anndemeulemeester.com
T +82 234 422 570

141 House of Dior Seoul
en.store.dior.com/253775-seoul-house-of-dior
T +82 202 3480 0104

144 Seoul National University Museum
snumoa.org
T +82 2880 9504

145 Transportation Centre, Incheon International Airport
airport.kr
T +82 1577 2600

147 Busan Cinema Centre
dureraum.org
T +82 517 806 000

150 Water Museum
biotopiamuseum.co.kr
T +82 107 145 2366

151 Podo Hotel
thepinx.co.kr
T +81 647 925 200

153 Stone Museum
biotopiamuseum.co.kr
T +82 107 145 2366

154 Wind Museum
biotopiamuseum.co.kr
T +82 107 145 2366

Japan

155 Aomori Contemporary Art Centre
acac-aomori.jp
T +81 177 645 201

156 Towada Art Center
towadaartcenter.com
T +81 176 201 127

157 Kanno Museum of Art
T +81 223 611 222

158 Sendai Multimedia Centre
smt.jp

160 Museum of Hiroshige Ando
hiroshige.bato.tochigi.jp
T +81 287 921 199

163 Tomihiro Art Museum
city.midori.gunma.jp
T +81 277 956 333

164 Yokohama International Passenger Terminal
osanbashi.jp
T +81 045 211 2304

165 Tama Art University Library
tamabi.ac.jp
T +81 426 795 609

167 Za-Koenji
za-koenji.jp
T +81 332 237 500

169 Sumidai Hokusai Museum
hokusai-museum.jp
T +81 366 588 931

170 Mikimoto Ginza 2
mikimoto.com/jp/stores/direct/ginza2
T +81 335 354 611

172 Tokyo Plaza Ginza
ginza.tokyu-plaza.com

175 Nezu Museum
nezu-muse.or.jp/
T +81 343 002 436

176 SunnyHills
sunnyhills.com.tw
T +81 334 087 778

177 Miu Miu Aoyama Store
miumiu.com
T +81 364 348 591

178 TOD'S Omotesando Store
tods.com
T +81 364 192 055

179 Christian Dior Building
en.store.dior.com/239562-dior-tokyo-omotesando
T +81 354 646 260

180 hhstyle Retail Store
hhstyle.co.jp
T +81 357 721 112

181 Gyre Shopping Centre Omotesando
omotesandohills.com
T +81 334 970 310

184 21st Century Museum of Contemporary Art
kanazawa21.jp
T +81 762 202 800

186 Museum of Modern Ceramic Art
cpm-gifu.jp
T +81 572 283 100

190 Sfera Building
ricordi-sfera.com
T +81 755 321 070

191 Kansai-kan National Diet Library
ndl.go.jp
T +81 774 981 200

192 Shiba Ryotaro Memorial Museum
shibazaidan.or.jp
T +81 667 263 860

195 Abeno Harukas
abenoharukas-300.jp

197 Sayamaike Historical Museum
sayamaikehaku.osakasayama.osaka.jp
T +81 723 678 891

198 Setre Chapel
hotelsetre.com
T +81 787 083 331

200 Teshima Art Museum
benesse-artsite.jp
T +81 879 683 555

202 Chichu Art Museum
benesse-artsite.jp
T +81 878 923 755

203 Inujima Seirensho Art Museum
benesse-artsite.jp
T +81 869 471 112

204 Shimane Museum of Ancient Izumo
izm.ed.jp
T +81 853 538 600

205 Island City Central Park
ic-park.jp
T +82 926 615 980

206 Komyo-ji Temple
komyoji-kamakura.or.jp

208 Oita Prefectural Art Museum
opam.jp
T +81 975 334 500

209 Oita Stadium
oita-sportspark.jp
T +81 975 287 700

210 Soda Pop Spa
lamune-onsen.co.jp
T +81 974 752 620

Thailand

213 Central Embassy
centralembassy.com

Vietnam

216 Hanoi Museum
baotanghanoi.com.vn
T +84 462 870 604

Philippines

219 Church of the Gesù
ateneo.edu
T +63 426 6001 4076

Singapore

223 Church of St Mary of the Angels
stmary.sg
T +65 6567 3866

225 Expo Transport Station
singaporeexpo.com.sg
T +65 6403 2160

226 ION Orchard
ionorchard.com
T +65 6238 8228

228 ArtScience Museum
marinabaysands.com
T +65 6688 8888

229 The Star Performing Arts Centre
thestar.sg
T +65 6636 0055

Indonesia

235 Ize Hotel
ize-seminyak.com
T +62 361 846 6999

Europe

Norway

238 National Tourist Routes
nasjonaleturistveger.no
T +47 9138 7374

239 National Tourist Routes
nasjonaleturistveger.no
T +47 9138 7374

240 Romsdal Folk Museum
romsdalsmuseet.no
T +47 7120 2460

241 Lillehammer Art Museum Extension
lillehammerartmuseum.com
T +47 6105 4460

242 Borgund Stave Church Visitor Centre
stavechurch.com
T +47 5766 8109

244 Norwegian Museum of Architecture
nasjonalmuseet.no/en
T +47 2198 2000

245 Norwegian National Opera and Ballet
operaen.no
T +47 915 161

246 Mortensrud Church
kirken.no/klem
T +47 2362 9980

247 Porsgrunn Maritime Museum
du-verden.no
T +47 9542 8959

248 Seljord Watchtower
visittelemark.no
T +47 3505 0400

249 Vennesla Library and Cultural Center
venneslakulturhus.no
T +47 3813 7200

250 Kilden Performing Arts Center
kilden.com
T +47 9058 1111

251 The Arch Cultural Center
buenkulturhus.no
T +47 3827 3111

Sweden

252 Väven
vaven.se/sve
T +46 9016 3300

253 Arlanda Airport
swedavia.se/arlanda
T +46 101 091 000

254 Victoria Tower
scandichotels.com/victoriatower
T +46 851 753 300

255 Quality Hotel Friends
nordicchoicehotels.se
T +46 8705 7000

257 KTH School of Architecture
kth.se/en/abe
T +46 8790 6000

258 Sven-Harrys Konstmuseum
sven-harrys.se
T +46 851 160 060

260 Örsta Gallery
galleriorsta.se
T +46 7958 2404

262 Facts Tåkern Visitor Centre
lansstyrelsen.se
T +46 144 535 155

265 Kalmar Konstmuseum
kalmarkonstmuseum.se
T +46 480 426 282

266 Halmstad Library
bibliotek.halmstad.se
T +46 3513 7181

269 Emporia Shopping Centre
se.club-onlyou.com/Emporia
T +46 4036 3600

Finland

270 Kärsämäki Church
karsamaenseurakunta.fi
T +358 453 488 145

271 St Henry's Ecumenical Art Chapel
taidekappeli.fi
T +358 2265 7777

272 Sibelius Congress and Concert Centre
sibeliustalo.fi
T +358 600 393 949

273 Lohja Main Library
libraries.fi/buildings/lohja

274 Suvela Chapel
espoonseurakunnat.fi/web/
asiointi/suvelan-kappeli
T +358 980 503 963

276 Kamppi Chapel of Silence
helsinginseurakunnat.fi

277 Laajasalo Church
helsinginkirkot.fi
T +358 923 405 757

278 Vuotalo Cultural Centre
vuotalo.fi

Denmark

279 Vendsyssel Theatre
vendsyssel-teater.dk
T +45 9892 4711

282 Herning Museum of Contemporary Art
heartmus.dk
T +45 9712 1033

286 Your Rainbow Panorama
en.aros.dk
T +45 8730 6600

287 Aarhus Library
dokk1.dk
T +45 8940 9200

288 Moesgaard Museum
moesgaardmuseum.dk
T +45 8739 4000

289 Kongernes Jelling
en.natmus.dk
T +45 4120 6331

292 UN City
un.dk
T +45 4533 5000

293 Opera House
kglteater.dk
T +45 3369 6969

294 Tivoli Concert Hall
tivoligardens.com
T +45 3315 1001

295 Black Diamond
kb.dk
T +45 3347 4747

298 DR Koncerthuset
drkoncerthuset.dk
T +45 3520 6262

299 AC Hotel Bella Sky
marriott.com/hotels/travel/cphac-
ac-hotel-bella-sky-copenhagen
T +45 3247 3000

302 The Blue Planet
denblaaplanet.dk
T +45 4422 2244

305 ARKEN Museum of Modern Art
uk.arken.dk
T +45 4354 0222

306 Danish National Maritime Museum
mfs.dk
T +45 4921 0685

308 Fuglsang Art Museum
aabne-samlinger.dk
T +45 5478 1414

309 Danfoss Universe Exhibition Centre
universe.dk
T +45 8881 9500

United Kingdom

311 New Library
abdn.ac.uk/library
T +44 122 427 3330

315 The Seona Reid Building
gsa.ac.uk
T +44 141 353 4500

316 Riverside Museum
glasgowlife.org.uk
T +44 141 287 2720

318 Edinburgh Sculpture Workshop
edinburghsculpture.org
T +44 131 551 4490

319 Scottish Parliament
parliament.scot
T +44 131 348 5000

322 The Hepworth Wakefield
T +44 192 424 7360

325 Imperial War Museum North
iwm.org.uk/visits/iwm-north
T +44 161 836 4000

326 Museum of Liverpool
liverpoolmuseums.org.uk/mol
T +45 151 207 0001

327 Winter Gardens and Millennium Galleries
museums-sheffield.org.uk
T +44 114 278 2600

328 Nottingham Contemporary
nottinghamcontemporary.org
T +44 115 948 9750

329 New Art Gallery Walsall
thenewartgallerywalsall.org.uk
T +44 192 265 4400

330 Selfridges Birmingham Department Store
selfridges.com/birmingham
T +44 800 123 400

332 The Balancing Barn
living-architecture.co.uk

333 The Dune House
living-architecture.co.uk

335 Henry Moore Studios and Gardens
henry-moore.org/
T +44 127 984 3333

337 London Aquatics Centre
londonaquaticscentre.org
T +44 208 536 3150

338 Rivington Place
autograph-abp.co.uk
T +44 207 749 1240

339 Idea Store Whitechapel
ideastore.co.uk
T +44 207 364 4332

342 20 Fenchurch Street
skygarden.london
T +44 207 337 2344

344 The Shard
the-shard.com
T +44 844 499 7111

346 Switch House
tate.org.uk
T +44 207 887 8888

349 Great Court
britishmuseum.org
T +44 207 323 8181

351 The Photographers' Gallery
thephotographersgallery.org.uk
T +44 207 087 9300

352 Serpentine Sackler Gallery
serpentinegalleries.org
T +44 207 402 6075

354 Newport Street Gallery
newportstreetgallery.co
T +44 203 141 9320

357 Chiswick House Café
chiswickhousecafe.com
T +44 208 995 6356

358 Sackler Crossing
kew.org
T +44 208 332 5655

359 Bombay Sapphire Distillery
distillery.bombaysapphire.com
T +44 125 689 0090

360 Turner Contemporary
turnercontemporary.org
T +44 184 323 3000

361 The Shingle House
living-architecture.co.uk

363 Downland Gridshell
wealddown.co.uk
T +44 124 381 1363

364 East Beach Café
eastbeachcafe.co.uk
T +44 190 373 1903

365 SeaCity Museum
seacitymuseum.co.uk
T +44 238 083 4536

366 The Eden Project
edenproject.com
T +44 172 681 1911

367 National Assembly for Wales
assembly.wales
T +44 300 200 6565

368 Great Glass House
botanicgarden.wales
T +44 155 866 7149

369 The Skainos Centre
skainos.org
T +44 289 045 8560

370 Lyric Theatre Belfast
lyrictheatre.co.uk
T +44 289 038 1081

Republic of Ireland

371 Model Arts and Niland Gallery
T +353 719 141 405

372 Solstice Arts Centre
solsticeartscentre.ie
T +353 469 092 300

374 Sean O'Casey Community Centre
seanocaseycommunitycentre.ie
T +353 1850 9000

378 Crawford Municipal Art Gallery
crawfordartgallery.ie
T +353 214 805 042

380 Glucksman Gallery
glucksman.org
T +353 214 901 844

Netherlands

384 De Verbeelding Centre for the Arts
deverbeeldingzeewolde.nl

388 EYE Film Institute
eyefilm.nl
T +31 205 891 400

392 The New Rijksmuseum
rijksmuseum.nl
T +31 206 747 000

393 LJG Synagogue
ljgamsterdam.nl/en
T +31 205 400 120

396 Dutch Reformed Church
haarlemmermeer.ngk.nl

399 City Hall and Theatre
fulcotheater.nl
T +31 306 884 230

400 National Heritage Museum
openairmuseum.nl
T +31 263 576 111

401 Cultural Centre Rozet
rozet.nl
T +31 263 543 100

403 Saint Mary of the Angels Chapel
begraafplaatslaurentius.nl
T +31 104 136 308

404 Centraal Station
ret.nl
T +31 307 515 155

405 Markthal Rotterdam
markthal.nl
T +31 302 346 486

406 Boijmans-van Beuningen Museum
boijmans.nl
T +31 104 419 400

408 De Rotterdam
derotterdam.nl
T +31 102 614 040

412 Book Mountain and Library Quarter
deboekenberg.nl
T +31 181 616 622

413 Exhibition Building
nmkampvught.nl

414 Popstage Mezz
mezz.nl
T +31 765 156 677

417 Stedelijk Van Abbe Museum
vanabbemuseum.nl
T +31 402 381 000

Belgium

419 Concert Hall
concertgebouw.be
T +32 5047 6999

424 Buda Art Centre
budakortrijk.be
T +32 5622 1001

427 MAD Brussels
new.mad.brussels
T +32 028 808 562

428 Le Toison d'Or
toisondor.be
T +32 2735 8190

Luxembourg

429 National Museum of History and Art
mnha.lu
T +352 479 3301

France

431 Lille Métropole Musée Extension
musee-lam.fr
T +33 320 196 868

432 Louvre-Lens
louvrelens.fr
T +33 321 186 262

433 Musée Matisse
museematisse.lenord.fr
T +33 359 733 806

434 Sports Palace
kindarena.fr
T +33 232 107 373

435 Zénith de Rouen
zenith-de-rouen.fr
T +33 232 919 292

437 Centre Pompidou-Metz
centrepompidou-metz.fr
T +33 387 153 939

439 Philharmonie de Paris
philharmoniedeparis.fr
T +33 144 844 484

440 Fondation Louis Vuitton
fondationlouisvuitton.fr
T +33 140 699 600

441 Department of Islamic Art
louvre.fr/en
T +33 140 205 050

444 Jérôme Seydoux-Pathé Foundation
fondation-jeromeseydoux-pathe.com
T +33 183 791 896

446 La Seine Musicale
laseinemusicale.com
T +33 174 345 400

448 Montreuil Coeur de Ville
grandangle-montreuil.fr
T +33 185 607 070

449 Le Château
fraciledefrance.com
T +33 176 211 341

450 Sénart Theatre
theatre-senart.com
T +39 160 345 360

451 Le Signe National Centre for Graphic Design
centrenationaldugraphisme.fr
T +33 325 357 901

452 FRAC Centre
frac-centre.fr
T +33 238 625 200

453 Sarrebourg Museum
ville-sarrebourg.fr
T +33 387 080 868

455 Frac Bretagne
fracbretagne.fr
T +33 299 373 793

457 Cite des Arts et de la Culture
citedesartsetdelaculture.fr
T +33 381 878 740

458 Vulcania Museum
vulcania.com
T +33 473 197 000

460 Lucie-Aubrac Media Library
bm-venissieux.fr
T +33 472 214 554

461 Musée des Confluences
museedesconfluences.fr
T +33 042 838 1212

462 Bordeaux Stadium
matmut-atlantique.com

464 Musée Jean Cocteau
museecocteaumenton.fr
T +33 489 815 250

465 Conservatory Darius Milhaud
aixenprovence.fr
T +33 488 718 420

467 Orange Vélodrome
orangevelodrome.com

468 Tour-Panorama, La Friche Belle de Mai
lafriche.org

471 FRAC PACA
fracpaca.org
T +33 491 912 755

472 Cité de l'Océan et du Surf
T +33 559 227 540

473 The City of Culture of Galicia
cidadedacultura.gal
T +34 881 997 565

474 National Museum of Science & Technology
muncyt.es

477 MUSAC Museum
musac.es
T +34 987 090 000

479 Altamira Museum and Research Centre
museodealtamira.mcu.es
T +34 942 818 005

480 Fundación Botín
fundacionbotin.org
T +34 942 226 072

481 Guggenheim Museum Bilbao
guggenheim-bilbao.eus
T +34 944 359 080

484 Parish Church of Santa María Josefa
sanadrian-miribilla.bizkeliza.net
T +34 944 662 662

486 Hotel at Marqués de Riscal
hotel-marquesderiscal.com
T +34 945 180 880

487 Contemporary Art Centre of Aragon, Beulas Foundation
cdan.es/en/museum-in-huesca-arts-territory
T +34 974 239 893

488 Forum 2004 Southeast Coastal Park
parcdelforum.cat
T +34 628 676 330

490 CCCB
cccb.org
T +34 933 064 100

494 Parc Esportiu Llobregat
parcesportiullobregat.com
T +34 934 753 577

495 Mercat Encants
encantsbcn.com
T +34 932 452 299

500 Terminal 4, Barajas Airport
aeropuertomadrid-barajas.com/terminal-barajas.htm
T +34 913 211 000

501 Museo ABC
museo.abc.es
T +34 917 588 379

502 Valle Inclán Theatre
cdn.mcu.es
T +34 915 058 801

503 Regional Library and Archives of Madrid
madrid.org/archivos/index.php/quienes-somos/conocenos/archivo-regional
T +34 917 208 850

504 Public Library at Usera
bibliotecasdemadrid.org
T +34 914 229 501

507 Cultural and Musical Centre
teatreelmusical.es
T +34 960 800 140

510 Canopy over a Roman Site
um.es
T +34 968 500 093

513 Centro de Arte Contemporáneo C3A
c3a.es
T +34 957 107 470

515 Doñana Visitor Centre of the Marine World
discoveringdonana.com
T +34 959 439 620

516 Baelo Claudia Visitor Centre
museosdeandalucia.es
T +34 956 106 796

518 Magma Art and Congress Centre
tenerifemagma.com
T +34 922 752 027

519 Municipal Library
biblioteca.cm-viana-castelo.pt
T +351 258 809 340

520 Centro De Artes Nadir Afonso
nadirafonso.com

521 Braga Stadium
scbraga.pt/estadio-lojas
T +351 253 206 860

522 MIEC
miec.cm-stirso.pt
T +351 252 830 410

523 Terminal de Cruizeiros
apdl.pt/terminal-passageiros-sul

524 Casa da Música
casadamusica.com
T +351 220 120 220

525 Igreja de Santa Maria
T +351 255 810 706

527 Adega Mayor Winery
adegamayor.pt
T +351 268 699 440

529 MAAT
maat.pt
T +351 210 028 130

533 Casa das Histórias Paula Rego
casadashistoriaspaularego.com
T +351 214 826 970

534 Museum of Mechanical Music
museudamusicamecanica.com
T +351 934 050 519

536 Museum of Luz
museudaluz.org.pt
T +351 266 569 257

537 Sines Cultural Centre
T +351 269 860 080

538 Volcanism Centre
grutasecentrodovulcanismo.com
T +351 291 280 147

Germany

540 Edel Music Headquarters
edel.com/de/home
T +49 4089 0850

545 Hamburg Elbphilharmonie
elbphilharmonie.de
T +49 403 576 660

546 Archaeological Museum and Park in Bramsche-Kalkriese
kalkriese-varusschlacht.de
T +49 546 892 040

547 Phaeno Science Centre
phaeno.de
T +49 536 189 0100

548 Biosphere and Flower Pavilion
biosphaere-potsdam.de
T +49 331 550 740

552 Museum for Architectural Drawing
tchoban-foundation.de
T +49 304 373 9090

554 Netherlands Embassy
sieunddieniederlande.nl
T +49 3020 9560

558 Jewish Museum Berlin
jmberlin.de
T +49 302 599 3300

559 Labels 2
T +49 302 757 1125

561 Museum Folkwang
museum-folkwang.de
T +49 201 884 5000

563 Jüberg Observation Tower
sauerlandpark-hemer.de/park/
fuer-naturliebhaber/juebergturm/
T +49 237 255 1616

565 Langen Foundation Art Centre
angenfoundation.de
T +49 218 257 010

566 Kolumba Museum
kolumba.de
T +49 221 933 1930

567 Wallraf-Richartz Museum
wallraf.museum
T +49 221 2212 1119

568 Bruder Klaus Field Chapel
feldkapelle.de

569 Arp Museum
arpmuseum.org
T +49 222 894 2516

570 Autobahnkirche Siegerland
autobahnkirche-siegerland.de
T +49 2736 6716

572 Synagogue Dresden
freundeskreis-synagoge-dresden.de
T +49 351 656 0710

574 Städel Museum Extension
staedelmuseum.de
T +49 696 050 980

576 Mensa Moltke
sw-ka.de/en/essen
T +49 721 690 9257

577 Museum of Modern Literature
dla-marbach.de
T +49 7144 8480

578 Mercedes-Benz Museum
mercedes-benz.com
T +49 711 173 0000

580 Museum of Granite
historyingranite.org

581 BMW Welt Exhibition Centre
bmw-welt.com

582 Church of the Sacred Heart
erzbistum-muenchen.de/
HerzJesuMuenchen
T +49 891 306 750

583 NS Dokuzentrum
ns-dokuzentrum-muenchen.de

584 The Jewish Center
bavaria.by
T +49 892 339 6096

586 Porsche Museum
porsche.com
T +49 711 9112 0911

587 Marktoberdorf Gallery
kuenstlerhaus-marktoberdorf.de
T +49 834 291 8337

588 Church for Two Denominations
kirche-im-rieselfeld.de
T +49 761 137 4310

589 Conference Pavilion, Vitra Campus
vitra.com
T +49 7621 702 3500

590 VitraHaus, Vitra Campus
vitra.com
T +49 7621 702 3502

591 Factory Building, Vitra Campus
vitra.com/en-gb/campus/visitor
T +49 7621 7020

592 Fire Station, Vitra Campus
vitra.com/en-gb/campus/visitor
T +49 7621 7020

593 Vitra Schaudepot, Vitra Campus
design-museum.de
T +49 7621 702 3200

594 Factory Building, Vitra Campus
vitra.com
T +49 7621 702 3502

Switzerland

603 Museum der Kulturen
mkb.ch
T +41 612 665 600

604 Kunstmuseum Basel
kunstmuseumbasel.ch
T +41 612 066 262

605 Basel Train Station
sbb.ch/de/bahnhof-services/
bahnhoefe/bahnhof-baselsbb

607 Schaulager
schaulager.org
T +41 613 353 232

609 Aarau City Museum Extension
stadtmuseum.ch
T +41 628 360 517

612 Freitag Flagship Store
freitag.ch/en/store/freitag-flagship-
store-zuerich
T +41 433 669 520

613 Swiss National Museum Extension
nationalmuseum.ch
T +41 584 666 511

616 Extension Centre Pasqu'Art
pasquart.ch

618 Friedrich Dürrenmatt Museum
bundesmuseen.ch
T +41 584 667 779

619 Zentrum Paul Klee
museen-bern.ch
T +41 313 590 101

620 Cultural and Congress Centre
kkl-luzern.ch/en
T +41 412 267 070

**621 Graubünden Museum
of Fine Arts**
buendner-kunstmuseum.ch
T +41 812 572 870

622 Bergbahn Arosa Chairlift
arosabergbahnen.com

624 Rolex Learning Centre
rolexlearningcenter.epfl.ch
T +41 216 934 237

626 ArtLab EPFL
artlab.epfl.ch
T +41 216 938 292

630 MAX Gallery
centroculturalechiasso.ch/m-a-x-museo
T +41 916 950 888

Liechtenstein

632 Liechtenstein Art Museum
kunstmuseum.li
T +423 235 0300

Austria

633 Kunsthaus Bregenz
kunsthaus-bregenz.at
T +43 557 448 5940

634 Bregenz Festival House
kongresskultur.com/en
T +43 5574 4130

638 Galzigbahn Lower Terminal
galzigbahn.at
T +43 544 623 520

640 Innsbruck Town Hall Gallery
innsbruck.gv.a
T +43 512 5360 1001

641 Bergisel Ski Jump
bergisel.info
T +43 512 589 259

642 Swarovski Kristallwelten
kristallwelten.swarovski.com
T +43 522 451 080

**644 Festival Hall Of The Tiroler
Festspiele Erl**
tiroler-festspiele.at

**649 Museum of Modern Art
Ludwig Foundation**
mumok.at
T +43 152 5000

654 Podersdorf Parish Centre
pfarre-podersdorf.at
T +43 2177 3285

**657 Franz-Liszt Chamber
Music Hall**
erzdioezese-wien.at
T +43 151 5520

**659 Fresach Protestant
Diocesan Museum**
evangelischeskulturzentrum.at
T +43 699 1106 3656

Italy

662 Vigilius Mountain Resort
vigilius.it
T +39 473 556 600

**664 Museum of Contemporary
Art**
gamtorino.it
T +39 114 429 518

**665 Pinacoteca Giovanni
e Marella Agnelli**
pinacoteca-agnelli.it
T +39 110 062 008

**668 Fondazione Giangiacomo
Feltrinelli**
fondazionefeltrinelli.it
T +39 249 5834

669 Galleria Lia Rumma
liarumma.it
T +39 022 900 0101

671 Fondazione Prada
fondazioneprada.org
T +39 256 662 611

672 Lido on Lake Segrino
parcolagosegrino.it/turismo/lido-aquilegia
T +39 331 902 5491

673 Church and Pastoral Centre
parrocchiaseriate.it
T +39 035 299 709

675 Enzo Ferrari Museum
musei.ferrari.com
T +39 594 397 979

676 MAST Foundation
mast.org
T +39 051 647 4345

678 San Michele in Borgo
turismo.pisa.it

679 Sandro Penna Library
turismo.comune.perugia.it
T +39 755 772 941

**681 MAXXI National Museum for
XXI Century Arts**
maxxi.art
T +39 6320 1954

683 Stazione Tiburtina
stazioneromatiburtina.it/it

684 Church of San Carlo Borromeo
sancarloroma.it
T +39 065 017 3095

685 Parco della Musica
auditorium.com
T +39 680 241 281

Estonia

691 Viimsi St James Church
viimsijaakobikirik.ee
T +372 566 17247

692 Kumu Art Museum
kumu.ekm.ee
T +372 602 6000

694 Museum of Occupations
okupatsioon.ee
T +372 668 0250

695 Pärnu Stadium
rannastaadion.weebly.com
T +372 525 3005

696 Estonian National Museum
erm.ee
T +372 736 3052

Latvia

**697 Art Academy of Latvia
Extension**
lma.lv

698 National Library of Latvia
lnb.lv
T +371 2202 2920

**700 Žanis Lipke Memorial
Museum**
lipke.lv
T +371 6720 2539

Lithuania

**702 Litexpo Exhibition
Pavilion**
litexpo.lt
T +370 5245 4500

Russia

**707 Garage Museum of
Contemporary Art**
garagemca.org
T +7 495 645 0520

Poland

709 National Museum
muzeum.szczecin.pl
T +48 912 004 315

710 Philharmonic Hall
filharmonia.szczecin.pl
T +48 914 309 510

711 CKK Jordanki
jordanki.torun.pl/pl
T +48 516 277 831

**712 Museum of the History
of Polish Jews**
polin.pl
T +48 224 710 301

**714 Artur Rubinstein Philharmonic
Concert Hall**
filharmonia.lodz.pl/en

Czech Republic

717 The Dancing House
tadu.cz

718 Nový Smíchov Shopping Centre
cz.club-onlyou.com/Novy-Smichov
T +420 251 101 061

Slovakia

722 Heat Exchanger Važecká
vymenniky.sk/vymennik-vazecka

Hungary

725 Füleky Winery
tokaj.org
T +36 4739 6478

726 Cultural Centre
makohagymahaz.hu
T +36 6221 2044

Slovenia

727 Cultural Centre of European Space Technologies
ksevt.eu
T +386 5993 4517

728 Celjska Koca Hotel
celjska-koca.si
T +386 4171 8274

Greece

733 Cultural and Recreation Centre
sxoliaristotelous.gr/en/center.htm
T +30 233 204 3437

734 Athens Olympic Velodrome
martialway.gr
T +30 210 683 4060

Turkey

736 Minicity Model Park
antalyacentral.com/attractions/
minicity-antalya

Africa

South Africa

739 Freedom Park
freedompark.co.za
T +27 123 364 000

742 South African Apartheid Museum
apartheidmuseum.org
T +27 113 094 700

743 Maropeng Visitor Centre
maropeng.co.za
T +27 145 779 000

744 Northern Cape Legislative Building
ncpleg.gov.za

745 Denis Hurley Centre
denishurleycentre.org
T +27 313 012 240

746 Nelson Mandela Museum
nelsonmandelamuseum.org.za
T +27 475 019 500

747 Thusong Service Centre
thusong.gov.za
T +21 483 3839

748 Zeitz MOCAA
zeitzmocaa.museum
T +27 214 187 855

Morocco

749 Menara Airport
marrakech.airport-authority.com
T +212 524 447 910

Senegal

751 Thread
thread-senegal.org

Egypt

753 Bibliotheca Alexandrina
bibalex.org
T +20 3483 9999

Middle East

Israel

755 Terminal 3, Ben Gurion Airport
iaa.gov.il/he-IL/airports/BenGurion
T +972 3975 5555

756 Palmach Museum
palmach.org.il
T +972 3643 8460

757 Amir Building, Tel Aviv Museum of Art
tamuseum.org.il
T +972 3607 7020

760 Peres Center for Peace
peres-center.org
T +972 3568 0680

761 Design Museum Holon
dmh.org.il
T +972 732 151 525

762 Cymbalista Synagogue and Jewish Heritage Center
en-heritage.tau.ac.il
T +972 3640 8020

763 Yad Vashem Holocaust Memorial
yadvashem.org
T +972 2644 3400

Lebanon

767 Aïshti Foundation
aishtifoundation.com
T +961 471 7716

Palestine

770 The Palestinian Museum
palmuseum.org
T +970 2294 1948

Saudi Arabia

771 King Fahad National Library
kfnl.org.sa
T +966 114 186 111

772 Kingdom Centre Building
kingdomcentre.com.sa
T +966 112 112 222

United Arab Emirates

773 Concrete
alserkalavenue.ae
T +971 505 569 797

776 Hazza Bin Zayed Stadium
hbzstadium.ae
T +971 9612 0801

North America

Canada

777 National Music Centre of Canada
nmc.ca
T +1 403 543 5115

779 Squish Studio
fogoislandarts.ca
T +1 709 266 1248

780 Bridge Studio
fogoislandarts.ca
T +1 709 266 1249

781 Fogo Island Inn
fogoislandinn.ca
T +1 709 658 3444

782 Long Studio
fogoislandarts.ca
T +1 709 266 1250

786 Bibliothèque du Boisé
bibliomontreal.com
T +1 514 855 6130

788 Vaughan Civic Centre Resource Library
vaughanpl.info/libraries/view/11
T +1 905 653 7323

789 Aga Khan Museum
agakhanmuseum.org
T +1 416 646 4677

790 Renaissance ROM Galleries
rom.on.ca
T +1 416 586 8000

792 Sharp Center for Design
ocadu.ca/about/sharp-centre-for-design.htm
T +1 416 977 6000

USA

795 Experience Music Project
mopop.org
T +1 206 770 2700

797 Seattle Central Library
spl.org
T +1 206 386 4636

798 Bellevue Arts Center
bellevuearts.org
T +1 425 519 0770

799 Tacoma Art Museum
tacomaartmuseum.org
T +1 253 272 4258

800 Portland Aerial Tram
gobytram.com
T +1 503 494 8283

801 United States Courthouse
utd.uscourts.gov
T +1 801 524 6100

802 Marcia and John Price Museum Building
umfa.utah.edu
T +1 801 581 7332

803 Frederic C Hamilton Building, Denver Art Museum
denverartmuseum.org
T +1 720 865 5000

804 Denver Union Station
rtd-denver.com/UnionStation.shtml
T +1 303 299 6000

806 Robert Hoag Rawlings Public Library
pueblolibrary.org
T +1 719 562 5600

807 Aspen Art Museum
aspenartmuseum.org
T +1 970 925 8050

808 Nevada Museum of Art
nevadaart.org
T +1 775 329 3333

809 Jan Shrem and Maria Manetti Shrem Museum of Art
manettishremmuseum.ucdavis.edu
T +1 530 752 8500

810 Berkeley Art Museum and Pacific Film Archive
bampfa.org
T +1 510 642 0808

811 SFMOMA
sfmoma.org
T +1 415 357 4000

812 Contemporary Jewish Museum
info@thecjm.org
T +1 415 655 7800

813 Federal Building
gsa.gov/portal/content/227903
T +1 415 625 2755

815 California Academy of Sciences
calacademy.org
T +1 415 379 8000

817 Stanford Apple Store
apple.com/retail/stanford
T +1 650 798 6180

818 Windhover Contemplative Centre
windhover.stanford.edu
T +1 650 723 1762

822 Inner-City Arts
inner-cityarts.org
T +1 213 627 9621

823 Emerson College
emerson.edu/ela
T +1 323 498 0600

824 Matthew Marks Gallery
matthewmarks.com
T +1 323 654 1830

825 Petersen Automotive Museum
petersen.org
T +1 323 932 277

826 Our Lady of the Angels Cathedral
olacathedral.org

827 The Broad
thebroad.org
T +1 213 232 6200

828 Walt Disney Concert Hall
laphil.com
T +1 323 850 2000

833 Mii Amo Spa, Enchantment Resort
miiamo.com
T +1 844 993 9518

834 Phoenix Art Museum
phxart.org
T +1 602 257 1880

835 Health Sciences Education Building
http://phoenixmed.arizona.edu/contact/health-sciences-education-building

836 Sandra Day O'Connor US Courthouse
azd.uscourts.gov/locations/phoenix

837 Stone Ridge Church
stoneridgechurch.com
T +1 928 314 4410

838 Walker Art Center, Expansion
walkerart.org
T +1 612 375 7600

839 Guthrie Theater
guthrietheater.org
T +1 612 377 2224

840 Des Moines Public Library
dmpl.org
T +1 515 283 4152

842 Figge Art Museum
figgeartmuseum.org
T +1 563 326 7804

843 Writers Theatre
writerstheatre.org
T +1 847 242 6000

844 The Godfrey Hotel
godfreyhotelchicago.com
T +1 312 649 2000

847 McCormick Tribune Campus Center
web.iit.edu/event-services/meeting-spaces/mccormick-tribune-campus-center
T +1 312 567 3000

849 Nelson-Atkins Museum of Art
nelson-atkins.org
T +1 816 751 1278

850 Contemporary Art Museum St Louis
camstl.org
T +1 314 535 4660

853 Speed Art Museum
speedmuseum.org
T +1 502 634 2700

854 Eli & Edythe Broad Art Museum
broadmuseum.msu.edu
T +1 517 884 4800

855 Driving Park Branch, Columbus Metropolitan Library
columbuslibrary.org
T +1 614 645 2275

856 Toledo Museum of Art Glass Pavilion
toledomuseum.org
T +1 419 255 8000

857 Akron Art Museum
akronartmuseum.org
T +1 330 376 9185

858 Corning Museum of Glass
cmog.org
T +1 800 732 6845

861 Tang Teaching Museum and Art Gallery
tang.skidmore.edu
T +1 518 580 8080

862 Tozzer Anthropology Building
library.harvard.edu/toz
T +1 617 496 4454

863 Renovation and Expansion
harvardartmuseums.org
T +1 617 495 9400

864 Honan-Allston Branch, Boston Public Library
bpl.org
T +1 617 787 6313

866 Institute of Contemporary Art
icaboston.org
T +1 617 478 3100

867 Grace Farms
gracefarms.org
T +1 203 920 1702

868 Roy and Diana Vagelos Education Center
educationbldg.cumc.columbia.edu

870 Rose Center for Earth and Space
amnh.org
T +1 212 769 5100

871 Alice Tully Hall Lincoln Center
aboutlincolncenter.org
T +1 212 875 5456

876 The Westin Hotel New York at Times Square
westinny.com
T +1 866 837 4183

878 Morgan Library Extension
themorgan.org
T +1 212 685 0008

880 David Zwirner 20th Street
davidzwirner.com
T +1 212 517 8677

882 The High Line
thehighline.org
T +1 212 500 6035

883 Whitney Museum of American Art
whitney.org
T +1 212 570 3600

887 New Museum of Contemporary Art
newmuseum.org
T +1 212 219 222

891 World Trade Center Transportation Hub
wtc.com/about/getting-here

896 Stapleton Branch, New York Public Library
nypl.org/about/locations/stapleton
T +1 718 727 0427

897 Queen Library at Glen Oaks
queenslibrary.org
T +1 718 831 8636

898 Parrish Art Museum
parrishart.org
T +1 631 283 2118

900 Krishna P Singh Center for Nanotechnology
nano.upenn.edu

902 The Barnes Foundation
barnesfoundation.org
T +1 215 278 7000

905 NMAAHC
nmaahc.si.edu
T +1 844 750 3012

906 Francis A Gregory Library
dclibrary.org
T +1 202 698 6373

907 Hunt Library, North Carolina State University
lib.ncsu.edu
T +1 919 515 7110

908 Bechtler Museum of Modern Art
bechtler.org
T +1 704 353 9200

909 The Wieland Pavilion
woodruffcenter.org
T +1 404 733 4200

910 Flint RiverQuarium
flintriverquarium.com
T +1 229 639 2650

911 Florida Polytechnic University
floridapolytechnic.org
T +1 863 583 9050

912 The Dalí Museum
thedali.org
T +1 727 823 3767

913 The Center for Asian Art
ringling.org/asian-art
T +1 941 359 5700

915 Pérez Art Museum Miami
pamm.org
T +1 305 375 3000

916 Miami Dade College Academic Support Center
mdc.edu
T +1 305 237 8888

917 Faena Forum
faena.com
T +1 305 534 8800

919 New World Center
nws.edu
T +1 305 680 5866

922 Louisiana State Museum and Sports Hall of Fame
louisianastatemuseum.org
T +1 504 568 6968

923 Webb Chapel Park Pavilion
T +1 214 670 4100

924 Nasher Sculpture Center
nashersculpturecenter.org
T +1 214 242 5100

925 Perot Museum of Nature and Science
perotmuseum.org
T +1 214 428 5555

926 Modern Art Museum of Fort Worth
themodern.org
T +1 817 738 9215

927 Kimbell Art Museum Pavilion
kimbellart.org
T +1 817 332 8451

930 Sicardi Gallery
sicardigallery.com
T +1 713 529 1313

931 Hobby Educational Center for the Performing Arts
thehobbycenter.org
T +1 713 315 2525

932 Museum of Fine Arts
mfah.org
T +1 713 639 7300

934 Moody Center for the Arts
moody.rice.edu
T +1 713 348 2787

935 Wagner Noël Performing Arts Center
wagnernoel.com
T +1 432 552 4430

936 Inde/Jacobs Gallery
indejacobs.com
T +1 432 386 0044

Central America

Mexico

940 Américas 1500
marriott.com
T +52 331 253 9800

942 Museo International del Barroco
mib.com.mx
T +52 222 326 7130

943 Museo Soumaya
soumaya.com.mx
T +52 5616 3731

944 Museo Jumex
fundacionjumex.org
T +52 555 395 2615

951 Cineteca Nacional Siglo XXI
www.cinetecanacional.net
T +52 554 155 1200

952 MUAC
muac.unam.mx
T +52 555 622 6972

954 Sunset Chapel
capilladelatardecer.com
T +52 555 536 8834

955 Fundación Casa Wabi
casawabi.org
T +52 954 582 2840

South America

Colombia

959 Library of Spain
sanantoniodeprado.co/bibliotecas/
T +57 319 691 0236

960 The Wishes Urban Complex
T +57 4380 6964

963 Gabriel García Márquez Cultural Center
fcecol.info/CCGGM
T +57 1283 2200

Brazil

966 Arena da Amazônia
amazoniaarena.tk
T +55 922 126 1260

967 Fortaleza Maritime Passenger Terminal
T +55 853 266 8828

969 Galeria Adriana Varejao
galeriadaarquitetura.com.br

970 Teatro Popular Oscar Niemeyer
teatropopularoscarniemeyer.art.br
T +55 212 613 2734

971 Museu do Amanhã
museudoamanha.org

976 Cidade das Arte
cidadedasartes.org
T +55 213 325 0102

977 Museu de Arte do Rio
museudeartedorio.org.br
T +55 213 031 2741

980 Praca das Artes
theatromunicipal.org.br
T +55 113 053 2092

982 Casa Triângulo Gallery
casatriangulo.com
T +55 113 167 5621

983 Nova Leme
galerialeme.com/en
T +55 113 093 8184

984 Vitra
jhsf.com.br
T +55 113 702 1900

986 Museum Oscar Niemeyer
museuoscarniemeyer.org.br
T +55 413 350 4400

987 Aeromovel Porto Alegre
aeromovel.com.br
T +55 513 077 4636

988 Fundação Iberê Camargo
iberecamargo.org.br
T +55 513 247 8000

Chile

989 Hotel Explora, San Pedro de Atacama
explora.com
T +56 223 952 800

990 ESO Hotel and Information Centre
eso.org
T +56 224 644 100

992 Viña Las Niñas Winery
vinalasninas.com
T +56 722 978 060

993 Viña Pérez Cruz Winery
perezcruz.com/en/vina
T +56 228 242 405

994 Hotel Remota
remotahotel.com
T +56 612 414 040

Argentina

995 Museum of Latin American Art
malba.org.ar
T +54 114 808 6500

997 Fondación Proa
proa.org
T +54 114 104 1000

999 Museo MAR
gba.gob.ar
T +54 223 471 7695

Uruguay

1000 Carrasco International Airport
aeropuertodecarrasco.com.uy
T +598 2604 0329

Phaidon Press Limited
Regent's Wharf
All Saints Street
London N1 9PA

Phaidon Press Inc.
65 Bleecker Street
New York, NY 10012

phaidon.com

First published 2017
© 2017 Phaidon Press Limited

ISBN 978 0 7148 7535 4

A CIP catalogue record for this book
is available from the British Library
and the Library of Congress.

Publisher: Emilia Terragni
Commissioning Editor:
    Virginia McLeod
Project Editor: Belle Place
Picture Research: Nicole Alber,
    Nabil Butt and Electra Simon
Production Controller: Lisa Fiske
    and Matthew Harvey

Cover design by Hans Stofregen
Artworked by Chris Lacy

The publisher would like to thank
Emma Barton, Clive Burroughs, Alison
Cowan, James Greig, Taahir Husain,
Isobel McLean, João Mota, Rebecca
Roke, Sarah Scott, Amelia Stevens
Greenhalgh, and Tom Wainwright for
their contributions to this book.

Printed in China